1991

ETHICAL DILEMMAS IN THE MODERN CORPORATION

GERALD F. CAVANAGH
ARTHUR F. McGOVERN

University of Detroit

PRENTICE HALL
Englewood Cliffs, New Jersey 07632

Library of Congress Cataloging-in-Publication Data

CAVANAGH, GERALD F.
   Ethical dilemmas in the modern corporation.

   Includes bibliographies and index.
   1. Business ethics. 2. Corporations—Moral and
ethical aspects. I. McGovern, Arthur F. II. Title.
HF5387.C38 1988   174'.4   87-25726
ISBN 0-13-290058-0

Editorial/production supervision and
   interior design: Mary A. Bardoni
Cover design: Ben Santora
Cover photo credit: Marc Anderson
Manufacturing buyer: Margaret Rizzi

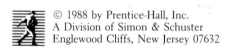

© 1988 by Prentice-Hall, Inc.
A Division of Simon & Schuster
Englewood Cliffs, New Jersey 07632

Printed in the United States of America

10 9 8 7 6 5 4 3 2

ISBN   0-13-290058-0

Prentice-Hall International (UK) Limited, London
Prentice-Hall of Australia Pty. Limited, Sydney
Prentice-Hall Canada Inc., Toronto
Prentice-Hall Hispanoamericana, S.A., Mexico
Prentice-Hall of India Private Limited, New Delhi
Prentice-Hall of Japan, Inc., Tokyo
Simon & Schuster Asia Pte. Ltd., Singapore
Editora Prentice-Hall do Brasil, Ltda., Rio de Janeiro

CONTENTS

PREFACE

Businesspeople prefer to act ethically; they also want to be successful in their careers. They would like to contribute to the good of society, but not at the expense of their own enterprise. Good ethical actions most often are also good business. Fair treatment of employees generally leads to better quality goods and services. However, good ethics and profitability can be in conflict. A healthy environment requires limits on pollution, but controls can be costly.

Ethical dilemmas nearly always involve conflicting values. Social values, which look to the good of society as a whole, can conflict with traditional business values that focus on efficiency, self-interest, and competition. In Chapter Two we present two sets of values; we call them social values and traditional business values, and we argue that both should be considered whenever business policies or governmental economic policies are being formulated.

We take a position and make ethical judgments on the many issues discussed in this book. Our judgments are based on the two sets of values and the model set forth in Chapter Two. Others may not agree with our judgments. Indeed, when using the book, an instructor might be well advised not to indicate her or his own judgment, so as not to foreclose discussion. The book thus features: many examples of problems that face the businessperson, an ethical values and norms model, and an application of these values in making ethical judgments.

We offer these two sets of values as a simplified ethical framework for use by corporate executives and others who are concerned with business and society. We do not deal with many theoretical issues that a more philosophical text on ethics might include, for example, about contending views on the ultimate grounds for morality or all the elements of the process of moral reasoning. We focus instead on a straightforward presentation of two sets of values that we believe offer a healthy balance between broad social concerns and legitimate business interests. This book thus presents ethical norms, not as merely a set of constraints, but as goals that can motivate and empower people.

This book began as a project that would treat important issues and problems that were not being covered by *Economic Justice for All*, the Catholic Bishops letter on the United States economy. Michael Lavelle, who was on the Committee that wrote the letter, helped conceive and worked on portions of the project. We hope this book will provide language, method, and a model that will be useful to the worker, the businessperson, and the student. The problems discussed here are faced by businesspeople every day. The book is intended to aid those who face these ethical dilemmas.

We are indebted to many who helped us during the three years it took to complete this book. The University of Detroit has been generous in providing us with physical, moral, and spiritual support over this period; we thank faculty, students, administrators, and friends who gave that help and encouragement. Boston College also provided much support for Cavanagh and the project, during 1986–87. At B.C. capable graduate students Brenda Baars, James Weinberg, and Jennifer Lau searched references, read proofs, did the index, and many additional tasks. At the University of Detroit Joseph Daoust worked with us in planning the project; Jennifer Coury, Thomas Renn, Tracy White, and Ann and James Reilly researched, proofed, and helped.

Many generous people provided helpful critiques of early drafts. Robert Betz, a successful businessman of Fairbanks, Alaska, read the entire manuscript and gave us detailed and useful comments. To him we are especially grateful. We would also like to thank those who provided very helpful comments on one or more chapters: John Staudenmaier, Leonard Weber, Margaret Betz, Joseph Raelin, Richard Dempsey, Florence Graves, Michael Bernacchi, Oswald Mascaranas, Richard Nielsen, Sandra Waddock, Walter Klein, Mary Lou Caspers, Michael McFarland, Theodore Moran, Amata Miller, James Halpin, Phil Chmielewski, Garth Hallett, Robert A. Cooke, Bruce Landesman, and Michael Payne. We thank you for catching unclarities and inconsistencies and for your many suggestions. Thanks also to Joseph Heider, Linda Albelli, and Mary Bardoni of Prentice Hall for their capable and sensitive assistance; it was invaluable.

Chapter One
THE CORPORATION: ITS VALUES AND INFLUENCE

The U.S. corporation today faces serious problems—lower productivity gains and poor-quality goods and services, which in turn result in difficulties selling goods overseas. A vital aspect of these problems is understood when we examine the ethics of the corporation and the values of its managers. The impact of ethics and values on these and a variety of other corporate problems are examined in the following chapters.

Values are an essential part of each person's working and daily lives. The ethical dilemmas that are faced on any work day are many. The purpose of this book is to examine some of those daily decisions and activities that have an ethical or moral content.

Ethical and moral values in the Western world have been heavily influenced by the Judeo-Christian tradition of care and concern for other people. Values and ideology are understandably becoming more important to many, as demonstrated by increasing numbers of fundamentalists, libertarians, right wingers, social-justice advocates and many others who call for a return to ethical values—sometimes rigid ethical values. Lest single minded ideological groups have an undue influence on our values and ethics, or, on the other hand, lest we end up with no ethics at all, it is vital that we make explicit the values and ethics that are most appropriate for ourselves, for business, and for life.

This book examines the values and ethics of the corporation and the people who inhabit the firm. It is not intended to be a traditional business ethics text. More thorough treatments of business ethics theories and models are available.[1] It is rather an overview of ethical situations that the average corporate manager faces. The major objectives of the book are (1) to examine some of the ethical dilemmas that corporations and managers face, (2) to help us to recognize the corporation that operates ethically, and (3) to learn more about our own values, goals, and ethics. We intend to present a number of ethical situations faced by managers, along with some basic ethical norms that will be helpful to those managers.

ETHICS, VALUES, AND THE CORPORATION

 The corporation is probably the most influential institution in contemporary U.S. society. It provides jobs, goods, income, and wealth. The corporation also profoundly affects our attitudes and values in the work setting and through its advertising. Each of us are touched many times daily by the corporation. Corporate leaders such as Lee Iacocca, Ross Perot, and James Burke are pictured and quoted in newspapers and magazines. Corporate executives have great influence on our thinking and on our government. Presidents, governors, and legislators rightfully seek the opinion of such able, informed, and experienced men and women. It is the corporation that we wish to examine, as it intersects so pervasively with society.

Before proceeding, let us present some operating definitions. *Ethics* provides the ability to decide right from wrong. *Values* drive an individual's decisions, emotions, and actions. Values are learned through the experiences of life. We are often unaware of the values that drive our decisions and our actions. Ethical (or moral) *norms* derive from our values and provide criteria whereby one can make ethical decisions. A *corporation* is an association of individuals treated by law as having powers and liabilities independent of those of its members.

Free Enterprise and the Profit Motive

Business and the corporation have been very successful in the United States. The conscientious manager is primarily concerned with the quality of the product, the people who work with her or him, and the needs of the people who will use the product. Note the leadership of Thomas Watson of IBM, Sam Walton of Walmart, Irwin Miller of Cummins Engine, William Norris of Control Data, and Robert Anderson of ARCO. These corporate statesmen created firms that produce quality goods, and the firms have been successful over an extended period of time. These firms all have a special concern for their workers (or associates) and are responsible citizens in their communities. Control Data and ARCO also have had business problems, however—an ethical corporation is not immune from difficulties.

There is also a less attractive side to corporate life and free enterprise. Recall the excesses of Andrew Carnegie and John D. Rockefeller two generations ago, and of Ivan Boesky and Dennis Levine of Drexel Burnham Lambert more recently. Carnegie and Rockefeller underpaid workers and drove competitors out of business, but they did create jobs, income, and goods. Boesky and Levine made millions personally while contributing little in the way of jobs, income, and goods that would benefit others. The excesses of Carnegie and Rockefeller brought on antitrust and other legislation to curb monopolistic power. The activities of financial manipulators are also likely to trigger legislative curbs.

For corporate managers to be concerned with social issues beyond the workplace is relatively new. Opportunities for black Americans in the corporation opened only in the mid 1960s, and for women in the 1970s. Trying to clean up pollution also emerged as an issue in the 1970s. In the late 1970s, corporations increased the size of their lobbying staffs in Washington and attempted to have greater influence on legislation.

Large firms today are enmeshed in the fabric of society. Chief executive officers see themselves and their firms as being responsible to more stakeholders than did their predecessors. *Stakeholders* are all those who hold a "stake" in the corporation: employees, customers, shareholders, suppliers, government, and the local community. Successful managers today claim that their primary purpose is not the maximization of profits.[2] While they understand that their survival and growth depends on profitability and return on investment, they see these as coming from a more basic concern for a quality product, wholehearted participation of employees (or associates), and attentiveness to customers. To say that the purpose of the firm is to generate profits is like saying that the purpose of living is to eat. Surely one must eat to survive, but living involves much more than just eating.

Business school faculty, especially those trained in economics and finance, will sometimes present profit maximization as the primary goal of the firm and its managers. The model is elegant: simple and consistent, it enables prediction and comparison. For most purposes this is extremely useful; it directs attention to generating additional revenues or cutting costs.

When profit maximization is over the long term, it can handle most, though not all, of the problems considered in this book. The major difficulty is that the model points the manager in the wrong direction for some of the most important decisions that the manager faces. Moreover, corporate executives tell us that profit maximization is not their primary goal. Yet business school students readily incorporate an exclusive use of profit maximization into their own thinking, because of its simplicity and elegance. For a few, it even becomes an ideology. When profit maximization crowds out other considerations, business schools do a disservice to the business community in the

United States. Business students entering a corporation with such a narrow view of the purpose of the firm and the role of the manager are a menace to contemporary business firms. Such thinking drags the corporation back to the values of the 1920s.

Historically, business leaders were opposed to most social legislation in the United States; they initially lobbied against minimum wage, product and workplace safety standards, truth in advertising, and early anti-pollution legislation. Yet in the 1980s, when federal officials proposed to rescind regulations on solid waste disposal and on requiring firms to provide data to support advertising claims, business leaders lobbied in favor of retaining those regulations. Corporate executives know they operate and can plan more effectively if the legislative parameters are clear. They realize that fair pollution control regulations force everyone to pay their fair share. Reasonable regulations protect the honest businessperson from a dishonest counterpart, who without those regulations would not hesitate to make or save money by taking unethical shortcuts. Law and regulations provide a floor for acceptable business activities. Ethical business behavior demands acts and policies well above that floor.

Changed Values and Poor Productivity

The values generally referred to as the Protestant Work Ethic (hard work, self-reliance) have shifted in the last two decades to a new sense of entitlement and self-fulfillment (see Figure 1-1). Supervisors encourage these values at the workplace, yet the same firm's advertisements and the climate of the nation encourage self-fulfillment. The disciplined, delayed gratification necessary for work then conflicts with the short-term, self-centered values of the consumer. This causes stress for the individual and problems at the workplace. This value shift touches each of us. Yet we are often not fully aware of these major values that have such a profound influence.[3]

Compounding the difficulties that we face in attempting to examine the ethics and values of the firm is the fact that we in the United States have

FIGURE 1-1   Shift of Values Underlying the Business System

PROTESTANT ETHIC . . .HAS SHIFTED TO. . . PLURALISM AND SELF-FULFILLMENT

1. Hard work	1. Salary and status
2. Self-control and sobriety	2. Self-fulfillment
3. Self-reliance	3. Entitlement
4. Perseverance	4. Impatience, short-term view
5. Save and plan ahead	5. Consumption: buy on time, save little
6. Honesty and observing the "rules of the game"	6. Obey the law; in any case, don't get caught

Source: Gerald F. Cavanagh, *American Business Values* (Englewood Cliffs, N.J. Prentice Hall: 1984), p. 163.

a bias against universal moral norms. We have little patience with tradition. Relativism, pluralism, and individualism are very strong among us. My values must be *my* values, and they are as good as anyone else's. Who is to judge that one person's values are better than another's? Thus we find it difficult to obtain a majority for anything but complaint. So there is a consensus in the United States on few important policy issues. Because of this individualism, relativism, and confusion, it is more difficult to deal with ethical dilemmas.

Legislation and regulations stem from the values and goals of a society. They seek to penalize and thus discourage seriously unethical acts. Yet all ethical problems cannot be solved by government legislation. Even clearly unethical activities, such as the overcharges and bribery we have witnessed at General Dynamics and the insider trading at Drexel Burnham Lambert, cannot be eliminated by legislation and regulation. While legislation is necessary, providing guideposts and sanctions, good ethics cannot be legislated—they are voluntary. Good ethics stem from values, and values are learned early in life from family, friends, schools, and places of worship. Good values can develop into good ethics given sensitivity, reflection, and education. This book intends to aid that process.

The Ethical Corporation

When managers and workers are not ethical, they focus on the short term and have little respect for other persons. This sets a climate concerned with the bottom line, self-centered and careless about ethical questions. The ethical corporation has a climate that is characterized by good ethics. People in such a work environment are able to distinguish right from wrong, and are encouraged to follow their consciences. Those who have worked in an ethical corporation can readily detect that climate—they need only observe the attitudes and actions of people around them. When managers and workers are ethical and considerate of others, that firm then develops an ethical climate.

CRITICS AND INFLUENCE

We will focus on the activities and ethics of the large corporation, since it is so dominant and influential in American business and life. Critics point to many perceived failures of the large corporation. In spite of the counterclaims of corporate executives, critics see maximization of profits (accruing mostly to a wealthy elite) as the firm's primary goal, to which social concerns are subordinated. Multinational corporations are charged with exploiting other countries, using their political power to influence U.S. foreign policy, defeating democratic movements in poor countries, and buttressing oppressive right-wing dictatorships. They are charged with concentrating wealth and decision-making in the hands of a small minority and creating great inequalities of wealth and income. Critics say that the corporation encourages a hedonistic materialism and consumerism, treats workers as a mere cost of production, and leaves many people unemployed.

Defenders of free enterprise in the United States point out that this system has provided the highest standard of living of any nation in history. Thanks to the entrepreneurial drive of its owner–managers, it is an innovative and efficient system, providing an increasing number of jobs and wealth for the majority. Moreover, the ideology upon which free enterprise is based is realistic. Enlightened self-interest channels a basic human desire into productivity and benefits for all. Free enterprise creates a "larger pie" in which all can share. The economic system is also closely linked with American freedom and democracy. We enjoy political freedoms as well as economic prosperity. Government, far from serving business interests, often restricts and limits these interests to the detriment of the economic common good. Large corporations are essential to modern living. In creating jobs, goods, and wealth, they benefit all people.

When government is inefficient, we even seek to "privatize" the operation, as we have with the Post Office, health insurance, and some social services. We tapped the energies and efficiencies of the free market when we deregulated airlines, banks, and trucking. The next step is to make the publicly held railroads private again. Many urge that free enterprise be brought to subsidized, state-run monopoly schools, from kindergarten through college, to encourage innovation, efficiency, and more effective education.

Beyond the systematic critique, the corporation receives criticism on some specific issues: cost overruns on defense contracts, contamination of soil and drinking water by toxic waste, worker antagonism and alienation, garish and demeaning advertising, tax evasion, fraud, and kickbacks. Some of these criticisms are valid and some are exaggerated. But they all have contributed to the decline in trust that the average citizen feels toward the large corporation and its leaders. In any case, we in the United States have had little experience in making ethical judgments on these issues, and we have few consistent and universal ethical principles to help us in deciding what is right. When business firms are perceived to be acting irresponsibly, they invite restrictive regulation. In order to determine when government regulation is called for, adequate criteria are necessary. Financial norms are essential in deciding business success. But in a society that claims to be moral, *ethical norms* are also necessary. Furthermore, many people are searching for criteria to evaluate the actions of people, governments, and corporations. This book applies ethical norms to problems involving corporations, but we hope the ethical norms will also be helpful to people in a variety of other settings. We will discuss these norms in Chapter Two.

Ethics as Basic to Business

An ethical critique of the corporation will provide an important service both to citizens and corporate leaders. Trust, cooperation, honesty, and fairness compose the bedrock upon which our society and the business firm rest. Without these virtues, long-term success and growth of the firm are impossible, increases in productivity and product quality depend upon them. These virtues depend in turn upon the ethics of managers and the organizational climate that they inspire. Most managers in the United States want to act ethically. However, they are often limited by a lack of an articulated understanding of what is right and their ability to present that position intelligently. Ethical dilemmas arise when the manager finds herself pulled in two contrary directions. Profitability and growth may urge one decision (as with a layoff or a manipulative ad), whereas justice and concern for the individual may argue another decision.

The norms used in this book are built on the basic values of the dignity of the individual and the right to freedom. The norms, and various applications of them, will be explained in some detail in Chapter Two. We believe that the values that these norms express are shared by most Americans, though may have never articulated them formally.

The actions of corporations and the decisions made by corporate executives have a significant impact on many sectors of society—the corporation's own employees, customers, the environment, government, people in other countries, and the nearby community. Chapters Three through Eight will examine some of the ethical issues raised by the impact of corporate actions and decisions on some of their major stakeholders (see Figure 1–2). Specific cases will highlight ethically good and ethically poor actions by firms, compare the behavior of companies, and raise important public policy issues.

The widespread attention that the Catholic bishops' letter on the United States economy has received illustrates that interest in this sort of analysis is great. Newspapers, magazines, and professional journals, such as *Business Week* and *The Wall Street Journal* regularly run stories on the ethics of corporate mangers. The many new books on business ethics and the expanding corporate in-house ethics-training programs also attest to this interest.

Size and Influence of the Large Corporation

We will examine large corporations because they are so important to our society. Most of our examples will deal with the largest 1000 firms in the United States. These 1000 firms employ about 24 million people, or almsot one quarter of all working people in the United States.[4] These same firms account for about 40 percent of all business sales.[5] Yet these 1000 firms are a very small proportion of the total of 14 million businesses (corporations, partnerships, and proprietorships) in the United States—less than 1/100th of one percent.[6] Thus, a relatively small number of business firms contribute immensely to goods, services, jobs, and the total business activity. Moreover, as we will see in the following chapters, these large firms are more adept at dealing with government, citizen attitudes, and various stakeholders than are smaller firms.

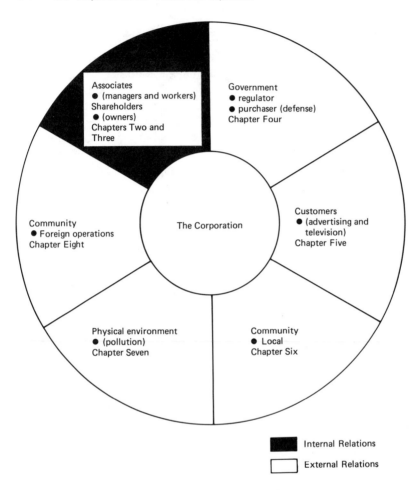

FIGURE 1-2 The Corporation and Its Stakeholders

The largest firms in the United States have become even larger in the last few decades, mostly through mergers and acquisitions. The Fortune 500 companies have absorbed 4500 other firms over the past 25 years. And 166 of the 500 companies listed as the largest in 1955 have been absorbed by other firms. For example, LTV absorbed five companies on the 1955 list; IT&T, Gulf + Western, Rockwell International, ARCO, and Conoco have all acquired four of the largest firms. Conoco itself was swallowed up by DuPont a few years later.[7] The total sales of many of these firms are larger than the total gross national product (GNP) of many nations. For example, the sales of General Motors and Exxon are more than the GNPs of all but 23 nations in the world. GM's sales are larger than the GNP of Turkey, Yugoslavia, Argentina, Austria, Korea, Nigeria, and Indonesia.[8] Hence we see that the large corporation is a dominant institution in the world.

When we examine the *world's* largest firms, we find that 12 of the largest 15 in sales are U.S.-based corporations. The 15 include 10 petroleum firms and 2 automobile firms. There are 5 manufacturing firms on the list, all U.S.-based: GM, Ford, IBM, duPont, and GE. Nevertheless, the dominance of U.S. firms among the world's largest is lessening. If we examine the largest 50 firms, we find that only 23 of that group are U.S.-based. Moreover, manufacturing (which traditionally has provided many jobs) is declining as a share of the United States GNP; it now accounts for only 22 percent, while services account for about 68 percent.[9]

The total number of jobs provided by the largest corporations remains relatively stable. The number employed by the Fortune 500 Industrials actually declined over the past few years, and this in spite of many acquisitions, mergers, and the recovery of the auto and auto-related industries. Yet the United States economy has doubled the number of jobs in 1950 to a total of 103 million in 1985.[10] Most of the new opportunities are generated in new and small firms.

Job creation and new products have traditionally been of concern to many Americans, and are of concern to us in this study. However, a new list of "The Top 1000 Companies" by *Business Week* does not provide the number of people employed by each company. To meet the needs of modern readers, the *Business Week* list emphasizes market value, profit margins, and earnings per share. It speaks to the new investor's need for information on potential investments. The investor is more concerned with net income and return on investment, and seems less interested in the longer-term issues of the physical impact of the corporation on people and jobs.

The corporation changes as it grows. As the corporation grows, there are fewer workers per machine and the hired manager has a different approach to ethical issues. Machines have replaced much manpower in the large corporation over the past few generations. This equipment requires large capital investment. Witness the current investment of U.S. business firms in labor-saving robotics. As the corporation is successful and grows, it gradually "replaces the entrepreneur, as the directing force of the enterprise, with the manager."[11] Note the effect of this: The large corporation's demand for capital increases, as does its total assets. Its share of output remains roughly stable. Its total number of jobs, both absolutely and as a percentage of those working, drops significantly. Moreover, the leader of the corporation is no longer the entrepreneur, founder, or owner-manager; it is the professional manager, who moves up through the bureaucratic ranks and often has a shorter planning horizon for the firm. This influences the ethical decisions made by corporate managers. While the hired manager often has a more professional or "statesman" view of social responsibilities, that same manager's planning horizon can be short term, both because of the individual's own career plans and because of the pressure of outside financial analysts.

SUMMARY AND CONCLUSIONS

In sum, the profit motive can be a powerful energizer, but it can also have unfortunate consequences. The free market model tells us that acting in one's self-interest automatically benefits all others. While true to some extent, such thinking can also narrow horizons and blind one to secondary consequences. Furthermore, the profit motive can also encourage selfishness and greed. One of the major goals of this book is to identify some managers and firms who are aware of secondary consequences of their acts (for example, pollution, abrupt layoffs, passing money to politicians) that are costly to others and avoid them even at some cost to themselves and their firms. Other managers seek profitability and do not realize, or, worse, care little about, these negative consequences.

The focus of the book will be on the ethical dilemmas that face the corporation. However, recognizing these responsibilities depends on the insight and the decisions of individuals within the corporation. So, where appropriate, we will offer practical recommendations for the individual citizen, worker, or manager. We hope to show that solutions to large problems can be brought about by the actions of individuals.

We will also examine the actions of corporate managers. Our purpose is to spotlight some major areas that have a substantial ethical component. We will not be able to discuss all the ethical dilemmas facing the corporation or the many profound influences it has on our lives; for example, we say little about discrimintaion in employment or energy conservation. Moreover, we do not intend to solve specific ethical problems, or enter into lengthy and abstract ethical reasoning that is not readily understandable or useful to most managers. Most decision makers do not make ethical judgments in that complex, abstract fashion. However, we will indicate where the ethical norms that we enunciate in Chapter Two will aid an assessment of the major dilemmas discussed in the following chapters. We hope that this will be of help to corporate managers.

DISCUSSION QUESTIONS

1.1. Outline the benefits of the profit motive. What are the limitations of the profit motive?

1.2. Is there evidence of a link between the economic problems that face the United States (poor quality goods, unemployment, lower rates of saving, unfavorable balance of trade) and personal and social values? Explain.

1.3. Is it in the long-term self-interest of a firm to be ethical? Is this *always* true? When?

1.4. What case can be made that good ethics are essential to long-term economic progress (a) for a firm? (b) for a society?

1.5. Explain the position stating that a narrow view of profit maximization is a menace to the free enterprise system. Do you think this is true?

1.6. Do you think we have a bias against universal ethical norms in the United States?

1.7. Have personal and work values shifted over the last generation? Explain.

1.8. What influences do the largest firms have on the United States? Compare the influence of the large corporation with small firms on influence on work values, attitudes, job creation, and national policy.

NOTES

[1]See, for example, Manuel Velasquez, *Business Ethics: Concepts and Cases,* 2nd ed. (Englewood Cliffs, N.J.: Prentice Hall, 1987); Richard T. DeGeorge, *Business Ethics,* 2nd ed. (New York: Macmillan, 1986); and Thomas Donaldson and Patricia H. Werhane, *Ethical Issues in Business: A Philosophical Approach,* 2nd ed. (Englewood Cliffs, N.J.: Prentice Hall, 1983); Norman Bowie, *Business Ethics,* (Englewood Cliffs, N.J.: Prentice Hall, 1982).

[2]Warren H. Schmidt and Barry Z. Posner, *Managerial Values and Expectations* (New York: American Management Association, 1982), p. 54.

[3]For additional material and references on the values of the business system, its historical roots, and how those values influence and are influenced by the organization, see Gerald F. Cavanagh, *American Business Values* (Englewood Cliffs, N.J.: Prentice Hall, 1984), Chapters 1–4.

[4]A total of 23.8 million people are employed by the *Fortune* magazine annual listing of the largest 1000 corporations in the United States. See *Fortune,* April 28, 1986 and June 9, 1986. The total employed for 1985 is from the U.S. Bureau of the Census, *Statistical Abstract of the United States: 1986,* (106th ed.), Washington, D.C. 1985, p. 390.

[5]*Statistical Abstract, ibid.,* p. 518; and *Fortune,* April 30, 1984 and June 11, 1984.

[6]*Statistical Abstract, ibid.,* p. 518. The 14 million include all corporations, partnerships, and proprietorships; individually owned businesses account for almost two-thirds of the total.

[7]"Fortune 500 Over 25 Years" *Fortune,* May 5, 1980, pp. 88–96; also Thomas C. Cochran, *The American Business System: An Historical Perspective—1900–1955.* (New York, Harper & Row, 1957), p. 179.

[8]*International Financial Statistics: Yearbook—1981; Statistical Abstract of the United States: 1980,* (101st ed.), Washington, D.C., 1979, p. 907; *Fortune,* August 13, 1979, p. 193.

[9]*Business Week,* March 3, 1986, p. 58.

[10]*Statistical Abstract, op. cit.* p. 390.

[11]John Kenneth Galbraith, *The New Industrial State* (New York: Signet, 1967), pp. 81–82.

Chapter Two
ETHICAL VALUES
AND NORMS

A breakfast cereal company gets an idea for a new sugar-coated cereal likely to be a winner with children. Should the company also consider whether the new product is healthy for children? A multinational pet food company considers establishing a fishery in Peru to produce cat food. Should the needs of the people in Peru for protein-rich fish deter the company? An auto manufacturer determines that relocation of plants in a different locale will enable it to cut costs by paying lower wages and taxes. Should the company also weigh the damaging effects such a move will have on the current work force and present locale?

These situations and questions typify many of the ethical dilemmas raised in this book. We believe they call for a different ethical approach from one used when confronting clear-cut cases of ethical misconduct; for example, defrauding customers or the government. In such cases, very basic and commonly accepted moral precepts apply: Deal honestly with others, do not cheat, do not lie, etc. Though we include some cases of obvious ethical misconduct in the book, we focus more on situations of *social responsibility*, in which strict business interests may conflict with the broader interests of society. From a short-term *business* point of view one might ignore the questions raised here and simply rely on the free market system, asking only about potential costs, markets, and profit rates. From a viewpoint of social ethics, however, the social consequences of corporate decisions become important.

This tension between narrow business factors and broad social concerns prompted the different approach to ethics we present in this chapter. This approach acknowledges the importance of the business values (freedom, individual responsibility, growth) that have traditionally supported business enterprises, and it recognizes the importance of the factors that corporations must attend to; for example, costs and potential sales. But it also calls for the inclusion of a broader set of social values (human dignity, community, justice) in forming and evaluating the policies and actions of business corporations. In the first part of this chapter, then, we present these two sets of values. In the latter parts of the chapter, we consider issues related to the "agents'" responsibility: whether, or to what extent, corporations should accept social responsibility, and where, within corporate structures, responsibility should be exercised. We discuss some specific cases in respect to this last point and offer some suggestions for achieving greater accountability.

As noted in Chapter One, we do not intend to offer a comprehensive treatment of business ethics. We assume that people using this book are able, if they choose, to supplement it with readings that deal more directly with ethical theories and the principles that enter into the process of moral reasoning. In addition to the textbooks cited in Chapter One, we have ourselves presented elsewhere some ethical "models," consistent with the approach used in this book, which can be applied to business practices and policies.[1] We also assume the validity of many time-honored, general moral precepts: It is wrong to kill, to steal, to lie, to cheat. Honesty, especially, is an essential value in ordinary business ethics.

Our main concern in this work is to raise ethical *questions* related to social responsibility. Where ethical misconduct is evident (for example, in cases of fraud) or where a corporation's policy clearly promotes some social good (for example, in improving owner-worker relations) we have not hesitated to make moral judgments. But many of the issues raised in the book concern broad and complex questions of social concern, such as the impact of multinationals on the economies of poor countries. In such instances it is impossible to determine *the* correct moral answer without taking into account all the attendant circumstances and factors. We have addressed ourselves primarily to conscientious and ethically concerned men and women. Anyone looking only to what they can legally "get away with" will not find our probing of issues to be of much value.

In most difficult ethical decisions, different values and norms come into play. Even on a personal level, managers working hard for promotion must weigh whether the overtime spent at work is taking too much time away from their families. Different business values enter into strictly business decisions; for example, stability versus the risk of a new venture. Different, and sometimes conflicting, values and norms are involved when deciding issues of social responsibility. These values and norms we wish now to consider (see Figure 2–1).

Values, such as freedom and justice, are concepts that indicate some object esteemed as good, worthwhile, or desirable. They express what a society believes "ought to be": People ought to be respected; they should be free; they ought to be treated fairly. To become operative, values must be appropriated, assented to, and esteemed by individuals in society. *Norms* are standards used to translate these values into principles for moral judgment. The norms we use here are intended as guidelines for generating questions regarding social responsibility. They do not constitute rigid standards or a code

FIGURE 2-1   Ethical Values and Norms

TRADITIONAL BUSINESS VALUES*	SOCIAL VALUES*
1. *Freedom of the Individual* NORM: Preserve and protect the freedom of all members. Political democracy, free enterprise, and a free market are institutions well suited to achieve this freedom.	1. *Dignity of the Human Person* NORM: Preserve and promote the dignity of all persons; deal honestly with others and treat others as ends, not means; enable people to meet basic human needs (life, health, safety, employment, etc.), so that a dignified human life may be realized.
2. *Individual Responsibility* NORM: Promote personal responsibility; institutions that encourage initiative and individual responsibility are favored. Enlightened self-interest is a useful and realistic motive for achieving this value.	2. *Community* (Common good; solidarity) NORM: Encourage people to care for others, for their neighborhood, work group, and society as a whole; enable all to have a sense of participation and belonging.
3. *Growth* (Productivity) NORM: Promote spirit and institutions that encourage the production of goods and services and economic health. Free enterprise, with its flexibility, competition, and legitimate striving for profits, best achieves innovation and productivity. "Consumer sovereignty" is the best means of distributing goods.	3. *Justice* (Equity) NORM: Strive for fair distribution of benefits, burdens, and power; deal fairly with all persons, including future generations; create structures that promote participation and the common good; change structures that discriminate against any group. Political democracy best achieves justice.

*Compare these sets of values with ethical models that stress rights, utility, and justice, respectively.[2]

of ethics, and some of the values overlap or intersect. But they do provide a framework for raising issues of social responsibility.

Responsibility implies accountability to others—an accountability that involves being able to justify personal actions in terms of their effect on others. Among the business values, we list *individual responsibility*. Stated as a business value, it stresses freedom to work for my own good with a conviction that doing my own work well will benefit others in the process. But individual responsibility, if taken in a narrow sense of self-interest alone, is inadequate as a basis of *ethical* responsibility. True responsibility is social; if I live in society I am accountable for the consequences of my actions as they affect others and society as a whole. Thus, even individual responsibility in a broader and truer sense links one to community and to social responsibility.

VALUES AND NORMS

The history of American business is a dynamic one. Thanks to this dynamism the people of the United States have enjoyed levels of prosperity unmatched by most other civilizations. The dynamism of American business is rooted in a number of important values. We have focused on three of them: freedom of the individual to pursue one's own goals, personal responsibility for one's own life, and growth/productivity. These values undergird the free enterprise system, but they find expression also in U.S. political democracy and the cultural ethos that has shaped life in the United States. To ignore the importance of these values and of the institutions that embody them would be blind and irresponsible. They form an integral part of any ethical questions about social responsibility.

Traditional Business Values and Norms

Freedom holds a place of incontestable importance in the American tradition. We take great pride in belonging to a free nation. Early American settlers came to this country because of the freedom of opportunity it offered; freedom to practice their own religious faith, freedom to own their own farm or trade, freedom to move on and upward in the pursuit of happiness. The Declaration of Independence declared that each individual has inalienable rights, rights that exist independently of any state. As the United States developed as a nation, its institutions became values in their own right. Political democracy, enshrined in the constitution, became valued as the means of guaranteeing political rights. Free enterprise and the market system became valued as embodying freedom of opportunity.[3]

Individual responsibility became a value closely linked to freedom of opportunity. Given freedom to pursue one's own ends, success in life was seen to depend on making good use of the opportunities this land provided. The Protestant work ethic stressed individual responsibility. The ethos of free enterprise, as articulated by Adam Smith, views acting out of self-interest as a legitimate way of exercising freedom to provide for oneself and to achieve success. Though he recognized the importance of civic virtue and benevolence, Smith accepted the fact that self-interest motivates humans. He believed that self-interest could be channeled to serve the good of all, since an individual's desire to make money by producing more would lead to more goods for all.[4] This stress on individual responsibility is closely related to a view of the state articulated by Thomas Jefferson and John Stuart Mill: a belief that a government is best that governs least—a government that leaves most responsibilities in life to the individual. This sense of individual responsibility carries over into international affairs as well. Each nation is deemed primarily responsible for its own interests, though the United States, especially in recent decades, has also viewed itself as the protector of the free world.

The third traditional business value could be stated in various ways, all of which are economic goals or objectives: growth, productivity, and prosperity. They represent concrete values or tests by which an economic system can be measured. Throughout its history the United States has generally fared quite well in realizing these values. It has done so, many would argue, because of free enterprise and the values that free enterprise encourages: hard work, risk-taking, innovation, and efficiency. Making profits is essential to achieving this prosperity. No economy can survive if its businesses, private or otherwise, lose money consistently. Profits used for new investment are essential to growth. The very drive to increase profits engendered the innovations and efforts that have moved our country forward. To limit freedom of opportunity is to suppress the force needed to achieve growth and prosperity. Freedom, then, in the economic sphere as well as in the political sphere, lies at the heart of these traditional American business values.

Social Values and Norms

For some Americans, faith in free enterprise and its values is so strong that they fear interference from any external influence or added norms. They believe that if free enterprise and the market system are permitted to follow their own course, the social goals that critics propose will be successfully realized. We question this faith in the autonomy of any economic system. Even writers like Michael Novak, who praise the values of democratic capitalism, acknowledge the need for moral virtue as a foundation for society. Thus, as Novak asserts, Adam Smith in his defense of free enterprise never stressed self-interest alone but acknowledged the necessity of sympathy and respect for others as fundamental for the good of society.[5] The values of free enterprise have never stood alone as expressive of U.S. culture. Social values (the dignity of every human person, a sense of community, justice, and equality) have prompted many important reforms in our economy; for example, the right of workers to form unions, regulation of monopolies, truth in advertising, and social security.

We acknowledge that many business leaders throughout U.S. history and in the present have incorporated social values into their perspective. But we perceive, as do many Americans, a great need for more ethical consciousness in today's society. This concern about ethics covers a broad spectrum of issues; for example, crime and violence, the breakdown of the family, and honesty in government. But our present concern lies with the world of business and corporations. Many business leaders, business periodicals, and business schools have acknowledged the need for inserting more ethical norms into decision making. In some instances specific scandals may have triggered this concern; for example, Ivan Boesky's dealings on Wall Street and charges of fraud in the defense industry (see Chapter Four). Whatever the immediate cause of such concern, the call for greater ethical consciousness has been sounded.

Some observers question the moral foundation of contemporary U.S. society. In *Habits of the Heart*, Robert Bellah and his co-authors raise this deeper concern. They believe that the balance between individualism and concern for the common good, a balance that once shaped America, has been lost. Individualism in different forms (freedom and self-fulfillment) now dominates our culture; a clear sense of the common good is missing.[6] We share this appraisal, and the social values we present may help to restore the balance.

Respect for the dignity of every person underlies all other social values. A person is an end and must never be treated merely as a means. Most people recognize that humans have a special value that we do not attribute to other things, so that humans ought to be treated with dignity. Society should seek, therefore, to encourage economic policies that promote human dignity and seek to challenge policies that may undermine that dignity. Respect for the dignity of others, however, means little if the basic needs of human life are not met. Without adequate food, no human being can live a dignified life or enjoy the rights of a free society. Without education and medical care, development of the person is impeded. We do not want to engage in a lengthy debate on whether basic needs constitute human rights.[7] We do assert, however, that society should *seek* to enable all its members to meet these needs as a base for a dignified human life. The opportunity for meaningful work is especially important, both as a means to meet other human needs and as a value in itself.

Community, which includes a sense of the common good, is intimately connected with human dignity.[8] Only with other people can individuals develop. We form governments and societies because of shared interests and goals—for example, safety and the exchange of goods—which constitute a common good. Translated into an ethical norm, community involves enabling all members of society to participate in political structures, but also to participate in the direction of economic organizations that deeply affect their lives. Those who belong to a community have some responsibility for the common good of the whole, and the whole includes those most in need. The broadest sense of community, moreover, would reach beyond national boundaries to include all members of the human family. But again, the value of community is best achieved when members of society are not simply "cared for" but able to work with others in fulfilling their own needs and the common needs of society.

Justice is the third social value we wish to highlight. Justice means rendering to others what is due to them. Justice in all its forms grows out of the values of human dignity and community.[9] Commutative justice calls for fairness in dealing with others. False advertising, cheating on contracts, and racial or sexual discrimination are all violations of this form of justice, which deals with relations between different parties. Distributive justice calls for an equitable distribution of income, wealth, and power. Responsibility for this form of justice falls chiefly on the state; for example, in determining the burden of taxes and the benefits of social security, or in assuring fairness in elections. But distributive justice also comes into play in corporate decisions determining executive salaries in relation to the salaries of subordinates or workers (see Chapter Three). Social justice concerns itself with organizing society *so that* all can participate fairly and benefit equitably. Laws and Supreme Court decisions aimed at eliminating racial segregation are expressions of social justice. Laws protecting the environment also deal with social justice. Human dignity calls for respect for others; community gives expression to concern for others and for the common good. Justice calls for equity and fairness toward all members of society.

Comparing the Two Sets of Values

Basically, everyone can agree with both lists of values, since values are generally universal. We all want people to be treated with dignity and to be able to meet their basic needs; we all want freedom. A sense of community and a sense of responsibility for oneself are both needed. We want a just, equitable society, but we do not want to share equally in poverty; we want a productive society, one that encourages innovation and a drive for achievement.

Problems arise, however, when it comes time to act upon the values—when the values are translated into norms for judging policies and implementing them. At that point conflicts arise because some values are stressed more than others. Stress on a particular value often reflects what one thinks should be the greatest concern of society. The social values are clearly altruistic, emphasizing concern for the "other" and most especially for those who are poor and powerless. Many who stress these social values see traditional business values as too individualistic, too materialistic, and too insensitive to the needs of others. The American business values, on the other hand, focus on the precious gift of freedom and on an ethic of responsibility for oneself. Many who stress these values fear they are being undermined by utopian do-gooders and social activists who stress state intervention.

Conflicts may especially arise between the priorities and perceived implications of these two sets of values. Differences in stress suggest that while all may accept both sets of values, priorities may differ. Those who stress the social side tend to view the fulfillment of these values as more urgent and important. Thus, for example, they may stress meeting human needs as more important than maximization of profits, the encouragement of consumer buying, and increases in military spending. Those, on the other hand, who stress the individual value of freedom may see its protection—politically, economically, militarily—as most important.

The social-value emphasis on meeting human needs is also perceived by many who value American freedom to imply greater state intervention. Many conservatives criticized the U.S. Catholic bishops' letter on the U.S. economy for relying too much on government action.[10] They believe that the government already spends too much on welfare and is too involved in regulating business, and with poor results. So they would view calls for even greater government involvement in the economy—for example, to reduce unemployment—as misguided and harmful. Indeed, some government legislation has proved counterproductive.

Clearly some balance is needed between government responsibility and responsibilities assumed by individuals or associations. At times the state must intervene to protect the common good. But it should not take over responsibilities that can be dealt with better by the private sector and smaller units of society. This position, however, puts greater responsibility on corporations. The more that corporations can do to create jobs, produce safe products, advertise honestly, protect the environment, and in general, promote the common good, the less government involvement will be needed.

Both sets of values, we believe, are essential to actions and policies regarding issues of social responsibility. A corporation that fails to be productive, that engenders losses rather than profits, and therefore fails at its primary objectives, will not survive. If it does not survive, society will lose the social benefits it contributes, including jobs and products. When we stress the social values and questions they engender, we do so not out of neglect or unconcern for traditional business values but because we wish to raise consciousness about issues that are often overlooked from a purely business perspective. However, we do not want to urge the better at the cost of sacrificing what is already good. Each set of values is needed as a balance and challenge to the other.

THE ISSUE OF SOCIAL RESPONSIBILITY

One ethical issue concerns what moral values and norms should be applied to a study of large corporations and the U.S. system. This application assumes some responsibility by the members of society for the common good of society as a whole. But that raises a second important issue: Where does responsibility lie for changing practices and structures that are deemed unethical or contrary to social values?

The Individual

An individual or group of individuals must ultimately be responsible for decisions that involve ethical issues. How to assess my own or others' responsibility requires some discernment. One way of discerning responsibility would be to imagine concentric circles corresponding to different degrees of responsibility. The inner circle would involve instances of primary responsibility. While primary responsibility suggests proximity ("charity begins at home"), it relates more to an individual's roles or positions in life. If I am a worker, I have a clear responsibility to carry out the work I agreed to do. If I am a manager, I have a responsibility to honor contracts my company has made. If I am a parent, I have a duty to care for my children. Even at this first level responsibilities may at times conflict, as with conflicts between social and business values. Rushing a sick child to the hospital takes priority over completing a job I agreed to complete on a given day.

The next circle broadens the areas of responsibility. (We offer these circles only as an aid; they do not represent neatly divided, clearly distinguished spheres. We recognize that use of such circles in any systematic ethics would require more work in defining phrases like "primary" or "direct" responsibility.) This circle includes situations that may not be defined by my position or role but that bear upon it. As a worker, I bear some responsibility for my co-workers; for example, to report unfair treatment or to support union efforts. As a parent, I bear some responsibility for challenging racial discrimination in my neighborhood or supporting the school my children attend.

In the broadest circle of relations lie problems of the city, country, and world. But how can one speak of personal responsibility for the problems of society or the world? Certainly I cannot be held responsible for hunger in Africa, for sexual discrimination, or for pollution, unless I personally helped cause the hunger, discriminated against women, or dumped waste in some river. If I define responsibility only in terms of strict obligations or not deliberately harming others, my sense of responsibility will not project beyond the inner circles. A broader sense of responsibility comes only with acceptance of, and a commitment to, the social values enunciated earlier. If I am not concerned about the dignity of all persons, and feel no commitment to peace and justice, my level of responsibility will remain minimal.

If I sincerely desire to do what I can to create structures that promote human dignity, to contribute to the common good, and to ensure justice, discernment will still be needed. I cannot take on all the problems of the world, and I need to weigh my other duties and the possible risks that my action might involve. Some practical questions might serve as partial guidelines in determining responsibility. How serious is the potential harm or injustice which may result from my action or failure to act? How certain am I that the harm is likely to occur? What difference will *my* contribution make? Will others act if I do not? If I am a secretary aware that my employer is engaged in fraud, my responsibility looms much larger than for a customer who suspects the fraud. If I am an executive with a multinational firm operating in South Africa, my responsibility for my company's influence on apartheid becomes greater than that of a concerned citizen. At every level of responsibility, but most especially in the outer circles, the degree of concern I experience will likely prove more decisive than the degree of strict obligation to which I may be bound.

Government

The state has some responsibility for the common good of its citizens. The state provides national defense and police protection; it passes laws to protect human rights. We expect it to provide certain services and resources; for example, sewage disposal, roads, parks, and libraries. But how far government responsibility should extend is the subject of much dispute. In recent decades in the United States we have come to expect a number of "entitlements," for example, social security and some covering of medical expenses. Corporations have become the object of considerable regulation. The less the state needs to intervene the better, but this depends upon members of society acting ethically and respecting others. Ethical behavior and social responsibility on the part of corporations will diminish the need for government action.

The government has a clear responsibility to intervene to rectify long-standing injustices. To determine other justifications for state intervention, we need to weigh in each case the positive and negative effects of government action. But here a conflict between social and business values often arises. In Chapter Four, on "Corporations and the Government," we take up some of these conflicts; for example, government regulations concerning business. Numerous other examples could be added, such as how much, or in what way, the government should be involved in dealing with the problem of unemployment. The government, because of its duty to promote the common good, is certainly an important agent of social responsibility whatever disputes may arise concerning the applications of its duty.

The Corporation

To what extent should corporations accept, or be held to, social responsibility? If we attempted first to resolve all the theoretical disputes about the nature and purpose of corporations, efforts to answer this question would become difficult or stymied. Instead we will state briefly our position and arguments in order to reach some guidelines for action. Some have questioned whether corporations as such can be considered "persons" in any real sense, so that ethics applies to them.[11] It may be more appropriate to fix final responsibility for corporate actions on persons within the corporation rather than on the corporation itself. But we do speak of corporations in personal terms. They are said to *plan* a new line of products, to *consider* relocating a plant and to *block* takeover attempts. They are held legally and morally responsible for defective products, for pollution, for failure to honor contracts, and so forth. At times personal responsibility for failure or success may be "shared" by many within the corporation; at other times circumstances beyond anyone's control or foresight may be the cause. This holds true also for the individual responsibility discussed earlier.

Milton Friedman, years ago, raised another much-disputed question: Should corporations accept the demand of social responsibility?[12] Friedman argued that they should not, that to accept such responsibility would in fact be unethical. He argued as follows. Corporate executives are employees of owners. While they are expected to conform to the basic rules of society, their purpose and primary responsibility is to make as much money as possible for their investors. For corporate executives to go beyond this and, for example, to keep prices down to help check inflation, would be to misuse the owners' money and to make themselves into unauthorized, unelected public officials.

Friedman's position, however, involves assumptions that have been challenged on several counts.[13] Corporate managers are expected to run the business well and to return a profit. But investment does not carry a promissory note that requires managers to maximize profits in whatever way they can and to disregard any higher needs of society. Moreover, investors can withdraw their investment if they feel a company is inefficient and not achieving a desired return. Neither can it be shown that corporate managers are simply agents for investors without responsibilities to other groups in society, any more than parents could be said to have responsibilities only to their children. Society certainly views corporations as legally and morally responsible for their products, as liability cases demonstrate; to their locale, as pollution charges show; and to their employees. Moreover, the alternative to viewing corporations as socially and morally responsible would be to treat them as irresponsible mechanisms *requiring* social and governmental control.[14]

We, along with most corporate leaders, believe that the correct issue is not *whether* corporations should be socially and morally responsible, but *when* and *to what extent* they should accept such responsibility. Just as individuals are involved in different circles of relationships, with corresponding degrees of responsibility, so also can corporate responsibility be viewed in terms of similar circles (see Figure 2–2). The inner circle of direct responsibility involves not only investors, but customers and employees as well. The line between the first and second circles of responsibility cannot always be clearly drawn. By including suppliers, environment, and the company's locale in the second circle, and by speaking of secondary responsibility, we do not mean to exclude important instances of direct moral responsibility. Corporations may have a greater responsibility toward their employees than to suppliers, but not cheating suppliers is certainly a direct moral responsibility. Similarly, protection of the environment in general may be a secondary responsibility, but avoiding deliberate pollution of the environment bears directly on the corporation. The outer circle comprises problems faced in the country or world as whole.

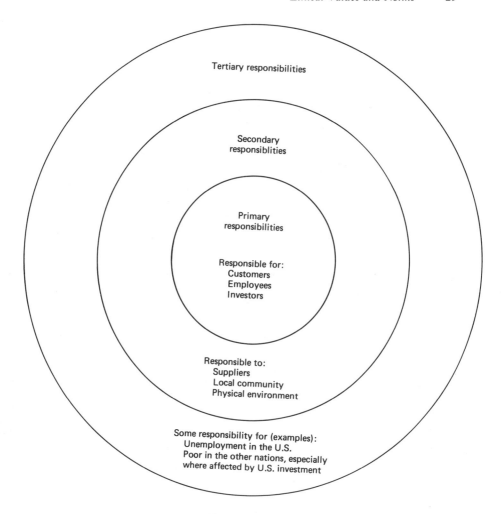

Tertiary responsibilities

Secondary
responsiblities

Primary
responsibilities

Responsible for:
Customers
Employees
Investors

Responsible to:
Suppliers
Local community
Physical environment

Some responsibility for (examples):
Unemployment in the U.S.
Poor in the other nations, especially
where affected by U.S. investment

FIGURE 2-2   Responsibilities of the Corporation

We can agree with Friedman that the purpose or primary goal of business corporations is not to solve national and world problems. When a firm contributes funds to a university, it may do so out of civic-mindedness or to increase its own pool of future executives. While its action can certainly be judged socially responsible, it is not morally obligated to contribute to the university. When Control Data developed teaching hardware and software for prisoners, or when Levi Straus kept open unprofitable plants in a poverty section of San Francisco, they were not obligated to do so, and they could not have done so if they were not already successful. On the other hand, we believe that corporations have indirect responsibilities regarding the influence of their hiring policies on minorities and the poor, the effect of their advertising on peoples' values, and the effect of their investments in a Third World country.

Corporations are made up of individuals, and it is the individuals who make the decisions. A corporation's ethics are heavily influenced by its managers and its chief executive officer. If good ethics and a sense of social responsibility are encouraged over a period of time, they will shape the climate of the organization. That climate will undoubtedly already recognize the traditional businesss values of freedom of the individual, individual responsibility, and growth or productivity. The extent to which its managers also recognize the social values of the dignity of the person, community and justice will determine the level of ethics within the corporation.

Adding urgency is the recognition that, precisely because of the corporation's large impact and its special expertise, it has greater responsibilities than do individuals. Putting it another way: We should expect a higher level of ethical behavior and a greater sense of social responsibility from corporations than we do of individuals. Ethically conscious individuals can do much good; ethically oriented corporations can multiply the good. Deviant and callous individuals cause harm; deviant and callous corporations generate far greater harm.

RESPONSIBILITY WITHIN CORPORATIONS

We have examined the norms (see Figure 2-1) by which actions and policies of the corporations may be ethically assessed. The next question is: Where does the responsibility rest for making decisions within the corporation? How are these decisions made and who makes them? How do we account for such widely disparate ethical behavior among different corporations? Is a better system of accountability needed? Following are three examples of how firms, faced with much the same type of evidence of wrongdoing among their own executives, reacted to that evidence.

Three Different Responses to Unethical Activities

During the 1970s, under pressure, a large number of U.S. corporations confessed to previously undisclosed and "improper" payments to political figures and parties both overseas and at home. Most of the "contributions" to U.S. politicians and political parties were illegal, as were many of the foreign payments. Some of these payments involved extortion. Most were an attempt to seek special privilege, and hence were bribes. Among the firms, which were each involved in more than $10 million worth of off-the-books political payments, were Gulf Oil, Lockheed, and Northrup. The corporation's board of directors bears ultimate responsibility in such cases; each of these boards handled the situation differently.

When evidence of the ethically questionable behavior became public, Gulf Oil set up a special committee of its board of directors to investigate, under the chairmanship of experienced outside director John McCloy.[15] When the report was presented, chief executive officer (CEO) Bob R. Dorsey claimed that he knew nothing of the illegal payments. The board decided that he either did know, or he did not. The noted that if he did, he was responsible for not preventing the payments. If he did not know, as CEO it was his responsibility to have known. In either case he was fully responsible for Gulf's activities. After a long meeting at which this ethically difficult problem was thoroughly discussed, the board fired the chief lobbyist, Claude Wild, and CEO Bob Dorsey. Gulf Oil's board did a thorough and conscientious job of investigating, evaluating, and attempting to remedy the situation.

Bribery is not only illegal, it is also unethical. It is unjust since it tries to influence an individual to extend special favors, not based on the merits of the case, but because the purchaser, broker or government agent receives some personal favor. Bribery violates the public or common good because it creates a climate of dishonesty. It also lowers productivity (a business value) by adding to costs.

Carl Kotchian was president and CEO of Lockheed Aircraft Co. when Lockheed acknowledged its overseas payments.[16] A a result of the revelations, the former Prime Minister of Japan, Kukeo Tanaka was arrested and eventually convicted of taking bribes from Lockheed. Tanaka's successor as Prime Minister was ousted because he was accused of complicity. In the Netherlands, Prince Bernhard was forced to resign from numerous governmental positions as a result of taking payment from Lockheed to facilitate sale of aircraft to the Dutch government. Carl Kotchian resigned under pressure of the board, but he continued to receive his full salary. Lockheed's board evidently considered the public dismissal to be sufficient punishment; cutting off or reducing Kotchian's salary was considered too severe. Perhaps the board reasoned that, since the bribery was for the sake of the corporation and not for personal gain, the penalty should not be too severe. Bribery is ethically wrong for the reasons given earlier. At Lockheed, however, the signals as to how wrong it was were at best mixed. In this case, also, Lockheed acted unjustly in paying the bribes, and added to its costs at the same time.

Northrup Corporation, another aircraft manufacturer, also paid about $30 million in "questionable overseas payments" in an attempt to gain overseas orders.[17] Thomas V. Jones was chairman and CEO of Northrup and denied any guilt. Northrup's board did nothing to remove or even penalize Jones or any other corporate officers. So a group of shareholders, along with the Securities and Exchange Commission, filed suit against Northrup asking the firm and its officers to return some of the millions of dollars that were misspent. Northrup and its officers settled with a consent decree. The consent decree required (1) new outside directors to constitute a majority of the board, (2) audit and nominating committees of the board to be composed of all outside directors and (3) that Jones step aside as president within 18 months. What the *board* had failed to do, to penalize Jones and to set up structures to lessen the chance of such a thing happening again, the courts were forced to do. Jones stepped aside as president. However, a few months later, the board reelected Jones as chairman and CEO of Northrup. While the literal requirements of the consent decree were met, its intent was circumvented by the board's action. Moreover, it signaled to Northrup's managers that they might continue to use such methods in selling military equipment, as long as they were not caught. Northrup and its board of directors did not take a stand on how such bribery was to be prevented. They never acknowledged that such bribery violated the norms of justice, the common good, and productivity, norms stemming from both social and business values.

These three contrasting cases focus our attention on ways of evaluating the actions of a chief executive officer and the values of the firm. They show how a corporation is influenced in its ethical climate at the highest level—board, CEO, and top management. Gulf, Lockheed, and Northrup reacted quite differently to much the same information on their executives' unethical and illegal payments of millions of dollars to politicians. To better understand why, let us examine the structure of the corporation, the role of its managers and directors, and how decisions are made in the corporation.

Structure and Decision Making

The theory as to who bears responsibility in the corporation, and what is actually the case, are quite different. In theory and in law, shareholders of the large publicly held corporation are the owners, so the board of directors and management are responsible to them. Shareholders elect individuals to the board of directors, and board members in turn select the chief executive officer (CEO) of the firm (see Figure 2–3). The CEO is then immediately responsible to the board of directors, and is charged with looking to the long-term best interests of the shareholders.

In practice, shareholders elect the members of the board of directors, but they have little choice in the selection of candidates. For example, if GE has three directors to be elected this year, shareholders are presented with only three candidates. The only choice is whether to vote or not to vote; the candidates are certain to be elected. The candidates are nominated by the board itself, and are most often suggested by the chief executive officer. At best, a nominating committee made up of outside directors presents the candidates to the shareholders. So the board perpetuates itself. The election of directors appears all too much like elections in the U.S.S.R. "Elections" are held, but there is only one candidate for each position. Moreover, in practice shareholders have shown little interest in the internal decisions of the firm; they seem content as long as they receive what they consider to be sufficient dividends or return on investment.

The board of directors thus has ultimate authority and responsibility for what happens within the corporation. The president of the firm is a member

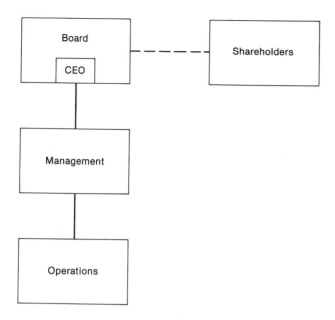

FIGURE 2-3 Corporate Responsibility and Accountability

of the board. Generally, several other major executives of the firm are also members of the board. In U.S. firms, the chairperson of the board is generally chief executive officer of the corporation. We think there is a conflict of interest here. We believe that changes in the composition and selection of the board are needed to avoid the potential injustices stemming from that conflict of interest. The size of the board varies, as does the number of full-time employees of the corporation (*insiders*) who are on the board (see Figure 2–4). *Outsiders* are directors who are not in the employ of the firm. Note that one-half of the Goodyear board are insiders, while the CEO is the only insider on the Merck board.

The principal responsibilities of the board of directors are: (1) select, and, when necessary, dismiss the chief executive officer of the firm and (2) approve major policies of the firm. This last item would include new products, acquisitions, and major expenditures. In the Gulf, Lockheed, and Northrup cases cited earlier, both of these major responsibilities were involved. Each corporation was guilty of illegal and unethical behavior. It was the responsibility of the board to assess the CEO's involvement and responsibility for that behavior. Each board reacted to the behavior differently. Gulf acted ethically and responsibly and sent clear signals to corporate officers that ethical behavior was important. During this same period the board of American Airlines reacted with as much integrity as did Gulf's board: They fired their CEO after it was disclosed that the firm had illegally contributed to the Republican Committee to Reelect President Nixon. 3M and several other firms also acted ethically

FIGURE 2-4   **Composition of Selected Boards of Directors**

CORPORATION	NUMBER ON BOARD	INSIDERS*	OUTSIDERS
Amoco	17	7	10
General Mills	17	5	12
Coca-Cola	14	2	12
Ford Motor	18	9	9
General Electric	16	3	13
General Motors	19	7	12
IBM	18	7	11
Merck & Co., Inc.	15	1	14
Goodyear	16	8	8
Proctor & Gamble	16	7	9
Raytheon	13	4	9

*Insiders often include retired company executives.
SOURCE: 1986 Company Proxy Statements and Annual Reports

in the face of similar information. On the other hand, a number of other boards, like Northrup, chose to ignore the information, and they thus damaged the ethical climate of their firms.

In order for the board to do its job, it must have all the relevant information. But the CEO, as chairperson of the board, generally determines what issues go on the agenda of the board meeting and what supporting information goes to the board. Even the best-intentioned CEO is going to have his or her own bias as to which items should be discussed and what information to provide to the board. Moreover, most CEOs would prefer that the board meeting go smoothly, both for their own credibility and to enable the firm to have a favorable image among lenders. Hence another conflict of interest for the CEO.

Nevertheless, it is the responsibility of board members to raise critical questions so they can fulfill their own ethical responsibilities. If board members suspect that important information is lacking, they have a responsibility to ask for it. Even more, they have a responsibility to read background materials and to be prepared to ask relevant questions. Some board members wait for the meeting to read materials. When they do not sufficiently prepare for the meeting, they shirk their responsibilities.

Boards of directors have but a mediocre record of bringing about ethical accountability among top management in the corporation. Part of the difficulty is a lack of understanding as to whom top managment and boards are accountable. Traditionally we have understood that CEOs are responsible to their board, and that boards are responsible to the long-term interests of shareholders. This old theory is neither accurate nor realistic. Over the last generation that view of responsibility has been expanded to include the additional stakeholders (or constituencies) of the firm; for example, customers, employees, suppliers, the local community, and the physical environment. Roger Smith, CEO of General Motors, put it well:

> In discussion of corporate management nowadays, we often find the word "stewardship." And with good reason. Certainly, a corporation must serve the interests of its customers, employees and shareholders. But that is not enough. In the cities and towns where its facilities are located, it must also act with a sense of responsibility for the natural environment, for the economic health of the country, and ultimately, for the welfare of future generations.[18]

This broad sense of responsibility is appropriate. It acknowledges the social values of community and the dignity of each person. But how effective are company boards in exercising this stewardship? Is there any person or group that can call a board to account? In a word, generally not. Unless there is a flagrant violation of duty, where shareholders seek to oust the board or take directors to court—and such instances are rare—the board is relatively autonomous. Shareholders and citizens must rely on the knowledge, experience, and integrity of the board members themselves to exercise faithfully their responsibilities. In practice, board members are responsible largely to themselves, in spite of the demands of society for greater accountability. So, when board members are conscientious and ethical, the firm reflects those values. However, in some cases board members are too busy to do adequate homework, or they are personally too close to the CEO. They leave the CEO to manage without oversight, and the firm can then more easily slip into actions that are short-sighted and unethical. These problems are compounded when board members themselves are unconcerned or, more rarely, outright immoral.

If accountability is to be held, board members and corporate executives must acknowledge the conflict of interest created by having officers of a firm serve on their own board. It is difficult for a vice president to question a proposal made by the CEO, from whom he will be obtaining his own performance appraisal. Moreover, when the CEO is chair of the very group that oversees her own actions, that also presents a conflict of interest. And it makes it more difficult for the board to perform its function objectively and justly. During the last decade, suggestions to make the board more accountable have received considerable attention: (1) all board members, except for the CEO, should be outsiders (not in the employ of the firm) and (2) the chairperson of the board should not be the CEO, and should also be an outsider.[19] These initiatives are intended to lessen the conflict of interest, and to encourage more responsible governance of the corporation. Outside board members are less likely to be biased by the CEO when that CEO presents a proposal to the board. As outsiders, if they do not think the proposal is wise, they can say so more easily. Similarly, the chairperson of the board sets the agenda, determines which items come up and the time allocated to each, and directs the discussion. This is a critical position, and greater objectivity is achieved when the CEO is not the chairperson. Nevertheless, most U.S. firms have a large number of insiders on their boards, and generally the chairperson of the board is also the CEO.

SUMMARY AND CONCLUSIONS

We have addressed three related issues in this chapter: (1) the values and norms we believe should enter into decisions made by conscientious corporations (2) the different agents who should exercise social responsibility, and the levels or circles of their responsibility and (3) the exercise of responsibility by board members of corporations. On the first issue, we have not attempted to construct a model for ethical decision making, but we have argued that social values as well as traditional business values should enter into corporate decisions. For a set of questions derived from both sets of values, see Figure 2-5. On the second issue, we have stated that individuals, the government, and corporations all have ethical duties pertaining to social responsibility. Throughout the book we will note ways in which each of these agents can or should exercise responsibility. The circles of responsibility cannot be sharply separated, but they may serve as a practical guide. On the third issue, we have discussed with some specific examples how boards operate, and we have suggested ways in which boards might become more accountable. To this summary we add some concluding reflections.

A basic premise of the social values we have enunciated is that we ought to be concerned about the effect of our actions and policies on others. This does not deny the fact that people act often for their own self-interest. But we believe that truly ethical judgments also involve concern for doing the right thing and weighing how personal actions will affect others.

FIGURE 2-5   Specification of Ethical Norms

Does the *atmosphere* of the firm and this *policy* or *act* of a manager respect:

A. FREEDOM OF THE INDIVIDUAL
  • Does it encourage freedom?

B. INDIVIDUAL RESPONSIBILITY
  • Will it encourage or discourage personal responsibility?

C. GROWTH AND PRODUCTIVITY
  • Will it encourage growth and productivity?

D. DIGNITY OF THE HUMAN PERSON
  • Does it promote human dignity?

E. COMMUNITY AND COMMON GOOD
  • Does it take into consideration its effect on other individuals, other groups, and society as a whole?

F. JUSTICE
  • Does it embody fairness and equity for all?

We recognize that asking what is "right" or "what is best" does not always lead to conclusive answers. Ethically motivated persons may agree in condemning fraud but disagree on the social benefits of some regulation on pollution, given its cost. On some issues, we may even end up with what one moral philosopher calls "tied verdicts," in which careful weighing of evidence does not point clearly in any one direction.[20] We do not expect readers to agree with all the analys:.s or conclusions stated in this book. But we do hope that readers will recognize the importance of the issues and be willing to confront their ethical dimensions.

We reaffirm that social values and business values are both essential to ethical decisions and the exercise of social responsibility. Social values that go beyond strict justice are needed to achieve a just and good society. Just as a marriage has little chance of success if each partner only agrees to do what he or she *must* do, so also a society whose members draw the line at strict obligations will not be very humane. A society, on the other hand, that places undue moral expectations on one sector of society (for example, expecting corporations to make social responsibility a higher priority than productivity) may only harm itself. The tension between social and business values is real. We believe that the norms of profitability and productivity are not sufficient to promote human dignity and justice. We believe that no society can prosper in a fully human way unless altruism and *civitas* (a sense of public responsibility) are strongly in evidence. We believe that a greater priority should be given by society to meeting basic human needs than to improving the living standards of the already affluent. But we also realize that pure altrism and complete justice are ideals which can never be fully realized, and that to destroy or significantly undermine the political and economic freedoms which we have would lead to a less just society. We want the best of both worlds (social values and business values). We are admittedly reformist, working for the best approximations of justice we can achieve.

DISCUSSION QUESTIONS

2.1 Do traditional business values generally support social values? Give examples where they do. Give examples of where they conflict.

2.2 Is freedom the most important value for Americans? Would most Americans explain it as we do in Figure 2–1?

2.3 How are the values of individual responsibility and those of growth and productivity related?

2.4 Do Adam Smith and other defenders of traditional business values see the need for social values? How so?

2.5 Are the traditional business values more important than social values for most Americans? What is the effect of this? Give examples.

2.6 What is the common good? Is it an important notion? Do people you know have a sense of the common good?

2.7 Is justice attained at the expense of growth? Or is growth better attained when justice is present? Give examples.

2.8 Describe the sort of individual responsibilities that are primary, according to our outline. Give examples of responsibilities that are secondary.

2.9 How can ethical initiatives of the firm lessen the need for government regulation?

2.10 Can we expect a higher standard of ethical behavior of corporations than of individuals? Why?

2.11 Did Gulf's board act ethically? Which norms are most helpful here? Assess the actions of Lockheed's board. Assess the actions of Northrup's board, according to the norms in Figure 2–1.

2.12 Are board members elected? Describe the process.

2.13 Outline the principal ethical responsibilities of a member of a corporate board.

2.14 Explain what General Motor's CEO Roger Smith means by stewardship.

2.15 Give some suggestions to make corporate boards more accountable to all stakeholders. Are these suggestions practical?

NOTES

[1]See Gerald F. Cavanagh, *American Business Values* (Englewood Cliffs, N.J.: Prentice Hall, 1984), Chapter Five.

[2]For an ethical model using these three concepts (rights, utility, justice) which correspond roughly to points in each set of the values presented in our figure, see Cavanagh, *American Business Values*, pp. 129–35. For a somewhat similar table of values, contrasting traditional ideology, and a new ideology, see George Cabot Lodge, "Managerial Implications of Ideolgical Change," in *The Ethics of Corporate Conduct*, Clarence C. Walton, ed. (Englewood Cliffs, N.J.: Prentice Hall, 1977), p. 81.

[3]For a strong defense of the ethos and institutions of American democratic capitalism confer Michael Novak, *The Spirit of Democratic Capitalism* (New York: Simon & Schuster, 1982) and *Freedom with Justice* (San Francisco: Harper & Row, 1984). Novak not only defends the U.S. system but argues that it embodies Christian social values.

[4]Adam Smith, *An Inquiry into the Nature and Causes of the Wealth of Nations* (New York: Modern Library, n.d.), pp. 14, 423. See also Novak, *The Spirit of Democratic Capitalism*, pp. 77–80, 145–49.

[5]Michael Novak, *Freedom with Justice*, pp. 8–9, 63.

[6]Robert Bellah et al., *Habits of the Heart* (Berkeley, CA.: University of California, 1985), Chapter Six on "Individualism."

[7]For a discussion of the controversy over the inclusion of human needs as "rights" confer David Hollenbach, *Claims in Conflict* (New York: Paulist, 1979).

[8]The social values we propose echo the ethical norms expressed by the U.S. Catholic Bishops in their pastoral letter "Economic Justice for All: Catholic Social teaching and the U.S. Economy," published in *Origins*, November 26, 1986, vol. 16, no. 24. The link between human dignity and community is noted in paragraph 14. If the phrasing of the social values follows Catholic social thought, we believe the content of these values also reflects much of the Judaeo-Christian and humanistic heritage which has influenced American culture. Hence we have not hesitated to express these values as non-doctrinaire social values.

[9]For a fuller description of the forms of justice (commutative, social, distributive) see Hollenbach, *Claims in Conflict*, pp. 145–55.

[10]For summaries of reactions to one of the earlier versions of the Catholic Bishops' letter, see *The Religion & Society Report*, March 1985, and *Commonweal*'s editorial "Shortchanging the Pastoral", November 30, 1984, pp. 643–44. Concern about the danger of "statism" was voiced by some Catholic lay men and women in their letter *Toward the Future* published just prior to

the Bishops' first draft (New York: Lay Commission on Catholic Social Teaching and the U.S. Economy, 1984).

[11]Manuel G. Valasquez, "Why Corporations Are Not Morally Responsible for Anything They Do," in *Business & Professional Ethics Journal*, Spring 1983, vol. 2, n. 3. But in response, see Thomas Donaldson, *Corporations and Morality* (Englewood Cliffs, N.J.: Prentice Hall, 1982), Chapters 1–2.

[12]Milton Friedman, "The Social Responsibility of Business is to Increase Profits," in *Business Ethics, Readings and Cases in Corporate Morality*, W. Michael Hoffman and Jennifer Mills Moore, eds. (New York: McGraw-Hill, 1984), pp. 126–31. See also Friedman, *Capitalism and Freedom* (Chicago: University of Chicago, 1962).

[13]See Christopher Stone's response to Friedman, "Why Shouldn't Corporations Be Socially Responsible"? in *Business Ethics*, pp. 132–36, and his fuller study, *Where the Law Ends* (New York: Harper & Row, 1975). See also Donaldson, *Corporations and Morality*, Chapter 2.

[14]Donaldson, *Corporations and Morality*, p. 18.

[15]"Gulf: Its Troubles Get Deeper," *New York Times*, January 4, 1976, p. E1 and 11.

[16]For the CEO's position, see A. Carl Kotchian, "The Payoff: Lockheed's 70-Day Mission to Tokyo," *Saturday Review*, July 9, 1977, pp. 6–22.

[17]For a summary of the data, see S. Prakash Sethi, "Northrup Corporation, Los Angeles," *Up Against the Corporate Wall*, (Englewood Cliffs, N.J.: Prentice Hall, 1982), pp. 86–96.

[18]Roger B. Smith, "Humanities and Business: The Twain Shall Meet—But How?" Address at Conference on the Humanities and Careers in Business, Northwestern University, May 21, 1984. p. 1.

[19]Harold Williams, when he was chairperson of the Securities and Exchange Commission, 1976–80, made these suggestions. His intention was to encourage voluntary actions on the part of business firms in order to prevent government regulation. See, for example, his "The Role of the Director in Corporate Accountability" address to the Economic Club of Detroit, May 1, 1978; "Audit Committees—The Public Sector's View," *Journal of Accountancy*, September 1977, pp. 71–74; and "When Profits are Illusions," *Across the Board*, June 1978, pp. 71–75.

[20]Garth Hallett, *Reason and Right* (Notre Dame, IN.: University of Notre Dame, 1984), pp. 44–47.

Chapter Three
WORK AND JOB SATISFACTION

Few activities of men and women take more time and attention than their work. Work has its own reward: the thrill of mastery of a skill and the achievement of a task. Through work, people know personal success and find a measure of their own self-worth. Work also has an external reward—the paycheck. For most people the paycheck is essential, for paying their bills and to support their families. Through work one meets friends and can rise to the limit of one's abilities. So work can provide both joy and frustration.

Work is necessary; it is a part of being human. The work ethic is still strong in the United States, and we look down on people who do not work, are drifters, and do not contribute to society. Our religious heritage supports the importance of each person working. In recent years work has become physically easier with the introduction of labor-saving equipment.

Workers and managers who are not interested in their work and do not enjoy their work soon find it to be tiresome, discouraging, and frustrating. This results in a dread of going to work, a lack of interest in it, poor relations with others on the job, and even in physical ailments for the individual. Being able to support self and family contributes to a person's sense of being worthwhile, productive, and valuable. The job can provide integrity and a chance to succeed.

Consider the opposite. Unemployment brings idleness, loss of skills, plummeting morale, and can even result in family breakup and the decay of neighborhoods and even of entire cities. High unemployment contributes to high death rates, cardiovascular disease, alcoholism, drug addiction, suicides and homicides, mental illnesses, child abuse, infant mortality, crime, and imprisonment.

Unemployment remains an immense problem in the United States. Even though the national unemployment rate has decreased, the official figures do not take into account people so discouraged that they have stopped looking for work. Job creation is therefore important, because work contributes so much to the dignity of the human person. National unemployment should therefore be a factor in corporate planning, also. The Catholic bishops discussed the problem of unemployment in their *Catholic Social Teaching and the U.S. Economy.*[1] But we will not explicitly treat unemployment here.

Dissatisfaction with work hurts both the individual and the company. If workers are alienated from their work and are merely putting in time, the corporation will suffer. Through lower productivity and efficiency, lower quality goods and services will be produced, and the firm will lose out to competitors. Many U.S. businesses have experienced this. This chapter examines the importance of work in an individual's life. It also views the successes and failures of some firms that try to enlist the best efforts of workers and managers in their enterprises.

IMPORTANCE OF A JOB

The U.S. economy has produced a net increase of more than 30 million new jobs in the last 20 years.[2] The majority of new jobs have gone to women, as increasing numbers entered the workplace in the last two decades. While 53 percent of these new jobs were created in firms of fewer than 100 workers, the largest total number of employees still work for large corporations.[3] When a successful small firm grows to become a large corporation, it faces increasing alienation among workers. The challenge becomes how to encourage high motivation and job commitment after the founder loses influence due to the increasing size of the firm.

People who work for large business firms often feel that their best talents are not being properly used in the workplace. Their perceptions are often accurate. Those who do simple, repetitive tasks feel less involved with their work, less concern for the quality of the product, and less responsibility for their job. This alienation has been documented often over the decades.

Listen to several people who perform a variety of unskilled and semi-skilled work in large U.S. firms.

Jim Grayson, spot welder at a Ford plant outside Chicago: "You can work next to a guy for months without even knowing his name. One thing, you're too busy to talk. Can't hear. (Laughs). You have to holler in his ear. . .They put that trim in, they call it. The paint and all those little pretties that you pay for. Whenever we make a mistake, we always say, 'Don't worry about it, some dingaling'll buy it.' (Laughs.)"

Phil Stallings works at the same plant: "I don't understand how come more guys don't flip. Because you're nothing more than a machine when you hit this type of thing. They give better care to that machine than they will to you."

Mike Lefevre, a steelworker near Chicago: "You can't take pride any more. . . It's hard to take pride in a bridge you're never gonna cross, in a door you're never gonna open. You're mass-producing things and you never see the end result of it. I worked for a trucker one time. And I got this tiny satisfaction when I loaded a truck. At least I could see the truck depart loaded. In a steel mill, forget it. You don't see where nothing goes."[4]

William Flack works on a line assembling home appliances in a General Electric Hotpoint plant in Chicago:

It's just a job, because there's really nothing to it. Place the motor. Put the housing on, tighten it. A twelve-year-old could do it. It's very easy. . .I'm gonna look for a job somewhere else.

The attitude of the blue collar worker is summed up by Art Lewis, a union officer at the plant:

They don't feel a part of this operation. They don't get enough responsibility. In other words, they're just like robots, just like a machine. You come in, and you put a screw in. You do this constantly, day after day. I think there should be more informative meetings between the company and the people. I mean assembly hours. I mean you got to invent how important this product is to an individual, make him feel a part of it.

In addition to detailing the problem, Lewis makes suggestions as to how to provide greater involvement for the worker. These suggestions recognize the dignity of the individual worker and produce better results. Therefore, management now takes such suggestions more seriously than previously.[5]

Absenteeism, tardiness and turnover provide evidence that workers do not like their work. Absenteeism among the workers in the General Electric plant averaged almost five percent, and reached nine percent some weeks. Tardiness and turnover were also high, and show that these workers did not like their work. They said it was uninteresting and unattractive. Women and men working on an assembly line find that few of their abilities are challenged. They are used as a single purpose tool. Actions are repetitive and paced by the machine; one cannot set one's own work speed. Little of the distinctive human qualities, such as intelligence and imagination, are used while working in this type of job.

Physical Effect of Job Dissatisfaction

The physical and psychological effects of work on the individual person are dramatic, and have been demonstrated in academic studies and personal experience.[6] Job satisfaction has been found to be the best predictor of a long life. Persons with coronary heart disease were significantly less satisfied with their work.[7] A group of other studies shows that job participation is a very important determinant in job satisfaction.

Alienation from Work

These data on work and the lack of interest in it are described by industrial psychologists and sociologists as alienation. Alienation at the workplace consists of such feelings as:

- Powerlessness,
- Meaninglessness, and
- Isolation.

An individual worker feels powerless when he has little or no input on the design of the work, the workplace set-up, or the pace of the work. Such a worker then feels that he is used much like mechanical equipment; useful and paid for when productive, but a cost and to be disposed of when perceived as not working well. In such a case, the individual worker has little more discretion than does the piece of machinery that he tends.

Meaninglessness at work stems from the perception that what any single individual contributes is not very important. This happens when work is broken into component parts. No one operation seems very significant, and so these people have little opportunity to gain a sense of satisfaction from their work. Frederick Taylor, the author of scientific management, encouraged breaking work into parts, so that even the most dull-witted could perform a task. It takes minimal time to train that person, and the very best work flow could be structured by the brightest work planner available.[8] So, according to Taylor, in order to achieve greater productivity, the best method of doing a job should be taught to all; work is too important to be left to the random intuitions of each craftsperson.

Isolation thus results because work is divided and done separately by each individual. Often the speed of the work, the noise of the workplace, and the distance of workers from each other make communication difficult. There is little opportunity to cooperate or communicate on such a job. Note how such a system is contrary to business values of individual responsibility and freedom, and contrary to the social values of dignity of the individual and community (see Chapter Two).

The Industrial Revolution brought about these changes in work conditions. Before that the overwhelming majority of workers were skilled craftspeople, shopkeepers, and farmers. Each had significant control over the design, manner, and pace of work. The Industrial Revolution brought division of labor, mechanization, time and motion studies, and the variety of techniques that enabled low cost production for large numbers of tools, autos, appliances, and other consumer goods. The advent of Industrial Revolution techniques thus thwarted three of the primary needs of workers: (1) a need for autonomy and control (2) a need for task achievement and completion and (3) a need for co-worker relations. These conflicting factors and needs are diagrammed in Figure 3-1.

Let us examine these needs in more detail. In spite of data showing considerable dissatisfaction and alienation from work, the vast majority of Americans are satisfied with their jobs. When asked, "All in all, how satisfied are you with your job?," between 80 and 90 percent of Americans are satisfied.[9] Even assembly line workers, while often critical of the monotony of their work, are generally satisfied with their pay.

There is dissatisfaction with some work, but not all workers are dissatisfied. Some are satisfied with repetitive work—it does not demand their entire attention and they can save their energy for their own personal concerns. It should be noted that those who are dissatisfied with their work tend to be less satisfied with other aspects of their lives also; for example, with home, leisure, and recreational activities.[10]

Regarding the desirability of various occupations, when asked, "What type of work would you try to get into if you could start all over again?," only 16 percent of unskilled auto workers would choose the same occupation. Comparatively, 93 percent of teachers in urban universities would do it again. For blue-collar workers as a whole, only 24 percent would choose the same occupation again, and only 43 percent of the cross-section of white-collar workers would do so.[11] Note that American workers will often respond that they are generally satisfied with their work, but they are far less satisfied when asked about specific aspects of their work.

The most important element in job satisfaction is work autonomy or the degree to which workers feel they can make their own decisions and can influence what happens on the job. Studies show that income has no significant influence on job satisfaction, although people earning high incomes generally experience greater autonomy and this in turn leads to job satisfaction. However, people with equal levels of autonomy on the job are equally satisfied with their work. This is true regardless of income differences.[12]

There is disagreement among students of organizations as to whether job satisfaction always brings about greater productivity.[13] There are happy groups of workers who spend much of their time talking to each other rather than working. However, most of the studies have shown a positive relationship between job satisfaction and greater productivity.

Participation—having a say in various aspects of one's work—is of value, because it allows a person to have input in one of the more important parts

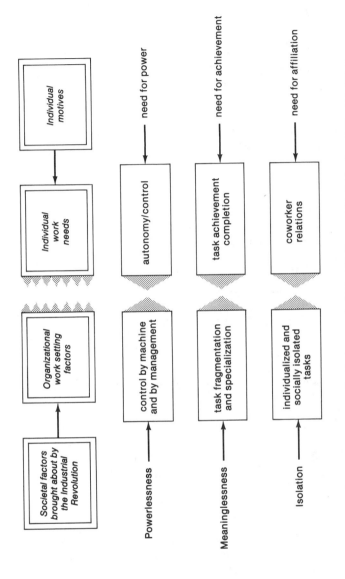

FIGURE 3-1 The Relationship between Individual Motives and Work Needs and Characteristics (*Source*: Reprinted, by permission of the publisher, from "Participative Management Is an Ethical Imperative," by Marshall Sashkin, p. 13, *Organizational Dynamics*, Spring 1984, © 1984 American Management Association, New York. All rights reserved.)

of one's life: work. Being involved in earning one's living was taken for granted before the industrial revolution. A person felt needed by family, tribe, or village. Today, when one is merely a cog in the production link, a person can feel useless.

The rest of this chapter will describe various methods for attempting to improve the participation and hence the autonomy of workers (see Figure 3-2). Participation at the workplace encourages communication and working together, and so respects community and the dignity of the individual (social values); it also encourages individual freedom and responsibility (business values). Thus, encouraging participation at work is ethically good. Nonetheless, not all the following cases were successes, either in attaining participation or efficiencies.

IMPROVING PARTICIPATION AT WORK

Worker dissatisfaction is now a major concern of many firms. The measurable problems of poor quality of American goods and services and failing productivity are related to feelings of powerlessness, meaninglessness, and isolation among workers *and* managers. Job satisfaction is essential for personal happiness, for an efficient organization, and for an ethical organization. Company executives now examine the problem of alienation among workers, and focus on the cost of such negative attitudes—the financial costs associated with poor quality and faltering productivity. The challenge of better quality goods at a lower price coming into the United States has sobered U.S. managers. Hence most U.S. firms have begun various forms of worker participation programs in an attempt to address these problems.

Quality of Worklife at GM

Perhaps mainly because of poor quality and productivity, GM management is now encouraging various methods of worker participation. GM's Pontiac Motor Division spent $300 million redesigning an old plant for greater efficiency, but more importantly, they instituted new cooperative work methods in building their Pontiac Fiero. The workforce is split into 150 teams, and each team is responsible for a certain section of a Pontiac Fiero's production. The workers themselves decide who works what assignment and how individual jobs are performed.[14]

Each of the 150 teams is made up of 8 to 12 employees, and they voluntarily meet weekly to solve production problems. Both Pontiac management and the United Auto Workers Union support the new program. Under the new arrangements, line workers deal directly with schedulers, maintenance, and quality staff. They are not restricted to going only to their supervisor. The workers themselves decide how to place the tools, machines, and robots to make the job easier and more efficient. The workers may reject substandard

FIGURE 3-2   Bringing Ethics into the Work Place

Methods of Recognizing Human Dignity, Responsibility, Freedom and Community:
Quality of Worklife Programs (QWL)
Scanlon Plan
Producer Cooperatives (PC)
Employee Stock Ownership Plans (ESOP)
Listening to Professionals
Unions and Worker Participation
Representation on Board of Directors
Job Security
Flexible Work Schedules (Flextime)
Empowering Management Style
Equitable Executive Pay

component parts, and even stop the production line when they see major problems. At this Pontiac Fiero assembly plant, the workers have a direct input into how the job is done, and how to improve it. It is not surprising that they experience less alienation and have a greater feeling of "ownership" of the plant and the individual automobile being built. Note how this method gives additional responsibility to each worker (business values) and at the same time encourages individuals to be concerned with each other and also respects the dignity of each worker (social values).

Wayne Johnson, 42, a welder on the Pontiac line, has been elected by 20 fellow workers as their group leader and link to management. He must report to work a half-hour early, at 5:40 am, to meet with other group leaders to plan the day. He himself is responsible for turning out 390 parts a day. A co-worker, a 62-year-old veteran, tires easily; he cannot keep up with the pace of the day. So, on his own time, Johnson performs an additional 10 operations for the veteran. Says Johnson, "If a fellow is a good hand but just getting old and tired, you try to help him out. We all get old someday."[15]

Because the Fiero was a new model, both management and the local UAW union felt that they could not afford to wait for comments from customers to filter back through dealers and service shops. That would take 6 to 12 months—precious time during which thousands of autos would be produced without this valuable input. A group of 50 workers volunteered to each call five randomly selected owners of new Fieros every three months for a year. These assembly workers call the customers on their own time; GM reimburses only their costs. Thus the information on potential bugs were delivered directly to those in the manufacturing units, and much time and money was saved and consumer satisfaction achieved.

Frank Slaughter, who was director of quality control when the program was designed, points out that there is a good cooperative relationship between salaried and hourly people at the plant. They all know that they must be able to put out a high quality product. They want their reputation to be: *We are concerned. We have ownership of what we do, and we are proud of it.*[16]

Another GM plant, Detroit Gear and Axel, is a 60-year-old facility in the heart of one of Detroit's older neighborhoods. It now serves as an example of a vastly improved quality of worklife. Earlier it employed 7000 people, but was not a profitable plant. The new plant manager was asked to use participatory methods to make the plant profitable, or failing that, to shut it down.[17] In order to simplify and to reduce overhead, he first cut his own management staff from 37 to 6. He then broke the 7000 person workforce into seven smaller business units. Each of these "small businesses" had its own marketing, financial, and other information needed for planning and to determine how well it was doing. The assembly line itself was broken into 65 teams, each of which put an entire brake system together and checked it for quality. The workers became concerned about the quality of their product.[18] Encouraging additional "ownership," and thus responsibility, brought about increased quality and efficiency.

In weekly meetings, workers now suggest improvements, and are encouraged to cost out their suggestions. A suggestion for a new 70,000 dollar grinding machine was not acted on at first—it was expensive—but was purchased when the team presented data showing how much it would save in the long run. Workers themselves watched the quality of parts brought in from outside, even when it was not their official responsibility. Thus, quality improved in the plant because the workers themselves see to it, both in their own work and in the quality of components that were supplied by outside vendors.

The workers decide the speed of the line itself. That way they are able to finish their quota as early as 2:15 p.m., rather than 3:00, the end of the shift. Quality increased and productivity jumped 12 percent, far more than management had hoped. When a person's full abilities are tapped, and she is given real responsibility, she then takes pride and ownership in her work. The results are increased quality and productivity. GM's problems with quality and productivity were not solved by such quality of work life programs. GM's failures are due more to an over reliance on quick fix robotic and high tech solutions, and too little reliance on the intelligence and abilities of its people.

The comments of the dissatisfied spot welders and the assembly line workers given earlier in this chapter are still characteristic of much work in the United States. But they represent declining numbers of workers. There are fewer repetitive jobs now and participation programs are spreading. Management recognizes that lack of responsibility encourages apathy and daydreaming; this in turn results in inefficiency and poor quality. Even if inefficiency and poor quality were not the result, a lack of participation does not respect the dignity of the person. If there is a reasonable alternative, a work setting without participation is not acceptable. It is unethical because it fails to recognize individual responsibility on a job, and it does not tap the best abilities of the individual over a major portion of one's life.

The cases we have noted indicate that positive results can be achieved with reorganization of work. Workers become less alienated. Their dignity is respected as they achieve a greater sense of autonomy and participation.

Other Plans for Worker Participation

Many U.S. firms have various other forms of shop-floor participation programs. In addition to General Motors, these firms include Lincoln Electric, Walt Disney, Proctor & Gamble, Polaroid, and Dana. Dana Corporation is a $2.5 billion a year manufacturer of automobile components and industrial equipment located in Toledo, Ohio. It uses an established form of participation called the Scanlon Plan. The Scanlon Plan was designed a half-century ago by Joseph Scanlon, a labor leader and cost accountant, who later taught at MIT. The Scanlon plan shares gains with employees. The plan is implemented in different ways in various locations; some companies use work teams, some have groups that discuss ways of improving quality. Although bonuses generated by the plan can bring a 10 to 25 percent wage premium, the bonuses are not the most important element to all participants. To many using the Scanlon Plan, having some say in the design of the work and the product is even more important.[19]

Disney World in Florida is a very visible example of teamwork, great attention to the needs of guests, and superb marketing. An essential element of the Disney approach is enlisting the enthusiastic cooperation of each of the members of its "cast." This takes sensitivity, patience, and money. Visitors to Disney World are impressed with the cleanliness of the park and the friendliness and helpfulness of its employees. Even temporary employees receive at least three days of training, especially on how to deal with customers. Customers are called *guests* by Disney people. The Disney organization does not *hire* people for a *job*, but it *casts* them in a *role* to help the *guests*. Everyone helps when the need arises. On particularly big visitor days, top managers and their entire staffs come to the park to sell tickets, work at information booths, and help the guests.[20] The Disney approach has high regard for each individual person; both guests and cast. They thus acknowledge the dignity of each person.

Lincoln Electric uses one of the best known bonus plans in the country to obtain greater worker motivation and commitment, while improving the quality of worklife. Located in Cleveland, Ohio, the firm is the world's largest producer of welding machines and of electrodes used in those machines. As early as 1915, Lincoln set up an Advisory Board of employees. They elected representatives to a committee that advises on company policy and practices. The Advisory Board meets with the chief executive officer twice each month.[21]

Traditionally, corporate managers have felt that their first responsibility was to shareholders. Lincoln is different. Customers come first, and employees are second in the thinking of the company and management.[22] There have been no layoffs at Lincoln Electric since 1949. A job is guaranteed after one year with the company. When business is slow, all employees work fewer hours.

Large year-end bonuses go to each employee. Bonuses are paid following a formula that includes base rate plus a series of performance appraisals. Items considered in the individual appraisal are output, ideas and cooperation, quality of product, and ability to work without supervision. The annual bonus generally is about as much as one's base salary. And base salaries are competitive with other firms.

There are few supervisors, yet supervisory orders must be followed without question. Change of work and overtime must be performed when they are demanded. While much of the management style is innovative, other aspects of plant life are quite traditional. The plant itself is old, dark, and cluttered. Employee morale and loyalty are high, despite the work setting. As evidence of satisfied workers, turnover is less than three percent per year.

Lincoln Electric's bonus plan does indeed increase motivation and commitment of workers. It measures and rewards the quality of work. In addition, job security is promised. The bonus plan itself builds on the individual's need for recognition and achievement. Job security and the way it is implemented—in down times all share fewer hours and lower pay—increase solidarity and contribute to the common good. Lincoln's program is rigid in some respects, and demands very hard work of its employees. It also respects the freedom and dignity of the person in its job security, design of the bonus system, and concern for employees. Moreover, workers can freely choose whether they want this sort of work environment.

The Scanlon Plan and other forms of participative management do indeed respect the dignity of the individual. Various Quality of Work Life (the GM term) and Employee Involvement programs (a Ford term) are being brought into manufacturing plants. When such programs are not manipulative and when management really is committed to participation, they support the individual and respect that person's human dignity and freedom.

Producer Cooperatives

In producer cooperatives (PCs) workers own their own firm; each worker has a strong input into corporate policies and actions. Producer cooperatives are thus the ultimate in worker control. PCs manufacture goods and are set up, owned, and operated by the workers themselves. PCs have been a part of the American tradition for some time. Beginning in 1860, they were initiated in several industries: plywood, foundry, shingles, and barrel making. Many of these PCs did not last long, some less than five years, while others lasted over 50 years. Even though many failed early, it is clear that they *can* survive for substantial periods of time.[23] Consumer cooperatives, which merely sell goods, are more numerous and simpler to operate.

Good comparative data is difficult to obtain when comparing the results of producer cooperatives with entrepreneurial firms. Because a firm is taxed on its profits and not on its wages, it is in the cooperative owners' best interest to pay themselves higher wages and have less left for profits. Nevertheless, producer cooperatives have been known to be 30 to 50 percent more productive than their privately held competitors.[24] Another study finds that the goals of cooperative members are to achieve a good level of income and job security. These goals can conflict sometimes, of course.

When we compare ordinary worker participation to what might seem to be a more developed form of participation, worker ownership, we find that worker *participation* has more of a positive influence on firm performance than does employee *ownership*.[25] When examining work attitudes and company performance, two conclusions emerge: (1) commitment appears to be a function of ownership, while (2) satisfaction and motivation are determined by feelings of participation in decision making.[26]

A comprehensive review article on U.S. labor-managed firms concludes:

> As a result of these analyses, there is no question that participation is highly related to individual motivation. The outstanding questions that remain unanswered are not whether or not there is a relation between participation and motivation in the U.S. labor managed firms, but rather (1) under what conditions will this relation be more pronounced, and (2) does individual motivation lead to organizational efficiency?[27]

Although early cooperative businesses were supported by such groups as the Knights of Labor (forerunner of The American Federation of Labor) and Christian Socialists, most soon collapsed. As a result, they were discredited until recently. Today there is a renewed interest in various participative plans. Assessing the data on performance for participative firms worldwide, there is apparently consistent support for the view that worker participation in management results in higher productivity.[28]

Producer cooperatives get mixed reviews. While many are begun in an overt attempt to respect the social values of the dignity of the individual, they often founder because they are inefficient. In theory they seem to unite business values and social values well (see Figure 2-1). For example, the Mondragon cooperatives in Spain have been remarkably successful by every measure, including both sets of values.[29] One feature of Mondragon that may influence its success is minority ethnic solidarity. Mondragon is a Basque enterprise within a larger Spanish culture. Like other new businesses, most producer cooperatives fail after a very short life. Thus, while PCs are not new and ideally bring together both sets of values, not many have lasted a long time, with the notable exception of the Mondragon PCs in Spain.

Employee Stock Ownership Plans

With an employee stock ownership plan (ESOP), a portion of the stock in the company is held by some or all of the workers and managers of the firm. Thus, these workers and managers have an additional stake in the success of the firm: They themselves are owners. More than 7000 firms and

10,000,000 workers are in employee stock ownership plans (ESOP). This number has increased 20-fold in the last ten years, because of tax advantages granted to ESOPs by the U.S. Congress. This rate is faster than in any other country in the world except Sweden. At this present rate, 25 percent of all U.S. workers will own some portion of their own firm by the year 2000.[30]

Workers who own a portion of their firm more readily feel that they have a stake in that firm. Their commitment to their jobs and to the organization is greater than that of workers who are hired at a simple salary or hourly wage. W. L. Gore & Associates has an ESOP in which all 3000 workers (called associates) own 10 percent of the company. It is a relatively young company, 30 years old, and makes *Gore-Tex* fabric and cable insulation.

The work atmosphere at Gore is informal and friendly. A visitor to a Gore plant is certain to be impressed with the fact that people seem to be working with great intensity and that supervisors are not in evidence. The workers have maintained this entrepreneurial atmosphere over the last three decades. Each plant is limited to 200 workers, so a friendly atmosphere is maintained in which supervisors know all the workers, and thus are able to treat them individually and fairly. Founder Gore acknowledges that it is less expensive to expand old plants than to build new ones. Expanding would raise the total number of workers above 200, so he opts to build new plants to keep each group of workers at a manageable size. Gore cites evidence to show that face-to-face relationships bring better overall performance for the firm.[31] Gore respects the existing relationships among workers; he encourages them. Thus he also acknowledges the dignity of the individual person. He also encourages a greater sense of responsibility among his "associates."

Some ESOPs have been initiated in threatening circumstances, for instance: (1) to prevent a plant closing, the workers purchase the facility (Weirton Steel, Hyatt Clark Industries, Rath Packing) and (2) to thwart an unfriendly takeover, management takes some of its stock off the market and sells it to workers (Dan River, Phillips Petroleum, National Can). Given some of these extraordinary conditions, it is not surprising that some ESOPs are not as successful as others.

Dan River, Raymond International, and Hyatt Clark Industries have not had happy results with ESOPs. A textile firm located in Danville, Va., Dan River faced a hostile takeover threat from corporate raider Carl Icahn. To prevent this, management proposed to workers that they purchase stock and thus make the firm private. Stock would no longer be publicly available, and Icahn could not purchase the shares. Management told the workers that they would lose their jobs if a takeover succeeded, so workers voted to terminate their own pension plan and replace it with an ESOP. This gave workers a 70 percent ownership in the firm for $110 million. A group of 26 managers received 30 percent of the firm for $4.3 million. Furthermore, as the value of the stock increases, the stock held by management increases at a much greater rate than that held by the workers.

The workers at Dan River now have little or no input to any management decisions. Because of the way the plan was set up, they cannot even vote their stock to elect the board of directors. Hence, the workers at Dan River are disillusioned. Now that the firm is private, it is not required to disclose earnings, sales figures, or profits—even to its own employee-owners; and so it does not. Even though Dan River's workers own their own plant, they are far less informed, committed, and motivated than they were when they were mere employees. Workers have been subjected to exploitation brought on by fear tactics.

Managers at Dan River took advantage of the workers for their own benefit. They not only failed to respect the freedom and dignity of the workers, but they will undoubtedly also cause decreased growth and productivity for the firm itself.

Several overall conclusions can be drawn from our experience with employee stock ownership plans: (1) when drawn up with the intention of bringing about greater participation, ESOPs generally bring greater commitment among members; (2) when an ESOP is proposed, employees should consider the proposal carefully and obtain financial and legal advice before signing into a plan; (3) because of the tax advantages of ESOPs and the sometimes narrow and self-serving goals of management, employees are not always better off as owners through an ESOP; and (4) as seen in the Dan River case, workers can be unscrupuously exploited.

When used as part of a larger pattern of participation in the firm, ESOPs build on the recognition of human dignity and community. At Gore & Associates, while the employees own a small share (10 percent), the ESOP is a part of a fabric of participation. As a real attempt to deepen the sense of ownership and participation, it is morally good. On the other hand, the Dan River ESOP violates the moral norms set forth in Chapter Two. The Dan River ESOP provides little participation for the employees, in spite of the fact that they have risked their savings to purchase the firm. Such a program is unjust and unethical.

Flexible Work Schedules

Flexible work schedules (flextime) allow people to report for work at varying times, not necessarily at the same time. Flextime is becoming increasingly popular; more than 11 percent of the full-time salaried work force use flextime.[32] Flexible work schedules allow individuals to choose—within limits—their hours for beginning and ending their work day, as long as the work week adds up to the required 35 or 40 hours. Generally there is a core time in the day, perhaps between 10 am and 3 pm, when everyone is expected to be present to enable people to communicate with one another.

Flextime increases job satisfaction and reduces absenteeism and tardiness. By allowing workers to be more flexible in choosing their own hours, it generally also increases productivity. When a family emergency, medical appointment, or other need arises, flextime eliminates the necessity to take a day off or to be tardy. A working mother can arrange to be home when her children arrive home from school. This results in less absenteeism and tardiness and greater job satisfaction. Flextime recognizes the need people have for some control over their time. It gives the individual greater responsibility and freedom in planning his own day and week.

Flexible work schedules are feasible when an individual's work is not totally dependent on another's. For example, it would be impossible to implement flextime on an assembly line, yet relatively easy in professional and office work. When flextime is used, it enables the individual to have more control over work times. Daily schedules are set by the individual worker so that family and other outside obligations can be accommodated without having to take a day off. Workers and employers both benefit from flextime.

Flextime gives the individual additional control over her own work environment. It thus respects both the dignity and the freedom of the individual. When properly implemented, flextime not only brings about additional efficiencies, but also respects justice and encourages participation.

Nevertheless, one caution is in order: If flextime is used as a quick fix for morale and/or productivity problems, it probably will not work. Most working groups have experienced dozens of programs that were introduced with great fanfare, only to fail after a short period. This has led to distrust. If flextime or any program is perceived by workers to be merely another management trick to get them to work harder, it will fail. Participative programs work best when they are a part of a larger set of management values. When management genuinely respects the freedom and need for responsibility of their workers (business values), and is concerned with them as persons and treats them with dignity (social values), then the participation program is more likely to succeed.

Listening to the Engineers

McDonnell Douglas provides an example of how listening to worker suggestions could have saved a firm's reputation and hundreds of lives. In the 1970s, McDonnell Douglas, Boeing, and Lockheed were all trying to sell similar large, wide-bodied jet aircraft. Most industry analysts agreed that sales could support only one American manufacturer of such planes. Competition was therefore intense, with major efforts to lower prices and costs.[33]

McDonnell Douglas was doing well in this competition. One of its best customers for the DC-10 was American Airlines. In 1972, an American DC-10 left Detroit airport, and at 11,500 feet the passengers heard a loud bang. Because it was not latched completely, the rear cargo door had blown out of the aircraft. This caused rapid decompression of the cabin as food trays, pillows, magazines, luggage, and cargo raced out of the gaping hole. The loss of pressure caused the floor to collapse, it severed many wire control cables and damaged the hydraulic lines that controlled the aircraft's rudder, horizontal stabilizers, and the control cable leading to the tail engine. The DC-10 went into a steep drive as the pilot fought to gain control of the plane. Because of his skill, the crippled plane was brought back to Detroit without any injuries to passengers or crew.

With the ongoing fierce competition for selling wide-bodied planes, McDonnell Douglas tried to minimize bad publicity from this dangerous incident. Convair was the subcontractor for the cargo doors, and its engineers had recognized the possibility of the cargo door not latching completely. Because of inside pressure, it could then blow out when the plane reached a certain altitude. In a test of the pressurized cabin in May 1970, the cargo door had actually blown out. Thus, McDonnell Douglas' own engineers recognized the potential problem.[34]

After the American Airlines aborted Detroit flight in 1972, the Director of Product Engineering at Convair wrote a memo to his superior:

> . . . Douglas has again studied alternative actions and appears to be applying more "band-aids". . . It seems inevitable that, in the twenty years ahead of us, DC-10 cargo doors will come open and I would expect this to usually result in the loss of the airplane. . . It is recommended that overtures be made at the highest management level possible to persuade Douglas to immediately make a decision to incorporate changes in the DC-10 which will correct the fundamental cabin floor catastrophic failure mode. . .[35]

The insight, courage, and acknowledgment of individual responsibility by the Director of Product Engineering should be noted. He here assumes his full professional responsibility, and is very much concerned for the lives of unknown and distant people. He acts out of the business value of professional responsibility and is also concerned for human lives.

Convair's management did not forward this memo or the concern it expressed, although "industry observers believe that those in the highest management position at McDonnell Douglas were aware of the long-term possible dangers of the cargo door design."[36] In December 1972, Turkish Airlines purchased two DC-10s; McDonnell Douglas officials assured them that the cargo door problem had been resolved. In March 1974, a Turkish Airlines DC-10 took off from Paris Orly Airport headed for London. Nine minutes later, at an altitude of 12,000 feet, the rear cargo door blew out, collapsing the floor. Out of control, the plane went into a steep dive. It crashed at 500 mph, instantly killing all 337 passengers and 11 crew members. The tragedy that was anticipated four years earlier by Convair engineers, but never forwarded to McDonnell Douglas, finally came to pass.

In this case, engineers were not adequately heard at either Convair or McDonnell Douglas when they warned of the safety of the aircraft. It appears that McDonnell Douglas executives were concerned about recouping their immense investment in the DC-10 project through additional sales, so they worked to eliminate negative publicity and did not give the safety-retrofitting project sufficient priority. Participation and listening to the informed advice of engineers at both firms was lacking. As a result, the DC-10 never did break even, and 348 lives were lost.

Engineers and other professionals at a firm have special knowledge and hence unique responsibilities.[37] It is not easy for such people to speak out when it would be in opposition to programs or positions that are generally accepted. In this case, it was the engineers who recognized the value of the dignity—the very life—of the individual person.

Unions and Worker Participation

The United Auto Workers, along with the Communication Workers of America, the United Steelworkers, and the International Brotherhood of Electrical Workers have all been active in cooperating with corporate management and have even urged participative programs at the workplace. On the other hand, many other unions and union members, most with good reason, perceive that their trust has been violated by previous actions of management. Promised programs and benefits never materialize, and workers then feel that they have been manipulated. At any work site that has a labor union, that union, its leaders, and members must be equal partners with management in participative programs. When such is the case, management recognizes both the need for freedom and responsibility (business values) and the dignity of the person and solidarity with others (social values).

When participative programs have been introduced and the quality of work life raised, the number of formal grievances drop dramatically. Grievances are often as much the result of frustration due to not being heard as they are the result of a specific complaint. When workers are listened to, their frustrations lessen and they feel respected and part of the team. Listening to workers and acknowledging their union tells those people that management recognizes that they have dignity as individuals and that they belong to a community.

In unionized plants the local union must support and help plan any participative program. Otherwise, it simply will not work no matter how good management's intentions. Some international and local labor unions have been quite helpful in these efforts, such as the United Auto Workers. Some other unions are less cooperative, and thus present a greater challenge to management.

Job Security and Representation on the Board

Holding onto one's job has become a very important issue with U.S. workers in recent years. Many unions now pursue greater job security as a goal. Although not unionized, Nucor Steel in Charlotte, N.C. has a "Share the Pain" program in which, at a business downturn, rather than layoff some workers, it reduces the hours that all work; this lowers everyones' total pay. Kenneth Iverson, president of Nucor, says, "The higher you go in the management scale, the greater the percentage loss in pay. But you still have a job."[38] Men and women at Nucor prefer it that way. Ray Strickland, a lathe operator, has worked 36-hour, 32-hour, and even 28-hour weeks at Nucor, cutting his gross pay accordingly. Says Strickland, "We weren't getting rich, but we were getting by. I certainly would rather have taken short time than see someone else laid off."[39] Increasing numbers of large U.S. firms now have no-layoff policies. Among them are Hewlett-Packard, Bank of America, Control Data, Delta Air Lines, Avon Products, and Xerox.[40] Ironically, most of these firms are not unionized. Workers perceive that there is little need for a union at these enlightened firms, which respect them as individuals.

In Japan, job security is guaranteed in most large manufacturing firms. Some U.S. firms just mentioned effectively guarantee job security also. When orders are slow, the entire workforce—especially management in the case of Nucor Steel—take a flat percentage pay cut. Guaranteeing jobs allows individual workers to make labor-saving suggestions without fear that the resulting increase in efficiency will place their own or their co-worker's job in danger. More than that, job security provides a firm foundation for looking to the long-term good of the entire enterprise and to the common good—and providing a spirit of solidarity for all in the firm.

West Germany has long had a substantial number of workers on each corporate board[41], but the trend is more recent in the United States. Most of the U.S. firms with worker representatives on the board of directors are those that were in financial trouble, and granted workers a board seat in return for wage and work rule concessions. Chrysler, Interstate Motor Freight, Pan American Airlines, Transscon, and Branch Industries all have a worker representative on their boards.[42] Observers agree that any worker representative on the board must know the business, have some objectivity, and be able to look to the interests of *all* stakeholders. They must be able to discuss company plans, policies and strategy intelligently, and they must be respected and listened to by their fellow board members.

Board representation sometimes follows an ESOP. Although establishment of an ESOP does not require that the workers have a representative on the board, this is often the case. ESOPs and having worker representatives on the board are new in the United States. Having representatives of the firm's own workers on the board of directors does violate the ideal of having only outsiders on the board (see Chapter Two). However, the firm will most likely have several inside managers on its board already. So if management objects on that basis to workers being on the board, they can hardly expect to be taken seriously.

SETTING THE CLIMATE

Let us examine the actions and attitudes of managers. Managers are ultimately responsible for product quality and productivity. Their role sets the tone and attempts to elicit the best efforts of all in the organization. When a firm is not productive, labor relations are poor, and goods are of poor quality, the responsibility must fall on management. W. Edwards Demming, the well-known management consultant who helped Japan increase its product quality and productivity, estimates that when a firm has poor quality goods and is not efficient, 85 percent of the blame goes to management.

Management Style

Most U.S. managers are not prepared for a program of participation by their workers. As one observer put it:

> Any collaborative system brings substantial changes to the roles of the managers involved. If a group makes a decision that a foreman thinks is wrong, he cannot simply reverse it without destroying the participative compact. Yet he dare not let it stand either. Nothing in his experience has prepared him to sit down with the workers and talk things out.[43]

American executives and managers generally have neither the patience nor the inclination to work through a decision with their subordinates. Managers are generally selected and promoted on the basis of their intelligence and their ability to make decisions, not on the basis of their consensus-building skills. With firms initiating worker participation programs, managers are now required to take the more difficult and time-consuming route of talking over major decisions with their subordinates. Executives now need greater sensitivity to others' reactions, coupled with the ability to lead others in a collaborative way.

Worker participation programs of all kinds have become popular in many industries in recent years—in newly formed firms and in those that must increase productivity. This has happened before. When profitability improves, management typically goes back to the older, easier, more autocratic forms of management: giving orders and having little patience for consultation and participation. Traditional, autocratic management supports the status and power of the supervisor. It is always easier for management to give orders than to consult. But people are not mere means to an end—they are ends in themselves. It takes patience, time, and skill to discuss major issues with one's subordinates. It also takes a more sensitive and subtle observer to recognize the potential leadership abilities of a man or woman and thus also recognize their dignity as a person. So, eliciting the best efforts of all in the organization demands the specific efforts of management. Such efforts do not come naturally to all managers, but they are the mark of a conscientious employer.

Executive Pay

Executive compensation is best designed to reward an executive based on corporate performance.[44] In order to motivate management, some recognition of superior performance is necessary. All people, including top managers, must have feedback on their work. Traditionally, the way to acknowledge superior performance among top managers in the United States has been through large salaries and bonuses. Now there is a growing consensus about the need to encourage cooperation and the best efforts of *all* in the organization. In good times all share rewards; in downturns, all share the pain. Yet executive pay and privileges are becoming increasingly disproportionate and inequitable. These two efforts run counter to one another.

In Japanese firms, including those on U.S. soil, executives have no special parking place, no executive dining room; their pay is not much out of line with the pay of hourly workers. In these firms, encouraging the best efforts of all in the firm takes priority over large salaries for executives. Large executive salaries encourage the hourly worker to be just as self-centered as he perceives his chief executive officer to be and thus to ask for more pay for himself. This attitude puts individual advantage ahead of the good of the group.

A lack of sensitivity to others' reactions is demonstrated by large salary increases and bonuses taken by top managers, after several years of asking blue-collar workers to hold the line on wage increases or even to take salary cuts. Most Americans know the free enterprise system and so acknowledge the need to reward performance and the need to keep top managers from going to competitors. However, most people also believe that top corporate executives receive too much in salaries and bonus compensation. James Baker, a corporate director and former university president, has written widely on executive compensation. He maintains that such executive self-seeking may diminish public trust to the point that "capitalists themselves will become a major force undermining capitalism." [45] Only TV stars, big-name entertainers, and star professional athletes are more resented by Americans because of their immense salaries.

A director of General Motors, Ross Perot, the founder of Electronic Data Systems, found fault with the excessive pay of managers and executives while GM was asking hourly workers to tighten their belts. Perot publicly and privately criticized GM as bloated and unresponsive to workers. GM bought out his $700 million interest for his promise that he cease criticizing GM, so he resorted to an analogy: "At Valley Forge, the troops were fighting barefoot in the snow. If George Washington had been out buying new uniforms with gold braid, it would have been hard to rally the troops."[46]

Middle managers also resent the excessive pay that many top executives receive. Over the past few decades, middle managers have been financially squeezed. Unionized blue-collar workers' salaries have risen substantially, while the managers' salaries have remained relatively stable, after being adjusted for inflation. These middle managers were told that costs must be contained, and so they received small salary increases. At the same time, top executives obtained large salary increases. Such large executive pay increases hardly provide the foundation upon which to build cooperation and a sense that "we are all in this together." Taking a large salary increase for oneself while asking subordinates to tighten their belts undermines trust, the foundation needed for people to live and work together.

Some European firms that want to stress cooperation have set limits to the income ratio between the highest-paid and the lowest-paid in the organization. This is in contrast to the United States, where the CEOs are the most highly paid in the world. For example, the CEOs of U.S. corporations receive almost twice as much compensation as CEOs in West Germany, the next highly-paid group of CEOs. CEOs in other countries are paid even less. Moreover, U.S. CEOs receive more pay proportionate to their own top managers' pay than in any other country.[47]

At the successful Mondragon producer-cooperative enterprises in Spain, top managers receive no more than three times the salary of the lowest paid workers. Some American cooperatives also try for a 3 to 1 ratio, while Yugoslavian firms are required to have no more than a 7 to 1 ratio. By comparison, the income differential between the CEO and the lowest paid worker in many American companies is 100 to 1.[48] Peter Drucker has urged executives to exercise self-restraint before legislation is proposed to limit executive pay.[49] He suggests that top managers' pay be limited to a multiple of 15 or 20 times the average wage in the firm; not an overwhelmingly egalitarian suggestion.

It is doubtful that higher pay is the reason that most executives work as hard and effectively as they do. Money, however, is often perceived as the easiest and most accepted way of telling a person he or she is doing well; such an attitude prevails in firms that do not give feedback and support to their managers. On executive pay, Peter Drucker suggests that beyond a certain top limit to executive compensation, the corporation could contribute the excess "in the form of a charitable contribution in his name to a beneficiary of his choosing."[50]

Such large salaries are seen by many as expressions of greed and abuse of power. Highly visible executive pay raises make it more difficult for the same executives to urge rank and file workers to restrain their wage demands in order to hold down costs. While preaching wage restraint, it is unjust that these same executives award themselves large salary increases. They should not be surprised when they lose credibility and create distrust. Moreover, many executives receiving disproportionate salary increases head firms that are not even performing well.

The large gap between the compensation of the top officers of a company and the average worker does not encourage a feeling of cooperation, and it can discourage the best efforts of others. Developing community and solidarity (see Chapter Two) within a firm is no easy task. In the short term it is easier to reward the performance of top management with dollars than to acknowledge the long-term divisiveness and mistrust that it creates, and therefore to seek other rewards.

Disproportionate salary increases for executives undermine the sense of solidarity in the firm. Whether fair or not, large salary increases look greedy to lesser-paid workers. Do executives contribute that much to the firm? How does one measure their contribution? Surely an executive's new product or marketing program can be worth far more than the individual's salary increase—or perhaps the entire annual salary. On the other hand, the negative effects on morale of a disproportionate salary increase can counteract the positive contribution of the executive.

Realistically and morally, an executive making $100,000 annually does not *need* a sizeable salary increase to live comfortably. While such a compensation policy encourages freedom and individualism (business values), at the same time it undermines cooperation, trust, solidarity, and community (social values). Here is a conflict, even in the short run, between the two sets of values. American life is strongly individualistic. Few would deny that we need more cooperation in our organizations, our country, and our world. From that standpoint alone, highly disproportionate executive salaries are a management mistake and are also unethical. They should not exist in a firm that wishes to be fair and to encourage the best efforts of its workers.

Japanese Social Values

Increasing productivity and product quality has become a top priority with most American businesses. The issue has been sharpened by the loss of market share by U.S. firms and the better quality of some foreign-made goods. A consensus is emerging that product quality and productivity increases cannot be achieved without the wholehearted support of the workforce. Quality and productivity cannot be controlled entirely by management. We have seen that management can create an environment so that all in the workforce can help to achieve both product quality and productivity.

American management has become well aware that the quick fix is no longer adequate. Seminars on "management by objectives" or "quality circles" can do more harm than good, if they are not a part of new attitudes that lead to a larger participative fabric.[51] What, then, do we know about an environment that will encourage product quality and productivity increases?

The success of Japanese firms reminds us of principles that we in the United States learned decades ago, but did not have the patience or the sophistication to consistently apply. Note how the highly successful Japanese industrial firms are managing their operations in the United States. Decentralized decision making and the notion that profit, earnings, and growth are all byproducts of a quality product are characteristics of Japanese management. An expert on manufacturing puts it this way: "It is easier for the American worker to appreciate what the Japanese manager wants above all else—quality—than it is for the American to understand what the American manager wants."[52] As a result, many Japanese-owned firms are outperforming their U.S. competitors in their U.S. facilities.

An early and astute viewer of Japanese managers, Richard Pascale, points out that Japanese managers distinguish themselves from American managers in the way that they interact with workers. He outlines three primary characteristics of the Japanese:

1. **A day-in, day-out presence by management on the work floor.** For example, the president and his managers at Nissan's Tennessee plant wear the same uniform as hourly workers as they conduct their rounds through the plant.
2. **A constant drawing on workers' knowledge.** The Japanese know that the worker is closest to the operation and thus is an extraordinary resource; she can make the best suggestions on how to improve quality and productivity. That worker is better at this than the production engineer in her distant office.
3. **Minimizing the gap between management and the workers.** Eliminating executive dining rooms, parking on first-come, first-served basis, and calling executives by their first names are all symbolic acts that reduce distance and stratification. Communication is easier and teamwork is more easily achieved without barriers.

Participation is made easier in smaller operations. Contrary to traditional biases toward economies of scale and thus larger facilities, we have come to recognize that small is beautiful. It is much easier to manage by walking around when you have a few hundred workers at one site than when you have several thousand. With large groups, it is impossible for management to know all by their first names, making it more difficult to consult and to establish teamwork and cooperation. Evidence on the shrinking size of new plants illustrates this. Plants built before 1970 averaged 644 workers. That number dropped to 241 for plants established in the 1970s and to 210 workers for operations begun in the 1980s.[53]

Urgent and quick-fix participative programs have often failed because they were perceived as manipulative. Nevertheless, carefully planned participation programs can do much to reduce worker alienation and to improve quality and productivity. More than that, they also respect the freedom and responsibility of the individual worker (business values), and support the dignity of the individual and the community of people living and working together.

Ethics of Work and Job Satisfaction

A job that is low paying and not attractive is better than no job at all for most people; their main desire is to be employed. Because of the importance of work for individuals and those depending upon them, it is generally better to have work at low pay than to be roaming the streets without a sense of purpose or self-worth. Yet even unskilled labor at low wage rates can benefit from the principles that we have presented in Chapter Two.

A work setting in which individuals are consulted and have their best talents challenged is better than work that is dangerous, repetitive, and where individuals are treated like extensions of machines.[54] The more innovative firms and those that produce better quality goods are those that encourage the best efforts of all of those in the workforce. Some participation by workers in their work and work design marks the most successful and the fastest growing firms in the United States. Genuine participation taps the best energies, imagination, and abilities of each individual person.[55] Participation enhances that individual's personal freedom and gives a sense of responsibility (business values). Moreover, it also enables the individual to maintain a sense of dignity and importance; this in turn builds up cooperation and community. Participation is also just, because the individual worker then has some direction over work in which he is engaged many hours per day.

Both sets of moral norms, business values and social values, must be respected by the firm (see Figure 2-1). Whether with flexible work schedules, employee stock ownership plans, or organizational climate, it is not only possible, but desirable—both morally and economically—to respect both the freedom of the individual and the dignity of the person. Morally, it is essential that neither the productivity of the firm nor the dignity of the individual be neglected. If too little attention is paid to efficiency, the firm founders and jobs are lost; if there is too little concern for people, workers are used and exploited.

On the other hand, a firm can—especially in the short run—coerce and take advantage of individuals working in it. Profits may be generated, but persons are abused and exploited. Such treatment does not respect workers' freedom, responsibility, or sense of dignity. It undermines solidarity and community. Such exploitation is immoral and unethical.

The norms for ethical judgment are such that work must support and respect the dignity, freedom, and the well-being of the worker. Productivity and efficiency are also moral considerations. They increase jobs and the life of the firm.

This chapter has not discussed hiring and promotion of minorities, women, or the elderly. Given the current concern with reverse discrimination and the resulting de-emphasis on affirmative action, this is a timely and important moral issue. After successful programs to relieve centuries of discrimination in the 1970s, there is now evidence that we are slipping backward. For a country that claims equal opportunity, this is not good news. Any discrimination against persons violates justice. When it is based on prejudice and bias against a group, it also undermines the community, solidarity, and the dignity of the individual person.[56]

Practical Recommendations

In this chapter we have examined ways in which a firm can encourage greater participation by its worker. The variety of programs that have proven successful have been detailed. It is true that the individual, whether as supervisor or citizen, has some influence over the work environment. If responsibility in an organization is greater, so too is an individual's ability to affect the quality of work and job satisfaction. At the risk of stating the obvious, we present some recommendations.

1. In so far as you can, choose work in which you can make a contribution, and work in which you can be happy. Find a *firm* that deals with a product or a service that is not trivial or harmful, but that is intelligently useful to people. Find a *job* in which you can use the best of your abilities.
2. View your work as a contribution to the betterment of others. Give yourself to the task with interest and enthusiasm, and encourage the interest and best contributions of others also. Work intelligently and hard to produce a good product or service.
3. Look for your rewards in a job well-done and recognized as such.
4. As a supervisor, give personal attention to each individual; encourage them to elicit their best abilities.
5. At work, encourage the initiation of and support existing well-designed forms of participation: employee stock ownership plans, flextime, quality of work programs, and other types of participation, such as we have discussed in this chapter.

SUMMARY AND CONCLUSIONS

It is through work that individuals support themselves and their families, and also obtain much of their own sense of self-worth. Because of the basic dignity of the human person, all individuals who are able to work should be able to find suitable work.

Moral analysis shows that the individual person has imagination, intelligence, and sensitivities that many jobs do not tap. Most firms now realize this, and redesign their work to utilize these many valuable human talents. Challenging individuals to become involved in product and production planning, a quest for quality, and even marketing not only generally improves the quality of the goods, but also improves productivity.

A variety of methods to improve personal involvement in work have been discussed in this chapter. When these forms of participation are part of a genuine attempt to build an overall spirit of cooperation, they recognize the dignity of the individual, build a spirit of solidarity, and contribute to community. Then one person's benefit at the workplace is not in competition with others. If others do well, the firm does well, and all benefit. Participative programs, when undertaken in order to encourage the involvement of all workers, have great moral value. Therefore, unless they would cause a serious financial loss for the firm—bankruptcy or close to it—encouraging the participation of workers is a moral obligation for any business firm.[57]

Note finally the happy coincidence: job satisfaction, good ethics, and efficient business practices support one another. Although worker participation has its short-term cost in time and resources, the long-term benefit is not only in good ethics but also in quality work and profits for the firm. This is not always so clearly the case with the other issues discussed later in this book.

We have seen the ethical importance of work and job satisfaction, along with programs that can encourage greater participation of workers. Often government regulations have vital impacts on the workplace. Our next chapter will examine the relation of the corporation and the government from an ethical viewpoint.

DISCUSSION QUESTIONS

3.1. Describe the importance of work in your own experience.
   (a) What do you (and others) expect from work?
   (b) What do you obtain from work?
   (c) What do you contribute to work?

3.2. How does the job satisfaction of workers affect managers and the firm? Give examples.

3.3. How did the industrial revolution change work? How did it affect peoples' satisfaction with their work?

3.4. Using the traditional business values and the social values of Chapter Two (Figure 2-1), assess:
   (a) redesigned work groups at Pontiac Fiero
   (b) Lincoln Electric, its work and bonus system
   (c) producer cooperatives
   (d) employee stock ownership plans—especially W. L. Gore & Associates and Dan River Co.
   (e) flexible work schedules.

3.5. Are there often conflicts between engineers and marketing people on safety and quality, as in the McDonnell Douglas case? Why?
   (a) How can the two sets of values (Figure 2-1) help to solve these conflicts?
   (b) How does one make a tradeoff judgment? Does one weigh the relative importance of a norm? The chance of an accident?

3.6. What role does a labor union play in job satisfaction and product quality?

3.7.   Describe the type of manager most able to improve job satisfaction, product quality, and utilization of ethical values in decision making (such as those in Figure 2-1).

3.8.   Compare the management style of American and Japanese managers.
(a)   What are strengths and weaknesses of each, using our values?
(b)   Why are the goals of the Japanese manager more easily communicated and understood?

3.9.   Assess executive pay in American firms using traditional business values and social values (Figure 2-1).

NOTES

[1]"Economic Justice For All: Catholic Social Teaching and the U.S. Ecnomy," U.S. Catholic Bishops. *Origins* (November 27, 1986).

[2]Table C-1, *Employment and Training Report of the President* (1981).

[3]See table "Small Companies Create Most of the New Jobs," *Business Week*, May 27, 1985, p. 90.

[4]The first three descriptions are classic and remain accurate today; they are from Studs Terkel, *Working* (N.Y.: Pantheon Books, 1972), pp. xxxi, 160, 165.

[5]The last two people were interviewed as part of a study of worker attitudes of black and white blue-collar workers; these attitudes have changed little since then. See Thedore V. Purcell and Gerald F. Cavanagh, *Blacks in the Industrial World: Issues for the Manager* (New York: The Free Press, 1972), pp. 73–74.

[6]For a summary of the data on the relationship between work and mental health, see Robert L. Kahn, *Work and Health* (New York: John Wiley & Sons, 1981).

[7]For data on medical and psychological effects, see Marshall Sashkin, "Participative Management is an Ethical Imperative," *Organizational Psychology* (Spring, 1984), pp. 5–22.

[8]See Daniel Nelson, *Frederick W. Taylor and the Rise of Scientific Management* (Madison: University of Wisconsin Press, 1980).

[9]Robert P. Quinn et al, "National Trends in Job Satisfaction, 1958–1973" in *Organizational Behavior: An Applied Psychological Approach*, W. Clay Hammar and Dennis W. Organ, eds. (Dallas: Business Publications, 1978), pp. 219–23.

[10]Barry M. Staw, "Organizational Psychology and the Pursuit of the Happy/Productive Worker," *California Management Review* 28 (Summer, 1986), pp. 40–53.

[11]"Work in America," James O'Toole, ed. (Cambridge: MIT Press, 1973), pp. 15–16.

[12]"Satisfaction on the Job: Autonomy Ranks First," *New York Times*, May 28, 1985, C4, p. 21.

[13]For a comprehensive overview, though biased against participation, see Edwin A. Locke and David M. Schweiger, "Participation in Decision Making: One More Look" in *Research in Organizational Behavior*, vol 1, Barry M. Staw, ed. (Greenwich, Conn.: JAI Press, 1979), pp. 265–339.

[14]*1984 General Motors Public Interest Report* (Detroit: GM, 1984), p. 46.

[15]"Who Says the Assembly-Line Age is History?," *U.S. News and World Report*, July 16, 1984, pp. 48–49.

[16]"A GM Plant with a Hot Line Between Workers and Buyers," *Business Week*, June 11, 1984, p. 165.

[17]John Simmons and William Mares, *Working Together* (New York: Alfred A. Knopf, 1983), pp. 49–71.

[18]*Working Smarter* (New York: Penguin, 1984), pp. 110ff.

[19]*Ibid.*, p. 112.

[20]*Ibid.*, pp. 173–74; also see also Thomas J. Peters and Robert H. Waterman, Jr., *In Search of Excellence* (New York: Harper & Row, 1982), pp. 167–68.

[21]William Serrin, "The Way that Works at Lincoln," *New York Times*, January 15, 1984, Business Section, p. 4.

[22]Michael Conte, "Participation and Performance in U.S. Labor-Managed Firms," in *Participatory and Self Managed Firms*, Derek C. Jones and Jan Svejnar, eds. (Lexington, Mass.: Lexington Books, 1982), p. 217.

[23]*Ibid.*

[24]*Ibid.*, p. 221.

[25]*Ibid.*, p. 222.; see also Frank Lindenfield and Joyce Rothchild-Whitt, eds. *Workplace Democracy and Social Change* (Boston: Porter Sargent, 1982).

[26]"Participation and Performance in U.S. Labor-Managed Firms," p. 232.

[27]*Ibid.*, p. 235.

[28]*Ibid.*, p. 11: Derek C. Jones and Jan Svejnar, "The Economic Performance of Participatory and Self Managed Firms: A Historical Perspective and a Review."

[29]See Ana Gutierrez Johnson and William Foote Whyte, "The Mondragon System of Worker Production Cooperatives," in *Workplace Democracy and Social Change, op. cit.*, pp. 177–98. Also, *Working Together, op. cit.*, pp. 136–44.

[30]William Foote Whyte, et al, *Worker Participation and Ownership: Cooperative Strategies for Strengthening Local Economies* (Ithica: Cornell, 1983); also "Popular ESOPs Get Tax Aid," *New York Times*, March 21, 1987, p. 37; and "Power-Sharing Between Management and Labor: It's Slow Going," *Business Week*, Feb. 17, 1986, p. 37.

[31]"ESOPs: Revolution or Ripoff?," *Business Week*, April 15, 1985, p. 94–107.

[32]Charles N. Greene, "Effects of Alternative Work Schedules: A Field Experiment," *Academy of Management Proceedings—1984*, pp. 269–73.

[33]Paul Eddy, Elaine Potter and Bruce Page, *Destination Disaster* (New York: New York Times Book Co., 1976), pp. 33–63.

[34]*Hearings Before the Subcommittee on Aviation of the Commitee on Commerce of the U.S. Senate*, March 26, 1974. (Washington: U.S. Government Printing Office), pp. 112, 152. See also, Brian Power-Waters, *Safety Last* (New York: William Morrow, 1976), p. 262.

[35]*Destination Disaster*, p. 184.

[36]Robert Orlando and Robert Dickie, "The DC-10, McDonnell Douglas and the F.A.A. (A)" Intercollegiate Case Clearing House, #9-380-780. See also *Hearings, op. cit.*, March 27, 1974, p. 110.

[37]See the excellent assessment of professional responsibilities in Joseph Raelin, *The Clash of Cultures: Managers and Professionals.* (Boston: Harvard Business School Press, 1986).

[38]John O. Whitney, "Effective Turnarounds Do Not Require Employee Turnovers," *Wall Street Journal*, January 12, 1987, p. 24; also "Unions' Latest Goal: A Job for Life," *U.S. News*, May 21, 1984, p. 75.

[39]*Ibid.*, pp. 75–76.

[40]"No-layoff Policy Spreads," *U.S. News & World Report*, Aug. 27, 1984, p. 14.

[41]W. Michael Blumenthal, *Co-determination in the German Steel Industry.* Princeton, N.J.: Princeton University Press, 1956.

[42]"Labor's Voice on Corporate Boards: Good or Bad?," *Business Week*, May 7, 1984, pp. 152–53.

[43]*Working Smarter*, p. 116.

[44]David H. Cliscel and Thomas Carroll, "The Determinants of Executive Compensation," *Research in Corporate Social Performance and Policy*, Lee Preston, ed. (Greenwich, Conn.: JAI Press, 1984), pp. 55–69. See also the balanced overview of these issues by GM vice president Elmer W. Johnson, "Million Dollar Executives," *Harvard Business Review* (May–June, 1985), pp. 211–13.

[45]"Top Executive Pay Peeves the Public," *Business Week*, June 25, 1984, p. 15. For the statement of John C. Baker, see his "Are Executives Overpaid?" *Harvard Business Review*, (July–August, 1977), p. 52. See also "Executive Compensation for Perquisites" in *Corporate Performance: The Key to Public Trust*, Francis W. Steckmest, ed. (New York: McGraw-Hill, 1981), pp. 159–66.

[46]"Smith and Perot, at Luncheon, Avoid Hostility Over Recent Buyout by GM," *Wall Street Journal*, December 9, 1986, p. 6.

[47]Survey of executive pay by Arthur Young & Co. and Business International; see "American CEOs Win the Paycheck Derby," *Business Week*, July 1, 1985, p. 16.

[48]Frank Lindenfeld and Joyce Rothschild-Whitt, eds. *Workplace Democracy and Social Change*. (Boston: Porter Sargent, 1982), pp. 3, 34.

[49]Peter Drucker, "Reform Executive Pay or Congress Will," *Wall Street Journal*, April 24, 1984, p. 34.

[50]*Ibid.*

[51]See, for example, Edward E. Lawler III and Susan A. Mohrman, "Quality Circles After the Fad," *Harvard Business Review*, Vol. 63 (January–February, 1985), pp. 65–71.

[52]Martin Starr, Professor of Production and Operations Management at Columbia University, as quoted in "How Japanese Work Out as Bosses in the U.S.," *U.S. News and World Report*, May 6, 1985, pp. 75–76.

[53]"Small is Beautiful Now in Manufacturing," *Business Week*, Oct. 22, 1984, pp. 152–56.

[54]For the Catholic tradition, see John Paul II, who encourages "proposals for joint ownership of the means of work, sharing by the workers in the management and/or profits of business, so-called shareholding by labor, etc.," *On Human Work (Laborem Exercens)* (Washignton, DC.: USCC, 1981) n. 14; The text of the encyclical and a lengthy commentary can be found in Gregory Baum, *The Priority of Labor* (New York: Paulist, 1982). See also John XXIII's statements on participation in *Mater et Magistra* (1961), pp. 32, 75–77, 91–103, found also in Joseph Gremillion, ed., *The Gospel of Peace and Justice* (Maryknoll, N.Y.: Orbis, 1976). See also U.S. Catholic Bishops, *Catholic Social Teaching and the U.S. Economy*, Chapter 4, "A New American Experiment: Partnership for the Public Good," nn. 295–325. Second draft (Wash: U.S. Catholic Conference, 1986).

[55]For a religious view that has been consistent over the last several generations on the importance of participation in the workplace, see *Catholic Social Teaching and the U.S. Economy, Ibid.*, nn. 96–101.

[56]For an overview and data on women in the workforce, see "Why Women Execs Stop Before the Top," *U.S. News & World Report*, Jan. 5, 1987, p. 72–73; also Phyllis A. Wallace, ed., *Women in the Workplace* (Boston: Auburn House, 1982). For the same on black white-collar workers, see John W. Work, *Race, Economics, and Corporate America* (Wilmington, Delaware: Scholarly Resources, 1984). An earlier study that details the issues involved in job discrimination is by Theodore V. Purcell and Gerald F. Cavangh, *Blacks in the Industrial World: Issues for the Manager* (New York: Free Press, 1972).

[57]See the carefully reasoned updated position, supported by research findings, by Marshall Sashkin, "Participative Management Remains an Ethical Imperative," *Organizational Dynamics*, Vol. 14 (Summer, 1986), pp. 63–78. Significant for our work here, Sashkin maintains that it is impossible to be "value free" on participative management, and that a person's position on it is heavily influenced by that person's own values.

Chapter Four
CORPORATIONS AND THE GOVERNMENT: MILITARY SPENDING, POLITICAL INFLUENCE, REGULATIONS

Governments are formed because people have some shared goals and interests, some common good that looks to what is best for all and that transcends particular interests. Government's primary duty is the promotion of the common good, a duty that includes overseeing the economic well-being of the nation. Corporations contribute to this common good primarily by producing goods and services needed in society, but we believe that they should also be conscientious about responding to other issues that affect the public interest. In this chapter we appeal at times to different ethical values, but the social value of the common good, the shared concern for what is best for society, underlies each of the three issues discussed in this chapter.

Military spending looks to the common good of defending our nation, but how the spending occurs can and often does run counter to our common good. We consider three different problems concerning military spending. The first is a moral problem which involves not only violations of the public interest but basic precepts of honesty and integrity: fraud on the part of defense contractors. The second problem, wasteful military spending, deals with ethical responsibility for the use of taxpayers' money. The third problem, the priority given to defense spending, raises a more controversial question about what is best for society, a question that also involves the business values of productivity and growth.

Two distinct but interrelated issues make up the second and third parts of this chapter. Some critics of corporations believe that big business exercises disproportionate influence in and on government. We will examine this charge since it implies a possible undermining of the value of democracy and a restricting of the broad and equitable participation promised by democracy. Some critics of government believe that government regulations have crippled growth and productivity to the detriment of the common good. Government regulations merit special consideration because they appear again as issues in, for example, Chapter Five on advertising and in Chapter Six on the environment.

MILITARY DEFENSE SPENDING

In the mid-1980s, some of the largest defense contractors were convicted of fraud or other forms of ethical and legal misconduct. The incidents were not isolated or exceptional. Forty-five of the top one hundred defense contractors, including some of the largest such as General Dynamics and General Electric, pleaded guilty to charges brought against them. These scandals, as newspapers accurately called them, involved serious violations of honesty and justice.

With these disclosures of fraud came accounts of exorbitant prices paid by the military for certain goods ($640 toilet seats and $30 screws), leading to more probing concerns about cost overruns and waste in defense spending. Wasteful spending violates justice since taxpayers' money is being misused. The problem of waste and inflated costs leads to another related issue, the priority in national planning given to defense spending. We recognize that moral consensus can be more easily obtained in calling for an end to fraud and waste than in urging a reduced defense budget—an issue where the values discussed in Chapter Two clash. But we believe that the issue of the defense budget should be raised since it does involve an important debate about the common good of society.

In the first chapter on ethics, we noted different "circles of responsibility" for the corporation (Figure 2-2). Here each of the three circles come into play. Fraud and ethical misconduct fall directly under the responsibility of the corporations involved. Controlling waste and inflated costs may be primarily the government's responsibility, but defense contractors have some secondary responsibility since they are collaborating in the expenditure of taxpayers' money. The question of how much the United States should devote to defense spending is a question of general public concern, perhaps falling into the third or outer circle for corporations. Involvement and responsibility for military spending are greater, however, for defense contractors, who lobby for expensive weapon systems.

We focus on military spending. We have not taken up other ethical issues that should also be seriously weighed by defense-industry corporations, particularly the morality of contracting to build nuclear weapons, napalm, and weapons for chemical warfare.

Fraud and Ethical Misconduct in the Defense Industry

General Dynamics currently bears an undesirable reputation as a corporation identified with fraud and other forms of ethical misconduct. Twice in 1985 it was suspended by the Navy from taking on new contracts because of allegations of "pervasive" misconduct. The indictments for misconduct involved many executives at General Dynamics, the second largest defense contractor in the nation. General Dynamics had sales of $7.8 billion in 1984; it has the contracts for the manufacture of Trident submarines, F-16 jet fighters and the Army's M-1 tanks.

The pervasiveness of General Dynamics' misconduct is evident from the incidents that follow. The first evidence of ethical wrongdoing came in 1983 through the testimony of P. Takis Veliotis, a former executive vice-president of the company. Veliotis headed Electric Boat, a division of GD that builds submarines in Connecticut. Electric Boat had been challenged by Congress about cost overruns in building attack submarines. Veliotis initially had defended the overruns in his testimony before Congress. But later, after being personally indicted for perjury on an unrelated kickback scheme, he changed his testimony. He contended that the overruns were fraudulent claims (for $843 million) made to make up for heavy losses on a submarine contract.[1]

Veliotis changed his testimony because he was offered immunity or special treatment in regard to the charges brought personally against him and another associate. The two were indicted on charges of receiving $2.7 million in kickbacks for awarding Frigitemp Corporation some $44 million in shipbuilding contracts. Frigitemp executives, in turn, were also charged with embezzlements which contributed to the company's filing for bankruptcy.[2]

The Veliotis affair led to further investigations of General Dynamics, investigations that uncovered many questionable acts by company executives. The company charged to the Department of Defense as expenses an $18,000 country-club fee, kennel fees for an executive's dog, and billed the government $9609 for a wrench. General Dynamics also pleaded guilty to a charge that its officers had given Admiral Hyman G. Rickover some $67,628 in gifts over a period of years. Rickover was chief of the U.S. submarine program and supervised the multi-billion dollar work at Electric Boat at the time. Also challenged was the top security clearance given to one of the General Dynamics' most powerful directors, Lester Cross. The Cross family owns about 23 percent—more than $840 million worth—of General Dynamics stock. Questions were raised about the propriety of giving Cross security clearance because he had been named as an unindicted conspirator in a 1974 Illinois bribery case in which he contributed to a fund to bribe Illinois legislators.[3]

The Pentagon's Inspector General also showed evidence that three top General Dynamics' executives—chairman David E. Lewis, finance officer Gordon MacDonald, and vice-president George Sawyer—had issued a press release concealing serious delays in Electric Boat's Trident sub program in order to prop up the value of GD stock.[4]

The evidence accumulated against General Dynamics led to a three-month suspension from new contracts, a fine paid for the Rickover incident, and the cancellation of $22.5 million in contracts. Two major charges against General Dynamics were later dropped by the U.S. Justice Department, because Navy officers knew of the falsifications and because of insufficient evidence. But dropping the charges also signaled defense contractors that "breaking the often-incestuous relationship between military contractors and their Pentagon overseers isn't a top priority."[5]

General Dynamics, unfortunately, is not an isolated example of ethical misconduct by defense contractors. In May 1985, General Electric pleaded guilty to defrauding the Air Force by filing 108 false claims for payment on a missile contract. The company was given the maximum fine of $1.04 million, and was ordered to pay back $800,000 for the false claims. The company initially denied any wrongdoing until a former G.E. manager, Roy Baessler, admitted his guilt in filing the claims, but stated that he was directed to mischarge by higher management. The mischarges involved the creation of a bogus research and development account to cover overruns from other accounts, and the altering of employee time cards.[6] Ethics in business requires honesty and condemns cheating; the evidence points to violations of these precepts by officials at General Electric and General Dynamics.

In July 1986, Litton Industries agreed to pay $15 million in restitution and penalties after pleading guilty to defrauding the Pentagon of $6.3 million in funds for military-electronic contracts. The fraud involved 45 contracts awarded between 1975 and 1984. The Justice Department also raised twenty-two charges of mail fraud and false statements against a former vice president of Litton, plus two charges against a former division manager. The former vice president, Michael Millspaugh, was charged with submitting false cost and pricing data to the military, in part by inflating prices of materials.[7]

A bribery scandal at the Defense Department's Industrial Supply Center in Philadelphia gave further evidence of the breadth of the scandals related to procurement. Through May of 1986, more than two dozen former center employees and company officials were convicted of, or pleaded guilty to, charges involving nearly $350,000 in bribes. Two more buyers at the center were indicted for allegedly accepting more than $240,000 in bribes. Prosecutors identified some $20 million in contracts awarded by the center to firms accused of participating in the bribery schemes.[8]

The government now recognizes how widespread the problem of kickbacks may be in the defense industry. Other investigations have resulted in the conviction of employees of several large corporations: Hughes Aircraft,

Northrup, Raytheon, and Teledyne. Suppliers who do not pay kickbacks risk being frozen out of business. One owner of a machine company in Massachusetts claims that when he refused to pay a military contractor a $45,000 kickback, his business with that contractor fell from $500,000 a year to less than $50,000.[9] Bribery and kickbacks are dishonest forms of cheating or coercion that violate the rules of fair competition.

Unfortunately, these examples represent only the tip of the iceberg. Rockwell International pleaded guilty to a 20-count indictment for submitting false labor costs on an Air Force contract. When a TRW manager was dismissed for inflating costs, he claimed that in doing so he was simply following the "standard operating procedure" of the company. United Technologies faced a series of charges on kickbacks, bribery, and cost mischarges. Lockheed and Boeing came under investigation in 1986. Some 45 of the top 100 contractors were under investigation.[10] Some companies may prove that they have done no wrong or may be able to cover up their wrongdoing. But the extensiveness of the investigations and the number of companies that have already pleaded guilty or been convicted indicate a problem of serious proportions.

What is being done to eliminate fraud in government procurement? Some corporations, stung by the scandals and fearing loss of reputation and business, have taken corrective steps. In response to the company's problems, General Dynamics appointed a new chief executive, Stanley Pace, to implement strong ethical guidelines and to define procedures more clearly so that incidents of ethical misconduct could be avoided. McDonnell-Douglas has instituted an in-house ethical training program for all its managers, and other companies have followed suit.[11]

The government must continue its investigations, however, to make certain that changes occur. In some instances it appears that penalties have been too light. General Dynamics lost $22.5 million in contracts as part of the penalty in its first suspension. That amounts to only 0.3 of one percent of its contracts. When General Dynamics was suspended again, the Navy extended indefinitely the bidding on new submarine contracts so that General Dynamics could compete after their suspension.

The government must also find ways to check loopholes that have enabled some suspended contractors to continue contracting. They now subcontract or create new corporations. One contractor, sentenced to jail for selling non-existent equipment, continued to do business from jail by starting a new firm operated by his wife and son.[12] The government has, on the other hand, put pressure on violators by applying the False Claims Act, which extracts double damages plus a penalty for every phony bill or report.[13] If corporations were to act conscientiously, adopting ethical codes and truly observing them, the need for such enforcement would end. General Dynamics is now training all its managers in ethics. It remains to be seen if the ethical climate will change there.

Responsibility for eliminating fraud rests not only with corporations and the government, but also with the military. Military personnel want the best; they want to stay with corporations they believe produce quality goods. Often there is only one contractor equipped to provide them with the weapons they want. But this overriding priority—evidenced by short suspensions and the extension of bidding deadlines to General Dynamics—unfortunately sends an all-too-clear message to corporations: We prefer that you act ethically, and public opinion can force us to crack down on you, but don't worry too much, you will get the contracts in any case. If we want corporations to act ethically, this message from the military must change.

Waste and Inflated Costs

The government has an ethical duty not to waste taxpayers' money; the military, as part of the government, shares this duty. Corporations remain ethically responsible for honesty in reporting costs and setting prices. Failures of these ethical responsibilities are evident in the following examples of scandal that have occurred concerning exorbitant costs and waste. The annual defense budget is over $300 billion, yet ironically it was relatively insignificant but graphic costs that awakened public concern. Lockheed sold $640 custom-made toilet covers for Navy planes. The Miramar naval station near San Diego paid Grumman $659 each for ashtrays, $404 apiece for socket wrenches, and $1143 for an indicator light that the manufacturers priced at $330.[14] The Air Force paid $9606 for a 12-cent Allen wrench. The Navy purchased $17 claw hammers for $435 each and 13-cent nuts for $2043 each. The Air Force bought plastic caps for $1118 each; these same caps cost 31 cents each when bought in bulk shipments.[15] The explanations offered for some of these exorbitant prices have not been too convincing: the screws required special metal; competitors priced the toilets only $100 lower; specific spare parts were difficult to obtain.

The cost of spare parts, however, only symbolizes the problem of exorbitant costs. Far more serious are the billions of dollars added each year by cost overruns and weapons that prove faulty or are abandoned. The cost of a single MX missile increased from $57.4 million in 1982 to $102.6 million in 1983, a 79 percent boost in a single year.[16] The Army's M-1 tank was predicted to cost $1.5 million in 1983; its actual cost was $2.5 million.[17] In a study of prices paid for aircraft engine parts, of some 15,000 components nearly a third had increased by 500 percent in just two years.[18] In 1985, *Business Week* claimed that Reagan's unprecedented 92 percent increase in weapons research and development was fostering "costly fiascos." It cited three high-tech weapons that have cost billions but which appear badly flawed or useless: a new submarine advanced-combat system (SUBACS), an advanced, medium-ranged, air-to-air missile (AMRAAM), and the DIVAD air defense gun, which has been abandoned.[19] Social responsibility demands that more conscientious care be taken in spending taxpayers' money.

One noted critic of military spending claims that the whole system of spending is structured to be cost-maximizing in contrast to the cost-minimizing which is more characteristic of U.S. free enterprise. With its logic of subsidy-maximization and non-competitive contracts, the Pentagon pays exorbitant amounts for military production. Compared to the cost per standardized unit of output in a competitive civilian industry, military production runs as much as twenty times higher. Defense contracts prove immensely profitable to contractors. In 1972, one hundred and thirty-one defense firms had after-refund profits of over 50 percent of net worth; twenty-two earned between 200 and 500 percent; four exceeded 500 percent profits.[20] These, we believe, are unconscionable profits.

Dealing with the Cost Factor

The public pays the tab for military weapons. Having a third party (the public) cover costs lessens the concern that the military or defense contractors might have for reducing costs. Getting the goods they want, not cost efficiency, appears to be a priority for the military. Selling more expensive weapons generally proves more profitable for the defense contractor. Analysts, however, see systemic features in the budget process as causes of high costs. They cite especially the non-competitive nature of defense contracts and the way in which costs are estimated.

Less than 7 percent of the Pentagon's contracts are competitively awarded. For most large contracts only a single company is considered, or one is chosen through negotiation with a selected group of major contractors. Prices, therefore, are often determined by government "cost estimates" rather than by competition between rival suppliers. Proponents of greater competition cite a study of 20 contracts where average savings of more than 50 percent were achieved by changing from sole-source to competitive bidding. When the Pentagon stopped purchasing door gaskets for $94.50 each under a sole-source contract, it was able to buy them through a competitively awarded contract for $5.69 each.[21] Present buying practices, in contrast, provide little incentive to cut costs.

The prevailing system of cost estimating, as opposed to competitive bidding, also opens the door to unethical behavior on the part of contractors. A primary defense contractor subcontracts the production of parts to other companies. In theory, the prime contractor should submit complete and accurate accounts of all subcontract costs. But at times the contract is negotiated before such information is complete. When this happens the prime contractor can negotiate subcontract prices considerably lower than the cost estimates submitted to the government. The result is a windfall profit. The General Accounting Office found that in 100 prime contracts negotiated before subcontract estimates were clearly priced, 87 of the contractors negotiated subcontract price reductions amounting to $42 million. In other cases prime contractors have misclassified subcontracts. For example, the FMC Corporation of San Jose misclassified non-competitive subcontract estimates as competitive; this enabled the firm to negotiate $3.7 million in price reductions with its subcontractors.[22] The GAO also found government agencies remiss in allowing too many overhead expenses. It noted that half of the defense contractor overhead charges challenged by the Defense Audit Agency were allowed by contracting officers. In one location, $31 million in costs were challenged, but the defense department contractors approved $16.5 million of these anyway.[23]

The Pentagon's budgeting process is often challenged for its "chronic tendency to underestimate prices" (the examples we have already noted). Studies show that the Pentagon has consistently underestimated inflation rates as well as the added costs of midstream design changes and operating costs.[24] Another contributing factor to high costs is that the present procurement system permits contractors to bid low but then to raise costs by introducing engineering changes after the initial award. Since the contractors are the sole source, the military will pay rather than lose the weapons they want. The lack of careful monitoring of costs and cost estimates by the Department of Defense also contributes to high costs.[25] Ethical responsibility for reducing costs lies primarily with the government, but the conscientious corporation will also recognize its duties of honesty and fairness in drawing profits from public money.

The evidence points to the need for change in the procurement process to assure more ethical conduct, but vested interests make the path to such change difficult. The leading defense contractors, who already have sole-source contracts and who profit from high cost estimates, will hardly lobby for change unless they are ethically motivated to do so. Military personnel find it easier to deal with one contractor whose products they know. It is also simpler for them to let the contractor deal with details like subcontracting. Military personnel appear to value quality more than cost-effectiveness. But high quality too often is equated with high-tech hardware—the flashiest and most impressive products. Since most research on new weapons is done within the industries (but paid for by the government), the contractors have a natural bias for selling the military on the most profitable equipment they can produce, not necessarily the best. The only real limits on cost are those set by Congress.[26]

The "revolving-door" syndrome, in which retired military personnel take jobs in the defense industry, also works against effective reform. In 1982, some 2600 senior military officials retired and went to work for defense contractors. Some took jobs with the very companies they were previously charged with overseeing. A former Air Force officer claims that Hughes Aircraft had "hired a small army of people" from the Pentagon office in charge of developing the problem-plagued Maverick missile manufactured by the firm. The revolving-door too often encourages Pentagon officials to worry less about the taxpayers' money and more about finding lucrative jobs in the future.[27]

Congress should be the natural place to find defenders for the uses of taxpayers' money. Indeed, most of the probes into the costs of military spending have come from members of Congress. But cutting back "in general" becomes a stickier issue when the cuts may affect one's own congressional district. Corporations know this and play on the parochial interests of the individual members. In many areas, defense companies employ more people than any other industry. Boeing is the biggest employer in the state of Washington; Bath Iron Works is the largest employer in Maine. General Dynamics is a dominant employer in Connecticut, and military companies are the most important source of employment in California. Defense industries influence Congress in other ways also. In the 1981–82 election cycle, the political action committees (PACs) of five defense contractors—Tenneco, General Dynamics, Grumman, General Electric, and Rockwell International— were among the 10 largest corporate PAC contributors. The Tenneco PAC, with expenditures of nearly $500,000, was the largest among all corporations.[28]

The natural forces at work in what one analyst calls "the iron triangle" (defense contractors, Congress, the Defense Department) will not produce significant reforms in defense spending.[29] Natural tendencies, which look to self-interest, need to be countered with social values that stress the common good of society.

Questioning the Priority of Military Spending

Ethically conscious Americans agree on the need to curb waste in defense spending. They differ in their priorities when the issue deals with determining how much of the federal budget should be allotted to defense as opposed to other needs. On this issue, the values we discussed in Chapter Two come into conflict. For some Americans protecting freedom is an all-important value, and money is no obstacle when freedom is at stake. Defense Secretary Caspar Weinberger expresses this view forcefully: "What can have a higher priority than peace with freedom. The answer, of course, is nothing."[30] The threat of the Soviet Union and the spread of world communism are stressed to show that freedom is indeed at stake. The alarm raised by the Reagan administration in the early 1980s, that the United States was falling behind in the arms race, fueled the buildup of defense spending.

Few Americans would downplay the importance of freedom, but many do question its use to justify current levels of defense spending. The U.S. buildup in spending was triggered in part by allegations that the Soviet Union was spending 50 percent more than the United States in order to surpass us. But a CIA reassessment in 1983 showed that Soviet expenditures had levelled off during 1977–81 and that the increase in overall Soviet spending was half of earlier projections. The earlier figure on Soviet spending had been reached by attaching U.S. dollar prices to Soviet expenditures (for example, assigning U.S. voluntary army wages to Soviet draftees). The Stockholm International

Peace Research Institute showed U.S. military spending running ahead of the Soviets in the 1970s, although it acknowledged that the Soviets had narrowed the gap.[31]

Evaluating the respective military strength of the United States and the Soviet Union, or the degree of threat posed by communism, would carry us far beyond the intended scope of this chapter. The priority issue, weighing defense needs against other national and global interests, should nevertheless be raised. Money spent on defense diverts funds that might be used to address many social needs related to the value of human dignity (food, housing, education, a clean environment, etc.). Ruth Sivard, a prominent analyst of military spending, presents the following items to provoke reflection about priorities in current (1985) world military and social expenditures:

> The megatonnage in the world's stockpile of nuclear weapons is enough to kill 58 billion people, or to kill every person now living 12 times.
>
> In the Third World military spending has increased fivefold since 1960, and the number of countries ruled by military governments has grown from 22 to 57.
>
> The budget of the U.S. Air Force is larger than the total educational budget for 1.2 billion children in Africa, Latin America, and Asia, excluding Japan.
>
> The Soviet Union in one year spends more on military defense than governments of all the developing countries spend for education and health care for 3.6 billion people.
>
> The developed countries on average spend 5.4 percent of their GNP for military purposes, 0.3 percent for development assistance to poorer countries.
>
> If the price of an automobile had gone up as much since World War II as the price of sophisticated weapons, the average car today would cost $300,000.
>
> It costs $590,000 a day to operate one aircraft carrier and every day in Africa alone 14,000 children die of hunger or hunger-related causes.[32]

In 1983, the Congressional Budget Office compared reductions on domestic programs versus weapons costs projected for the fiscal year 1984. Reductions in work incentive programs would be $153 million compared to the cost of $180 million for three C–5 aircraft. Reductions in student financial assistance were projected at $1080 million, compared to a cost of $1025 million for five B–1B bombers. Child welfare services faced a $29 million reduction, compared to $34 million to be spent on one F–18 fighter jet. Child nutrition would lose $1392 million compared to $1,620 million to be spent on the F–18 program.[33]

In addressing the question of military spending, we need also to consider how it affects employment and productivity. Does defense spending create jobs and boost the economy, or does it adversely affect jobs and economic growth? The Council on Economic Priorities found adverse effects predominating. Comparing 17 advanced industrial nations, the Council found that those devoting large portions of gross domestic product to arms typically had weakening economies, decreasing technological progress, and spreading industrial lethargy associated with low investment rates. The Council also showed that military spending is one of the least effective ways of stimulating job creation. About 28,000 jobs are created for every $1 billion spent on military procurement; the same billion dollars would create 32,000 jobs if spent for public transit, 57,000 if spent for personal consumption, or 71,000 if spent for education.[34] Military spending also exacerbates the national debt and makes capital less available for other business investments.

Questioning the level of U.S. military spending is an important ethical issue because it affects our whole economy and national priorities. We recognize, however, the conflicting values and data interpretation involved in this issue, so we focused primarily on issues of fraud and waste where we would hope to find a moral consensus. Conscientious corporate leaders, concerned with eliminating fraud and reducing military costs, could take significant steps toward making ours a more ethical nation.

POLITICAL INFLUENCE AND CORPORATIONS

Americans prize democracy. The freedoms and equality articulated in the U.S. Constitution and the Bill of Rights constitute an embodiment of important ethical values. We discussed these values in Chapter Two, under the heading of traditional business values. Some critics argue that big business (large corporations) undermines democracy by using disproportionate power in society and influence on government to achieve its own self-interests. This criticism is not new; large corporations have been attacked by leftist critics through most of modern history, but the issue does touch on fundamental values and should be considered.

Corporate Power, Wealth, and Politics

Charles Lindbloom presents a forceful challenge to corporate influence in his study on *Politics and Markets*. He defends free enterprise and the market system, but he questions the amount of power exercised by large corporations. He concludes with the strong judgment that corporations are "disproportionately powerful" on many counts and consequently do not fit well into democratic theory and vision.[35] Lindbloom argues, first of all, that business executives act as "public officials in the market system" because they make the policy decisions that most affect the welfare of the nation. The executives decide a nation's industrial technology, the way work is organized, plant locations, resource allocation, and executive compensation and status.[36] Their decisions, Lindbloom argues, affect people's lives—their jobs, homes, consumer goods, leisure—far more than decisions made by government officials. But citizens have no vote on these important economic policies.

When direct influence on government is considered, Lindbloom claims that business leaders hold a position different from any other group in society, since the functioning of the market system rests in their hands. Jobs, prices, production, growth, the standard of living and the economic security of everyone depends on how business performs. Business leaders are not just representatives of one or more interest groups; the whole welfare of society depends on what they do. They may not obtain all they ask for, but the state cannot risk ignoring their demands. When government officials talk about the need to adjust taxes or monetary policies to stimulate business, they are acknowledging the privileged position of business. Lindbloom also argues that large corporations have disproportionate lobbying power because of their extraordinary sources of funding, professional personnel, and special access to Congress and government officials.

Who runs the government of the United States? Wealthy white males, in comparison with other segments of the population, are disproportionately represented at the highest levels of the federal government. Most of the presidents of the United States over the past fifty years have been white male millionaires, with Democrats providing the wealthiest (Roosevelt, Kennedy, Johnson). At least 53 members of Congress in 1985 were millionaires; a study of the Senate seven years before showed the average senator to have a net worth of nearly one-half million dollars.[37]

The link between wealth and large corporations, on the other hand, is not so clearly drawn. Few presidents came from the ranks of large corporations; of the 53 millionaires in Congress in 1985, 33 amassed fortunes on their own and 11 inherited much of their wealth. Men with some significant corporate background do predominate, however, at top levels of the executive branch of the government. Some of the top officials and advisors in the Reagan administration were: George Bush, founder of Zapata Oil, George P. Shultz, president of Bechtel Corporation, Caspar Weinberger, vice-president of Bechtel, Edwin Meese, vice-present of Rohr Industries, Malcolm Baldridge, chairman of Scoville Corporation, Donald Regan, chairman of Merrill Lynch & Co.[38] The pattern of looking to big business to fill cabinet posts crosses political party lines. A study made of cabinet appointments between 1897 and 1972 showed that 78 percent of the 205 cabinet appointments came from the ranks of business or corporation-oriented law firms.[39]

The dominant presence of wealth in federal offices, even where it is closely linked to corporations, does not necessarily mean controlling power. G. William Domhoff, a well-known critic of wealthy elites, acknowledges that "no group or class has 'power' in America, but only 'influence'."[40] More importantly for our consideration, wealth and influence, or even power, are not in themselves ethically wrong or bad. Some of the finest officials in U.S. history have come from the wealthy class. We want successful people to be in government. Wealth and influence do, however, present a potential danger. They can be used unethically: to undermine democratic rules by buying influence; to make politics a tool for attaining one's own self-interest to the detriment of the common good of society. We will examine this danger more closely.

Congress enacted federal election campaign laws in 1971 and 1974 to limit the influence of money in politics and to limit the influence of any individual or organization on candidates for federal office. The influence of money in politics, one analyst of election laws observes, was evident during Richard Nixon's presidency:

> His major contributors, rightly or wrongly, were getting favorable consideration from government agencies. Clement Stone had given Nixon $500,000 in 1968 and was about to give him $2 million in 1972; at the same time, rate increases proposed by his Chicago-based insurance company were being considered by the Price Commission.[41]

Following Nixon's 1972 re-election campaign, 20 corporations and corporate officials were indicted on charges of making illegal corporate political contributions. Most pleaded guilty or *nolo contendere*.[42]

Columnist Jack Anderson drew national attention to another money-in-politics incident during this same period of the early 1970s. The Justice Department had filed an antitrust suit against the International Telephone and Telegraph Co. (ITT) but then backed off and reached a settlement. Anderson found evidence that suggested that the settlement was made as a "payoff" for a $400,000 pledge paid by an ITT subsidiary to help in bringing the 1972 Republican Convention to San Diego.[43] In some of the cases, guilt was not proven; but we cite them to dramatize the issue of using wealth and corporate power to influence politics.

Lobbies and PACS

How do groups "influence" government? Two legal and accepted ways of doing so are through lobbies and through some forms of fundraising for election campaigns. Lobbying is guaranteed by the First Amendment right of free speech. Both the style and amount of lobbying done in the United States have changed significantly in recent decades. Once it was possible to "buy" considerable influence by patronage, gifts, lavish entertainment, and other favors. To be effective today a lobbyist must be knowledgeable. Facts, analysis, and convincing communication are the keys to lobbying success. Congress faces nearly 15,000 proposals for bills each year. Legislators themselves have come to depend on lobbyists for their flow of information in dealing with these bills. The common perception of lobbying is influencing a legislator to vote one way or another on a bill already on the floor of Congress. Good lobbyists know that the more crucial stage comes at the level of subcommittees and that information, and even work on preparing bills, can be decisive.[44]

Lobbying has become a major business in its own right. By 1981 the number of lobbies in Washington had grown to over 8000. Over a thousand lawyers are paid to represent different interests. Labor and trade groups still have the largest number of lobbies, and special-interest groups have grown dramatically—for example, 102 lobbies represent different minority groups. Large corporations, noting labor's successful lobbying efforts and the proliferation of consumer-protection and other "issue-oriented" lobbies, developed their own successful lobbies. Few major corporations are without their own lobby. Most have offices in Washington; those who do not have offices there hire lawyers and professional lobbyists. Ford Motor Co. has a staff of forty in Washington. In 1980, the oil companies, represented by the American Petroleum Institute, had the largest budget ($40 million) and the largest staff (375) of any one industry. The iron and steel companies also had a $10 million-a-year-budget; the American Bankers Association had a $20 million annual budget. The U.S. Chamber of Commerce had a $85 million budget and a staff of 1600.[45] Grass-roots lobbying was once the special forte of labor unions. Business has now become one of the most effective lobby groups, as the Business Roundtable and the Chamber of Commerce demonstrated in rallying their constituencies to defeat efforts to create a Consumer Protection Agency. No other lobby group, however, seems to match the effectiveness of the National Rifle Association, which claims it can generate fourteen million letters of grass-root support within a few days.

Corporations do not compete on an equal footing with other contending lobby groups; they have distinct advantages. A popular-based, government-watchdog group like Common Cause cannot match through voluntary contributions the lobbying activities of corporations. Corporations can pass their lobbying costs on to consumers as a cost of doing business; Common Cause, with no product to sell, cannot. Wealth does make a difference. Corporations also have other means of influence. Corporate executives predominate in the numerous governmental "advisory" councils (for example, the Business Council, the Council on Foreign Affairs, the Business and Defense Services Administration), which affect policy formation long before lobbyists come on the scene.

The Business Roundtable represents a new style of advocacy, made up exclusively of chief corporate officers of major corporations. Members pay dues ranging from $10,000 to $45,000 to finance their efforts. The Roundtable was initiated in 1972 to counter the lobbying power of labor. It used its influence to help defeat Ralph Nader's effort to create a consumer protection agency. But it differs from older business groups, like the National Association of Manufacturers, in that it strives to go beyond narrow advocacy positions. It conducts its own research in the search for positive solutions to issues of national concern. While the Roundtable continues to represent the interests of big business, one of its stated goals is to concern itself with social responsibility. Its main successes, however, have come in "defeating" regulations and reform legislation aimed at corporations.[46]

If lobbying is a recognized means of exerting influence, so also is fund-raising to promote candidates viewed as favorable to one's interests. The Federal Election Campaign Act of 1971 stimulated corporations to make use of political action committees (PACs) like those which had been used by labor unions. In 1975, the use of PACs rose significantly after the Federal Election Commission ruled favorably on a case where company funds were used to solicit voluntary contributions for PACs from employees.[47] PACs have grown dramatically since that time. From 1974 to 1984 the number of PACs grew by 700 percent, from 608 to 4243, and the money contributed by PACs to congressional candidates jumped 800 percent, from $12.5 million to more than $100 million. Three months prior to the 1986 elections PAC contributions had jumped 32 percent over the comparable period in 1984.[48] PACs have also become the center of much controversy; we believe that they are proving detrimental to the political process of democracy.

Those who favor PACs say that they enable many dispersed individuals to channel their efforts and to tie their contributions more closely with their special interests. PACs give such groups more focus, greater visibility, and greater influence. But is the "buying of influence" ethically good? We believe it is not. Common Cause reported in 1986 that the National Rifle Association's PAC spent $1.1 million from 1981–1985 on House members, with the hope of defeating or weakening gun-control laws. Eighty percent of the House members who voted with the NRA had received financial support from the NRA's PAC; eighty percent who voted against the NRA position received no support. Common Cause also noted that, during the 1984 elections, contributions from thirteen major defense contractors' PACs totalled $2.1 million, up 132 percent over the 1980 elections.[49] Congressman Dan Rostenkowski (Dem, Ill.), chair of the House Ways and Means Committee, which writes tax legislation, collected $600,000 in 1983. Eighty percent of this came from PACs with special interests to protect in any new tax legislation.[50]

The fact that donors "get something for their money" is precisely the ethical concern of critics, a concern that legislation may go to the highest bidder or most affluent PAC. Since the Tilman Act of 1907, it has been illegal for business to make contributions from company funds to political campaigns for federal elections. The legislation was intended to avoid the buying of interest that PACs seem now to encourage. Corporations may still not use company funds for campaign donations; but crediting the corporation's PAC for contributions achieves the effect that the original 1907 legislation sought to avoid. Many firms with good reputations, such as DuPont, IBM, and Xerox, have not developed PACs. But many more corporations have. *Corporate* PAC affiliations increased more than 147 percent between 1977 and 1984 with a more than 700 percent increase in dollars contributed (as compared to a 67 percent increase in labor PACs and a 240 percent increase in the dollar contributions).[51] In elections from 1972 to 1976, Democrats received more than two-thirds of PAC money. In the 1980s Republicans came out on top. The top fund-raisers are ultra-conservative, pro-business PACs; Jesse Helm's National Congressional Club and the National Conservative PAC were the top fund-raisers in 1981–82. The top ten PACs also included the Fund for a Conservative Majority, Citizens for the Republic, and other conservative PACs.[52] Many fear that the PAC system is harmful to the political process by redistributing political strength from ideologically broad political parties toward ideologically narrow or extreme groups and special interests. This militates against the social value of participation (community).

Two other concerns have been raised about PACs. First, PACs have contributed to dramatic increases in election spending. Senate winners in the 1986 elections spent an average of $3 million each, five times more than winners a decade before. House winners spent an average of $340,000 each, four times the average spent in 1976. PACs poured $126 million into the campaigns, with $98 million going to the winners. The elections did suggest, however, that spending can reach a saturation point; several candidates who outspent their opponents were routed in the elections.[53] Second, PACs have also been shown clearly to favor incumbents. With their larger war chests, only six House incumbents were defeated in the 1986 elections. Before the 1984 elections, 87 percent of corporate PAC money went to incumbents; only 5 percent went to challengers, with the rest going to candidates in open elections.[54] The reason for the disparity seems clear. Incumbents have something to provide in return: their vote on vital interests. The moral concern here is evident. The PAC contributor wants to buy access to the officeholder or wants a vote on specific legislation. Buying influence subverts the ideals of democracy.

Some corporate executives recognize the danger of PACs. Irving Shapiro, retired CEO of DuPont Chemical calls PACs "an invidious thing" that corrupts and pollutes the political system. Stanley Marcus, retired CEO of Neiman-Marcus, considers them "dangerous as the devil."[55] Many members of Congress are now urging that PACs be curbed. Congressman Dan Rostenkowski, a recipient himself of $500,000 in his personal PAC, complained that he was "nauseated" at the influence that campaign money seemed to have on some members of his committee working on the tax revision bill. Two old-line conservatives joined in his complaint. Senator Barry Goldwater complained, "It is not 'we the people' but political action committees who are setting the nation's political agenda and are influencing the position of candidates on the important issues of the day." Senator John Stennis concurred: "We are gradually moving elections away from the people."[56] While getting more people into the political process is good, PACs tend to substitute special-interest pressures for attainment of the common good. Moreover, they bias the electoral process by making access to money an even greater determinator of success, money that too easily can be used to purchase access, or even votes, in a legislature.

GOVERNMENT REGULATIONS

Government, through regulation, attempts to keep the market competitive (antitrust laws) or otherwise protect the public interest (for example, health, safety, truth in contracts). Corporate executives in the past often viewed the government as an adversary attempting to regulate and constrain their efforts. Executives have blamed the government for economic woes that have often beset the nation—inflation, stagnation, loss of markets to other countries, and government spending that siphoned off money needed in the private sector and drove up interest rates. Many business leaders oppose government intervention because they believe free enterprise best serves the needs of the nation. They have been especially critical of many government regulations.

We believe that some of their criticisms are valid and need to be considered. We also recognize, however, that many regulations have been effective in protecting and promoting human dignity, the public good, and justice; they have also served to protect free enterprise itself and to support business values.

While government control of American industry began in colonial times, detailed price and entry regulations were first enacted in 1887. Through the next several decades regulation developed slowly. The Federal Communication Commission, The Interstate Commerce Commission, the Civil Aeronautics Board, and similar agencies were designed to protect competition and to guard against monopolistic control over prices. In more recent times public concern over social issues has led to a rapid growth in regulatory agencies. From 1965–75, twenty-six new government agencies were established, including the Environmental Protection Agency (EPA) and the Occupational Safety and Health Administration (OSHA).[57]

By 1980, these many agencies were issuing thousands of rules, covering almost every aspect of economic life—hiring, promotion, workplace conditions, product design, plant locations, pollution, and more. Critics pointed to the enormous costs of government regulations. The clamor for deregulation became strong in the business community in the late 1970s. The newer social regulations were a special target of criticism, especially the FDA (Food and Drug Administration), EPA, and OSHA.[58] Ronald Reagan was elected president in 1980, promising a return to a minimal government role.

Cost of Regulation

Critics figured that regulations were costing the nation between $100 and $130 billion dollars each year.[59] Environmental regulation alone was said to cost $50 to $60 billion annually. Dow Chemical estimated its own cost in meeting regulations at $186 million per year. Dow acknowledged that some government regulations benefited the public, but said that 45 percent of regulations did not. Dow canceled plans to build a $300 million petrochemical complex in California, despite consumer needs, because it could only obtain four of the sixty-five government permits it needed.[60]

One prominent critic claimed that safety regulations imposed on the auto industry added an estimated $666 dollars to the price of an average 1978 car, or $6.7 billion dollars for every ten million cars sold.[61] Similar regulations added $1500–$2000 to the cost of a typical new home. Time spent on paperwork and litigation was estimated to be 71,500 man-years of work. Regulations on the mining of coal led to a 32 percent drop in production from 1968–78, and lower productivity caused by overall regulations amounted to a $20 billion loss in the annual level of GNP.[62]

Regulations have protected lives, but at a cost of an estimated $170,000 to $3 million per life saved.[63] Regulations are aimed chiefly at large companies, but small businesses often suffer the most. Many small firms failed because they could not meet the costs needed to comply with government regulations.[64]

Cost is not the only reason for criticism of government regulation. The government often sent out conflicting messages: reduce pollution or improve safety conditions, but keep prices down; reduce energy consumption, but improve productivity. Government agencies made the electric utilities shift from coal to oil to reduce pollution, but then told them to shift back to coal to reduce dependency on oil imports. Regulations called for protection of children against flammable sleepwear. To meet requirements, several companies introduced a new flame-retardant chemical phosphate, called TRIS. But then TRIS was judged to be a carcinogen and was banned. Manufacturers lost tens of millions of dollars trying to meet a safety standard that had been imposed on them.[65]

The triviality of many regulations has also come under fire. One FDA committee deliberated over a period of years on whether peanut butter should be required to contain 87 percent or 90 percent peanuts. Another regulation concerned itself with the number of lemons that could be shipped from California to Arizona in January.[66] The effectiveness of many regulations was also questioned. New York City spent $200 million to reduce the level of sulfur in fuel burning by 0.3 percent, a negligible change.[67] The sheer number of regulations points out the scope of the problem. The 1980 *Federal Register* had more than 74,000 pages on regulations; forty agencies added 8000 new regulations in that year alone.[68] Corporation managers thus feel that the deck is stacked against them, and that they are faced with a frustrating burden of costly, conflicting, and often ineffective regulations.

To the extent that regulations are excessively costly, trivial, or contradictory, they violate our traditional business norms of individual responsibility and productivity. The regulations in these instances also fail to promote the public good.

Government Protects Business and the Community

Government has supported business throughout most of U.S. history. It offered numerous benefits to business: laws protecting private property and contracts, land grants and loans for the railway industry, the building of roads, government intervention to protect overseas investments, and tariffs to protect domestic industries. Antitrust regulations to assure competition came about through the insistence of the business community itself, albeit mostly small businesses. Even large corporations could hardly complain at the outset that the regulations undermined their efforts. Fifteen of the first sixteen cases reviewed by the Interstate Commerce Commission (ICC) in the 19th century were adjudicated in favor of the rail companies.[69] Many industries, moreover, have called on the government *for* regulations, since the advent of increased foreign penetration of the U.S. markets. Thus U.S. steel companies asked the government to check "dumping" practices by foreign companies (i.e. selling steel at lower-than-cost prices).[70] Corporations also retain a potent power to resist, contain, mitigate, and even to avoid regulation.[71]

Without government regulations we would not have clean air or water. Toxic materials would still be dumped in landfills, getting into drinking water. Without government regulations children might still be working 70 hour weeks, as they were at the time of the Industrial Revolution. The market alone does not ensure human dignity and the public good. Government needs to play a role; this general point businesspeople acknowledge and support. The ethical question is: Does the regulation indeed support justice, the public good, and the dignity of the human person without too great a trade-off cost of individual responsibility and productivity? We are willing to pay a considerable amount, for example, for clean water. Yet we are not willing to pay limitless sums for perfectly clean water.

An adversarial relationship between government and business is more of an American phenomenon than one common to free enterprise systems. In Europe, business and government work more closely together.[72] In Japan, corporations have cooperated in helping the government to shape national policies. The reluctance of U.S. corporations to accept social norms and social responsibility in the past often required government action. This will probably happen again, perhaps in such areas as control on financial "raiders," use of confidential information, equal employment opportunity, or cost over-runs on government contracts.

The total cost of regulation discussed earlier was not all wasted. Many of these dollars went to bring cleaner air and water and safer products and workplaces. Some of it surely went into record keeping. However, if the goals of regulations are good, and the regulations reasonable, why should record keeping be a waste? We do not consider financial accounting systems a waste, but a necessary cost of doing business. Moreover, for a fair analysis, one must subtract the avoided costs of medical bills, damaged crops, oil spills, and insurance claims. For example, it has been estimated that by preventing a single lost day of one manufacturing worker due to a work-related accident, a typical company saves $14,000.[73] Regulations have also been effective. Coal mining deaths have been cut in half; the quality of air has improved greatly, with a 46 percent decline in carbon monoxide.

Effective Regulations

As indicated earlier, regulations are intended to:

1. Protect the market system, or
2. Protect a public good that the market system neglects.

The ethical norm by which one judges whether a certain regulation is good is the extent to which it achieves its purpose at a reasonable cost. A regulation such as antitrust insures competition and therefore is supported by the traditional business norm of productivity and individual responsibility.

Deregulation of the airlines was brought about to achieve lower air fares. Regulation had led to artificially high prices.[74] The regulating agency, the Civil Aeronautics Board, (CAB) was also criticized for overprotecting existing airlines. Between 1950 and 1974, seventy-nine applications were considered from companies wishing to enter the domestic-scheduled airline industry. None of them was approved, and more than 90 percent of requests for new routes by existing airlines were turned down. The consequences of airline deregulation were positive. Even with higher fuel prices, lower ticket prices resulted.[75] A more recent concern is whether the current merger trend among airlines will result in monopolistic control, and eventually higher prices.[76]

Regulations to protect airline travel or for clean air and water are ethical when they are effective in achieving their purpose and at a price that is reasonable. Note that the ethical norm is also one that is practical and effective. Ethics is not an absolute or an unrealizeable ideal, but an aid to decision making when difficult trade-offs are necessary.

Deregulation or modification of regulations is called for when the regulations do not meet the parallel set of traditional business norms and social norms that were discussed in Chapter Two. The problem is to find the right balance in meeting the common good while maintaining efficiency and productivity. Airlines and trucking were good candidates for deregulation. Regulations were no longer effective in achieving the original goals and were costing the consumer and the economy immense sums of money to retain.

Let us examine pollution regulations more carefully. Pollution problems are serious enough to warrant government intervention, since corporations cannot be expected to invest heavily in voluntary control unless they know their competitors are required to do the same. Pollution regulations have proved very expensive and are not always effective. Rather than specify an absolute amount of pollution that may be generated, another option is to use incentives such as charges, taxes, and marketable rights. The EPA is already experimenting with a simpler and less costly rule on smoke pollution. Instead of a rule limiting the amount of emissions from each of a factory's smokestacks, the EPA places an imaginary "bubble" over the factory. The bubble states the *total* amount of pollution the factory can emit; the owner is free to determine how much pollutant each stack will emit. A similar standard can be set for a whole region, with incentives for companies that meet or improve on the standard and charges for those that do not.[77]

Trade-offs between costs and other social benefits are a major consideration here. The more that emissions are reduced, the more expensive the process. Take, for example, a meat packing firm that is trying to reduce the biological oxygen demand (BOD) that its processing plant discharges. (BOD refers to the oxygen that the discharge will demand from the water as it undergoes chemical change; the more oxygen needed by the discharge, the less that is available for plants and fish.) If the plant already removes 30 percent of the BOD, elimination of an extra pound of BOD might cost 6 cents; but if 90 percent is already removed, removal of one pound more would cost 60 cents, or 90 cents if 95 percent has already been removed. In more macroscopic terms, it may cost $61 billion over the next ten years to remove 85 to 90 percent of effluents from the nation's water supply. To eliminate *all* pollutants might cost an additional $200 billion.[78] The issue, then, is not *whether* pollution and safety regulations are needed, but finding a balance, and finding the most effective ways to reduce both dangers and costs.

In smaller social complexes, violations and unethical actions can be dealt with on an individual basis without writing detailed rules for all. As society becomes larger and more complex, the personal approach will no longer do. Rules and regulations become increasingly detailed and complex. More flexibility and use of incentives seem to be called for in the area of regulations. But so also does the need for more corporate responsibility become evident. When corporations ignore or pay little heed to public concerns, the government is forced to intervene for the common good. The more corporations regulate themselves—through company codes, industry-wide codes, high-level executives responsible for enforcing codes, social audits to evaluate implementation of codes—the less will government need to interfere.[79]

Government regulations are an instrument designed to achieve either (1) a more efficient operation of the markets, assuring competition and thus greater productivity, or (2) a protection of citizens and the public good. Most early regulations fell into the first category. Many of the recent regulations are in the latter group. Note that these groups parallel our two sets of ethical norms: traditional business norms and social norms. Both sets of goals should be kept in mind in evaluating each type of regulation. Regulations that protect the free market may also serve to promote justice and the public good. Social regulations generally cost something, yet that cost must not be excessive. The benefits to society must be worth the cost that is paid by all.

SUMMARY AND CONCLUSIONS

Voluntary steps taken by corporations to act ethically and to exercise social responsibility could solve many of the problems addressed in this chapter. Ethical integrity and social responsibility seem clearly to have broken down in the defense industry. Until greater integrity becomes more evident, the government will have to exercise its responsibility in eliminating fraud and controlling wasteful military spending. Individual citizens and public-interest lobby groups can help to make certain that the government remains vigilant.

The problem of political influence is more difficult to address. Democracy envisions a broad and equitable representation of different interest groups and promotion of the common good for all. Wealth and power used to "buy influence," and to achieve special interests in conflict with the common good, run counter to democratic ideals. Reducing the influence of PACs in federal elections may be one corrective step.

Government regulations are ethically and practically useful in protecting free enterprise and the public good. But they are ethically and practically useful to the extent that they achieve these goals at reasonable costs. Some regulations need stronger enforcement; others need modification. Cooperation between the government and corporations is needed to assure a balance that respects both business values and social values. Individual citizens and public-interest lobbies serve a constructive purpose in drawing attention to areas of public concern.

Conflicts of special interests will always remain in society. But we believe that the United States should move toward a more cooperative model of government, one in which all sectors of society may find greater voice and greater participation.[80] The Business Roundtable has sought to play a more constructive role in relating business and government concerns. We need a Coalition Roundtable of business, labor, consumers, and government to work genuinely for the common good of society.

DISCUSSION QUESTIONS

4.1. What are some of the most blatant examples of ethical misconduct in the defense industry?

4.2. Why does wasteful spending occur so frequently in respect to military goods, and how does wasteful spending violate the norms presented in Figure 2–1?

4.3. What are some of the main difficulties in attempting to reduce the cost of military spending?

4.4. Why does Lindbloom say that corporations are "disproportionately powerful" and do not fit well into democratic theory?

4.5. Assess the effect of PACs in the light of social values.

4.6. On what basis can one argue that PACs undermine democracy and harm the political process? How do they help?

4.7. Regulatory agencies are created to protect certain values. What are these values, and how are they operationalized in American society? (For example, consider the Environmental Protection Agency and some other regulatory body.)

4.8. Using the norms presented in Figure 2–1, how can we evaluate regulatory agencies?

4.9. How can one use ethical norms to judge the effectiveness of airline deregulation?

4.10. As summary questions: American society has developed strong business values. Identify them and comment on government's duty to protect those values.

4.11. Does American society have strong social values? Does government have a role to play in protecting them? Explain.

4.12. Describe ways in which large corporations have a greater affect on the individual than government does.

NOTES

[1]"Mr. Clean Charts a New Course at General Dynamics," *Fortune*, April 28, 1986, pp. 70–76.

[2]"Beware of Greeks Bearing Secrets," *Newsweek*, Feb. 20, 1984, pp. 58–61.

[3]"Mr. Clean Charts a New Course at General Dynamics", p. 70.

[4]"Waste, Fraud, and Abuse?", *Newsweek*, June 3, 1985, pp. 22–23.

[5]Paula Dwyer and Seth Payne, "The General Dynamics Case Sets a Bad Precedant," *Business Week*, June 8, 1987, p. 41.

[6]Jeff Gerth, "General Electric Admits Falsifying Billing on Missile," *The New York Times*, May 16, 1985, p. A-1.

[7]Eileen White and Debbie Goldberg, "Litton Pleads Guilty to Defrauding U.S. on Pentagon Work, Will Pay $15 million," *The Wall Street Journal*, July 14, 1986.

[8]Andy Pasztor, "Bribery Scandal at Defense Department Center Puts Focus on Problems in Military Procurement," *The Wall Street Journal*, May 28, 1986, p. 64.

[9]"Kickbacks Reported Widespread in Subcontracts for Military Work," *The New York Times*, April 26, 1986, pp. 1, 36.

[10]"Stepping Up the Attack on Contract Abuse," *Business Week*, July 1, 1986, p. 24.

[11]"Mr. Clean Charts a New Course," pp. 70–76.

[12]John Koten and Tim Carrington, "For General Dynamics, Scandal Over Billing Hasn't Hurt Business," *The Wall Street Journal*, April 29, 1986, pp. 1, 20, and Eileen White, "Suspended Contractors Often Continue to Get More Defense Business," *The Wall Street Journal*, May 6, 1986, pp. 1, 23.

[13]Lawrence J. Till, "Uncle Sam Vs. Chicken Fat," *Barrons*, August 18, 1986, pp. 27–29.

[14]"More High-priced Purchases Found at Miramar Air Base," *The Washington Post*, July 11, 1985, p. A-15.

[15]"Pentagon Bogs Down in its War on Waste," *U.S. News & World Report*, June 4, 1984, pp. 73–76. See also John Hanrahan, "Fat City," on Pentagon waste, in the *Common Cause* magazine, May/June 1983, pp. 44–55.

[16]Ibid.

[17]Michael R. Gordon, "Pentagon Cost Overruns, A Venerable Tradition, Survive Reagan's 'Reforms'," *National Journal*, Jan. 8, 1983, p. 58.

[18]"Pentagon Bogs Down in its War on Waste," p. 75.

[19]"Forget the $400 Hammers: Here's Where the Big Money is Lost," *Business Week*, July 8, 1985, pp. 48–50.

[20]Seymour Melman, *The Permanent War Economy* (New York: Touchstone, 1985, revised), pp. 43–44 (on units or outputs); p. 141 (on profit rates).

[21]"Pentagon Bogs Down in its War on Waste," pp. 73–76.

[22]Thirtieth Report by the Committee on Government Operations, House Report 99-562, April 29, 1986 (Washington, D.C.: U.S. Government Printing Office, 1986), pp. 5–6.

[23]Ibid., p. 8.

[24]"Pentagon Bogs Down in its War on Waste," p. 74.

[25]Gordon, "Pentagon Cost Overruns", pp. 55–57.

[26]Kenneth A. Bertsch and Linda S. Shaw, *The Nuclear Weapons Industry* (Washington, D.C.: Investor Responsibility Research Center, 1984), pp. 69–75.

[27]"Pentagon Bogs Down in its War on Waste," p. 74.

[28]Bertsch and Shaw, *The Nuclear Weapons Industry*, pp. 69–71.

29Gordon Adams, *The Iron Triangle: The Politics of Defense Contracting* (New York: Council on Economic Priorities, 1981).

30Caspar Weinberger cited in Bertsch and Shaw, *The Nuclear Weapons Industry*, p. 98.

31See the sources cited in the *Military Budget Manual*, A Report by the National SANE Education Funds, Washington, D.C., 1983, p. 3, and Ruth Leger Sivard, *World Military and Social Expenditures 1985* (Washington, D.C.: World Priorities, 1985), p. 17.

32Sivard, *World Military and Social Expenditures*, p. 5.

33Bertsch and Shaw, *The Nuclear Weapons Industry*, pp. 87–88 (for the Congressional Budget Office comparisons).

34Robert W. DeGrasse, Jr., "The Military: Shortchanging the Economy," in *The Nuclear Predicament, A Sourcebook*, Donna Gregory, ed. (New York: St. Martin's Press, 1986), pp. 163–164.

35Charles E. Lindbloom, *Politics and Markets* (New York: Basic Books, 1977), p. 356.

36Ibid., Chapter 13, "The Privileged Position of Business."

37"Congress's Millionaires—A Thriving Breed," *U.S. News & World Report*, June 3, 1985, p. 35; and Mark Green et al., *Who Runs Congress?* (New York: Dell, 1984), p. 298, on the 1978 Senate.

38Thomas R. Dye, *Who's Running America? The Conservative Years* (Englewood, N.J.: Prentice Hall, 4th ed, 1986), pp. 88–91 (from his table of officials).

39G. William Domhoff, *Who Rules America Now? A View for the '80s* (Englewood Cliffs, N.J.: Prentice Hall, 1983), pp. 139–41.

40Ibid., p. 8.

41Rodney N. Smith, "Federal Election Law Part II: What You Can Get Away With!," in *Campaign & Elections*, Fall 1982, p. 11.

42Ibid., p. 21.

43A lengthy history of "The ITT Affair" is given in S. Prakash Sethi, *Up Against the Corporate Wall, Modern Corporations and Social Issues of the Seventies*, 2nd ed. (Englewood Cliffs, N.J.: Prentice Hall, 1974), pp. 55–211.

44Most of the examples and statistics noted in this section on lobbying are taken from J. Ronald Fox, *Managing Business-Government Relations* (Homewood, IL.: Richard D. Irwin, 1982), Chapter 20.

45Ibid., pp. 310–12.

46Thomas K. McCraw, "The Business Roundtable," in John D. Aram, *Business and Public Policy* (Marshfield, MA: Pitman, 1986, 2nd ed), pp. 680–99.

47Joanna Banthin and Leigh Stelzer, "Political Action Committees: Fact, Fancy, and Morality," *Journal of Business Ethics* 5 (1986), pp. 13–14. The authors argue that PACs operate from principles and not just on the basis of a return on their investment.

48The statistic on the growth in number of PACs is taken from Aram, *Business and Public Policy*, p. 663; on the jump in money contributed, see Common Cause, "People Against PACs," a July 15, 1986 mailing; on the 32 percent jump in 1986, see *The Wall Street Journal*, Friday, August 1, 1986, p. 40.

49Common Cause mailing (July 15, 1986).

50Brooks Jackson, "PAC Funds Flowing to Congress," *Wall Street Journal*, February 23, 1984, p. 58.

51Aram, *Business and Public Policy*, p. 664 (citing a Federal Election Commission news release of Oct. 26, 1984).

52Joanna Banthin And Leigh Stelzer, "Political Action Committees . ..," p. 15, on the 1970s PACs that favored Democrats; Keith Davis and William C. Frederick, *Business and Society* (New York: McGraw-Hill, 5th ed, 1984), p. 192, on the top fund raisers.

53"New Congress Relied Heavily on PAC Donations, But Much of Spending Had Little Effect on Results," *Wall Street Journal*, September 24, 1986, p. 32.

54Ibid., on the 1986 elections. On the 1984 corporate PAC spending, see Aram, *Business and Public Policy*, p. 673.

[55]Nina Easton, "Swimming Against the Tide: Not All Business Executives Love PACs," *Common Cause Magazine*, September–October, 1983, pp. 13–15.

[56]Brooks Jackson, "Even the Beneficiaries Are Deploring System of Financing Elections," in *The Wall Street Journal*, Friday, July 18, 1986.

[57]On the different types of regulatory agencies, see Fox, *Managing Business-Government Relations*, pp. 142–43. See also Davis and Frederick, *Business and Society*, pp. 147–49.

[58]Aram, *Business and Public Policy*, pp. 202–4.

[59]"The Regulators: They Cost You $130 Billion A Year," *U.S. News & World Report*, June 30, 1975, pp. 24–28.

[60]Murray L. Weidenbaum, *The Future of Business Regulation* (New York: AMACOM, American Management Association, 1979), pp. 19–20.

[61]Ibid., pp. 12–13.

[62]Ibid., p. 17 on years of work; p. 20 on coal-mining losses.

[63]Aram, *Business and Public Policy*, p. 224.

[64]Weidenbaum, *The Future of Business Regulation*, p. 53.

[65]Thomas L. Beauchamp, *Case Studies in Business, Society and Ethics* (Englewood Cliffs, N.J.: Prentice Hall, 1983), p. 176.

[66]Stephen Breyer, *Regulation and its Reform* (Cambridge, MA: Harvard University, 1982), p. 347, on the peanut butter regulation; Weidenbaum, *The Future of Business Regulation*, p. 121, on the lemons shipped.

[67]Weidenbaum, *The Future of Business Regulation*, p. 121.

[68]Aram, *Business and Public Policy*, p. 209.

[69]Frederick D. Sturdivant, *Business and Society* (Homewood, IL.: Richard D. Irwin, 3rd ed, 1985), p. 88.

[70]Fox, *Managing Business-Government Relations*, pp. 94.

[71]Edward S. Herman, *Corporate Control, Corporate Power* (London: Cambridge University, 1981), pp. 182–83.

[72]Fox, *Managing Business-Government Relations*, Chapter 1 (from an excellent article by Alfred D. Chandler, Jr.).

[73]Aram, *Business and Public Policy*, p. 212.

[74]Breyer, *Regulation and its Reform*, p. 197.

[75]Ibid., pp. 197–98.

[76]"Gridlock: Airline Delays Are Going to Get Worse," in *U.S. News & World Report*, December 22, 1986, pp. 14–19.

[77]Breyer, *Regulation and its Reform*, pp. 272–73.

[78]Ibid., p. 264.

[79]See Norman E. Bowie, "Business Codes of Ethics: Window Dressing or Legitimate Alternative to Government Regulations?", in W. Michael Hoffman and Jennifer M. Moore, *Business Ethics: Readings and Cases in Corporate Morality*, pp. 374–79.

[80]For a new, more cooperative model, see The Catholic Bishops of the United States, *Economic Justice for All: Catholic Social Teachings and the U.S. Economy*, Chapter 4, "A New American Experiment: Participation for the Public Good," #295–325, in *Origins*, November 27, 1986, vol. 16, no. 24.

Chapter Five
ADVERTISING
AND TELEVISION

When examining the impact of the corporation on the values of people, no single influence touches us more obviously or more often than advertising. From the standpoint of the seller, advertising is a communication that attempts to persuade a prospective purchaser to buy a product or service. An ad is *effective* when it leads to sales of the product. This attempt to persuade can have a profound effect on a person's values; it sometimes supports traditional business values, but more often tends to undermine one or another of those values, as we will see in the following pages. An ad can be morally good, bad or neutral. An advertising program or an individual ad is *good,* in our definition, when it does not undermine traditional business values or social values, and supports values of community, justice, and the dignity of the individual person (see Chapter Two).

From the standpoint of the purchaser, advertising brings information about prices and product qualities. Obtaining information is essential if a person is to make informed purchase decisions. Advertising can help the purchaser obtain the information needed for an intelligent choice of product or service. In helping the purchaser, advertising contributes to the success of a free, competitive market system. Insofar as it informs, advertising supports freedom, individual responsibility, and the dignity of the individual person. However, note the tension between the two purposes: the purchaser needs information and the seller seeks to persuade.

⌐ əⁿⁱˣ

⌐This chapter will examine the long-term impact of advertising and television on the values, habits, and lifestyles of people.⌐ While acknowledging the importance of communicating price, product qualities, and information on use, we will also examine some of the undesirable effects of advertising; effects that are undesirable for citizens and also bad for business. In many cases, advertising undermines not only social values, but traditional business values. Some of advertising's negative effects arise because of unfair or deceptive persuasion techniques. Advertising is also sometimes targeted at vulnerable children or illiterate poor people. Advertising is also used to promote products that cause disease, such as tobacco, or have bad effects when used improperly, such as alcohol and infant formula. Each of these cases will be examined in this chapter.

SELLING ADS

Advertising is unethical if it is deceitful, manipulative, or undermines the self-confidence of individuals or the humane values of society. Advertising is often a lower-cost means of selling goods and services in a country where labor costs are high and distances are great. An effective vehicle for advertising products that are sold nationally is the mass media—newspapers, national magazines and the television networks. Our critique of advertising will include all the media, but our discussion of the media as such will be limited to television. While we are often critical of advertising, we recognize that it pays for most of what we see on TV. Because advertisers purchase time on TV, television stations can present news, entertainment, and public-service programming. Advertisers pay the bill for these services. This is worth recalling when we complain about the number and quality of ads on TV.

Advertisers generally stay within the bounds of what is truthful, tasteful, and legal. Government regulations, discussed in Chapter Four, have been necessary to insure that advertisers maintain truth in advertising. Good ethics and social values will encourage an advertiser to go beyond what the law requires. Yet advertisers often skirt or even break the law. If a product is advertised as 40 percent off, but is never sold at list price, this is not truthful advertising. If another product is advertised as "new and improved," and in fact little has been done to improve it, this is also deceitful advertising. The Federal Trade Commission (FTC) is charged with overseeing the truthfulness of advertising and demands that advertisers keep data that will substantiate their claims.

Sex and Puffery

Advertisers typically engage in what they call "puffery" or exaggeration of their claims. A *White Shoulders* perfume ad in a magazine shows several bare-breasted women around the main figure with the caption "The best the world has to offer." Clearly this is an overstatement. Or a skin cream ad will show a beautiful woman in the presence of an admiring man. The suggestion is that if one uses the skin cream, one will look like the beautiful woman and men will admire you. Rationally, we all know that neither the perfume nor the skin cream has such magical powers. Puffery is defended by advertisers— customers expect claims to be exaggerated. We know that goods are being sold and we expect exaggerated claims. The extent to which these claims are deceitful and manipulative is the subject of lively debate. A recent Seagram's gin ad in a teenage women's magazine shows a partially clad female being fondled by a male with the caption, "They also say it's improving your vocabulary. . .in body language." The implication: if you purchase and drink Seagram's, you will have satisfying sex and love. This is puffery. The Lucky Strike ad with a beautiful woman sensuously staring at you along with the caption "Light my Lucky" seems designed to give a double meaning.

Advertising has long used sex as an attention getter. A scantily clad female attracts the attention of the viewer, but often she has little to do with the product being advertised. A twosome in a suggestive pose is also common in ads. The use of nudity and suggestiveness in ads elicit strong physiological and cognitive reactions. Women, according to some studies, react even more strongly than men to suggestiveness in ads.[1] In recent years, many women have condemned such ads as exploitative of women. They point out that such ads use women as a means and encourage us to look on them as objects and not as intelligent, sensitive human beings; as such the ads do not respect the dignity of women. We agree with their judgment.

Influence of Ads

Advertising and television touch each of us every day in hundreds of ways. Commercial messages are constantly directed to our eyes and ears. Consider this: the average American sees about 1600 advertisements and several hours of television every day.[2] The number of hours that children watch television and its accompanying advertisements has increased each year. Over the last 10 years the number of hours that children two to 11 years old watch television rose 17 percent—up to 27.3 hours per week.[3] By high school graduation day, the average graduates have spent twice as much time watching television as they have spent in the classroom.[4] All of this exposure to TV and to the commercial messages of advertising have a profound impact on us and on our values. We will return to the issue of children and TV later.

Many TV and magazine ads encourage selfishness and materialism. They can undermine not only social values, but also business values such as individual responsibility. Ads sometimes challenge the self-esteem and generosity of adults and can be even more harmful to children, as we will see later in this chapter. In being both so visible and so open to criticism, advertising is the vulnerable Achilles' heel of business. The short-term benefits of an ad to one company's sales may be offset by the long-term harm that it does to business in general. Remedies for the abuses of advertising are also examined in this chapter by examining a firm and its manager's ethical values, customer wariness, ethical codes, and government regulation.

Information and Free Enterprise

Good ads are truthful, recognize ethical values, and provide the purchaser with useful information. Effective ads sell products. Good advertising enables us to check product information and prices before purchasing. It can direct buyers to the firm that offers the type and quality of product that they desire, thus enabling consumers to save time and to be more satisfied with their purchases. Without advertising the purchaser has a difficult time making buying decisions, the entire operation of the economy would be hampered, many products would not be purchased, and jobs would be lost.[5] The traditional defense used by advertising professionals maintains that advertising enables us to increase our standard of living. Any legal advertising strategy that will sell the goods to any prospective purchaser and by whatever means is generally considered effective advertising. We disagree with this assessment, as we will show in the following pages.

A classic, lengthy, ethical study of advertising[6] raises five crucial issues:

(1) What is meant by the standard of living?
(2) How does advertising propose to raise the standard of living?
(3) Why do advertising people believe this growth is necessary?
(4) Why do advertisers believe this growth must take place through the increased production of consumer goods?
(5) How does advertising propose to increase the importance given to material goods and services?

While we do not have the space to treat each of these issues, some attention will be given to the last two in the following discussion.

More than $60 billion is spent every year on advertising.[7] We purchasers pay that cost, so it behooves us to ask if advertising is working well for us. Does advertising provide us with the information that we need? Does it use selling techniques that most of us find helpful? Perhaps most importantly and yet hardest to grapple with: Is advertising having a long-term impact on our attitudes and values that the majority of us find acceptable? Or, is advertising's impact a subtle but real undercutting of the social fabric of our lives? Does advertising tend to undermine social values and sometimes even our business values? From the standpoint of the seller, is advertising accomplishing what the conscientious advertiser intends? Does it provide the information necessary for an intelligent purchase, and does it respect our traditional values? Or is it having a detrimental effect quite different from and beyond what is intended?

Industrial advertising, as opposed to consumer advertising, does spell out a product's qualities. Retail advertising, especially print ads, often do a better job of informing than TV ads. Slick consumer magazine and television ads often provide little helpful information. Advertisements for new products are often designed to stimulate a need where there was no prior explicit need. Hence the charge that such ads provide no net benefit to either the consumer or the economy, and that they substitute persuasion and emotional appeals for price competition. Such ads "seek to bypass the reflective powers. . .or render them inoperative to a greater or lesser extent." Such an ad is unethical not because it uses emotion, but "because it makes a person less a person and is an implicit act of contempt for a person's dignity." Such an ad is unethical when it (1) violates the reverence due to the individual person and (2) brings negative social consequences.[8]

Some ads provide a positive image not only of the product but also of the firm and people. Note IBM's ad showing systems-analyst Jim Caldwell, who is blind and in a wheelchair. He is presented as a professional who is proud of his work. He remarks that he could have spent his life in a hospital but chose to develop his talents. In the ad he says, "There is more than one way to get from here to there." A McDonald's ad features a family waiting for their child's surgery at a Ronald McDonald House built by McDonald's. Another McDonald's ad gives us no sound, only signing and captions. The ad points out that without the sound, we may achieve some understanding of how hearing impaired people feel.

A series of Gallo Winery ads feature family reunions, religious celebrations, anniversaries, weddings, births, and christenings. These ads have been successful in building a better image for Gallo wines, and they also support sharing and family values. A GE dishwasher ad promotes the athletic achievement of a woman in Olympic tryouts. The dishwasher, plus her loving husband, give her the time to compete. A Chrysler ad gives a wide variety of images of the U.S.—a pregnant mother, an Amish couple. . .—a cross-section of America. Each of these ads presents a person-centered message that respects individual responsibility and freedom, and promotes human dignity and community. These ads show how advertising can carry socially valuable messages. While these ads do not explicitly sell the product, the manufacturers are convinced that a positive general image will encourage the view that their product is trustworthy and of high quality. An overview of the various types of ads and the media used are shown in Figure 5-1.

Corroded Link in the Market System

Rather than provide useful product information, advertisers often attempt to build an image—how the product will make you feel happier, sexier, and more enviable. Leo Burnett, past president and chairman of the advertising agency that bears his name, spells this out in his checklist: "Don't tell people

FIG. 5-1 Types of Advertising and Vehicles

Type of Ad	Popular Media
Information on product	Print
Image building for product	Trade journals
Institutional: name of firm	Newspapers
Advocacy: taking position on	Magazines
public issue	News
Political: advertise political	Slick
parties, candidates, or issues	Teenage
Public Service: information on	Television
public issues (generally	Radio
provided at no charge)	

how good you make goods; tell them how good your goods make them."⁹ Burnett urges effective ads, not good ads.

To best aid the purchaser, advertising should help define product differences. What new information do the following advertising strategies provide: "You've come a long way, baby" (Virginia Slims), "Coke, the real thing," "When you say Budweiser, you've said it all," "Come to Marlboro Country"? Or consider cosmetics ads that appeal to our insecurities or desires for status— Oil of Olay, for example. The information that is communicated is often irrelevant, trivial, and not useful to an intelligent purchase decision.

Note the text of an ad seeking sales for *Fortune* magazine. The ad pictures a businessman with the quotation "I'd say we have a mature, responsible attitude toward our major competitors. We'd like *to see them dead.*" The text goes on: "Millions of dollars sometimes ride on fractions of a share point. For some marketers, stalking those fractions is *a blood sport.* In issue after issue, Fortune *takes dead aim on the strategies, tactics and technologies of the hunt.* Unlike other business publications that simply report the who and the what, Fortune *cuts it closer to the bone...*" (italics added). What values does this ad encourage? What values does it undermine? How does it affect respect for others, individual responsibility, and cooperation? Violence and killing are not a part of even the competitive American business scene. *Fortune* is trying to build an image; they should not be surprised if most business people reject that image and the magazine that presents it.

American people do not trust advertising. In a national public-opinion poll, more than two-thirds of Americans thought that "Advertising causes people to buy things that they don't need."¹⁰ In a more recent assessment of public attitudes toward advertising, more than 38 studies were reviewed. All those studies found a decidedly negative public opinion toward advertising. In almost every instance where a study was repeated, the later one shows an even more negative attitude.¹¹ A professor of marketing at a major university quotes his students as describing television advertising as "irritating, dumb, stupid, insulting, unethical, misleading, deceptive, worthless (in terms of influencing them), and generally disgusting."[12]

Critics of advertising maintain that it encourages dissatisfaction with present goods, status, and life, and thus brings about unhappiness. Moreover, advertising encourages excess and frivolous consumption, using scarce energy, materials, and capital on luxuries when other people are homeless and starving. Thus advertising encourages young men and women to be selfish and materialistic. In a study of the effects of advertising on adolescents, researchers concluded that "increased advertising exposure seems to decrease the person's likelihood of performing socially desirable consumer behavior" among those adolescents who initially are not inclined to be sensitive to others. Advertising seems also "to contribute to the development of materialistic values. . ." among less mature and impressionable young people.[13] Advertising with prosocial themes such as indicated in the last section could positively affect the values of young people toward community and respect for the dignity of the person.

It is not surprising that we are suspicious and cynical about what is said in advertising. Ads try to make us dissatisfied with what we have so that we will purchase products. This is often done with exaggeration and sometimes even deception. Deliberate deception is not acceptable; lying is unethical. Yet every day we are exposed to examples of distortion, manipulation, and even deception. Moreover, this distortion and deception is recognized as such by most Americans. What this does to the trust that is essential for persons, family, society, and business to grow is an important and open question.

PRODUCTS THAT HARM

The way some ads are presented can result in harm from otherwise safe products. For example, laxative and aspirin ads can give the impression that if you use these products your ailment will disappear. Constipation or a headache are often symptoms of something more serious. A current series of ads for Medipren, an aspirin substitute, has the theme in song, "If you haven't got time for the pain." Pain is most often an early warning of something more serious that could be neglected if the ads are taken at face value. A trusting person might mistakenly conclude that these pills are an easier means to feeling healthy than a good diet and exercise—a false and dangerous conclusion.

Some products that are widely advertised actually do cause serious harm to many people. Both tobacco and alcohol ads are not allowed on TV for this reason. Because they can damage health, we have asked the government to intervene with regulations. However, many argue that if a product is not illegal, it's advertising should not be curtailed, and they cite the First Amendment freedom of speech of the Constitution to defend their position. Such an argument is ethically indefensible; it presumes that all actions that are unethical have been prohibited by law. An additional argument, in the tradition of John Stuart Mill and the Utilitarians, is that the government should not interfere if the results of the action fall mainly on the self. This point is the center of much of the debate. Advertising tobacco and alcohol are controversial issues that are of interest to many people, so they will serve as useful examples of the role of advertising in a free economy.

Tobacco and Cigarettes

In recent years we have come to understand the increased risk of lung cancer, heart disease, and a variety of other ailments that directly result from smoking. Current government figures show that deaths related to cigarette smoking number more than 350,000 each year. It costs taxpayers an estimated $3.8 billion each year in Medicare and Medicaid payments alone because of diseases related to smoking.[14] The advertising expenditures of cigarette companies are an extraordinarily high percentage of sales compared to other firms. So an examination of the ethics of advertising tobacco products is intimately linked to the ethics of the product itself. Do tobacco products and advertisements for them respect the life and the dignity of the individual?

Tobacco producers disputed this data and used their economic power to continue to advertise their products for many decades after the first authoritative warnings in the 1950s. When *Readers Digest* printed an article warning about dangers related to smoking, the agency that handled their advertising cut them off. That agency also had the American Tobacco account, which was nine times more lucrative. When Arthur Godfrey said on his television show that smoking made him feel bad, Lorillard Co. (a cigarette manufacturer) stopped sponsoring his program.[15] This sort of pressure existed until the 1970s. Such conduct does not respect the lives or the dignity of people.

In 1969, the U.S. Congress banned radio and television cigarette advertisements and required a label on packages. Four warnings currently rotate on packages and advertisements. One of them states: "SURGEON GENERAL'S WARNING: Smoking Causes Lung Disease, Emphysema, and May Complicate Pregnancy." Congress also required the Federal Trade Commission to report annually on cigarette labeling, advertising and promotions, and the lethal consequences of smoking. Recent evidence shows that spouses and children of cigarette smokers also suffer an increased risk of smoking-related diseases. "Passive smoking," breathing other peoples' smoke, can cause lung cancer. The United States Surgeon General has asked employers to set up smoke-free workplaces, and governments at all levels to establish smoke-free public places.[16]

Advertising expenditures by tobacco firms are immense—an estimated $2 billion, or between 4.5 and 5 percent of net sales. Compare this to other large advertisers like automobiles (1.6 percent) and grocery stores (1.3 percent). The target audience of these efforts is determined by market research. This research shows that 75 percent of all smokers are regular smokers by age 21, and practically all are smokers by the age of 25.[17] In order to increase and stabilize sales, it is important to induce young people to begin smoking early. The magazines used by the cigarette firms for advertising demonstrate their marketing strategy. Magazines like *Playboy* and *Penthouse*, which are oriented toward young adults, get 25 percent of their advertising revenues from cigarette companies. Movie magazines, aimed at teenagers and young adults, also carry a large number of cigarette ads. By way of contrast, magazines given to airline passengers and magazines such as *Forbes* and *Fortune*, which young people do not generally read, have little or no cigarette advertising.

Tobacco firms have also been accused of focusing on women and blacks in their advertising. The percentage of blacks who continue to smoke is now higher than whites, as is their coronary disease and lung cancer. Moreover, the quit rate among both blacks and women is lower than that of white males.[18] Advertising dollars are targeted on inducing young people, women, and blacks to smoke.

Note also the content of the cigarette advertisements—young, handsome and athletic men and women climbing mountains, riding horses, or in romantic settings—all designed to appeal to the youth market. Some examples: Sterling cigarette ads picture an energetic young man riding the waves on a small boat. The caption reads, "Reach for the Exceptional." Vantage (another R. J. Reynolds product) pictures a racing sports car with the caption, "Performance counts—performance so good you can taste it in a low tar." One might ask: What do cigarettes have to do with exceptional acts and good performance? Perhaps people who would be willing to risk their life racing a sports car are also willing to risk it by smoking. Virginia Slims still advertises to women: "You've come a long way, baby." The percentage of women who are smoking has increased dramatically in recent years. Moreover, not as many women as men have stopped smoking. Is this ". . .a long way, baby?" It has been shown that smoking during pregnancy risks damage to the newborn baby. A medical doctor points out that lung cancer became the leading cause of cancer deaths among men in 1960 and of women in 1985:

> How much of the escalating lung-cancer epidemic will be due to the sex-appeal advertising of cowboys and liberated women? "You've come a long way, baby" and "The Marlboro Man" may look romantic today, but there is nothing romantic about being hooked up to an oxygen tank and dying of cancer.[19]

A Newport Lights ad got Lorillard Co. in trouble. It showed a woman who appeared pregnant with a cigarette. Medical people pointed out that cigarettes (and alcohol) can permanently harm an unborn child. Newport also advertises heavily in teenage girls' magazines with subtle, manipulative (and gross, if spelled out) sexual innuendo. It might be instructive for the reader to glance through several issues of *Mademoiselle, Cosmopolitan, Vogue,* or

Glamour to assess the advertisements that are being directed to young women. Many focus on superficial appearance and some are grossly sexual.

On related products: snuff and chewing tobacco have recently reentered the market and their sales are growing rapidly as a response to the anti-cigarette attitudes of thinking consumers. The caption on a current Skoal chewing tobacco ad says: "When you can't smoke, but you want to enjoy tobacco, try Skoal Bandits." These products dramatically increase the incidence of cancer of the mouth. But they have no warning label, since government regulations have not yet caught up with them.

Sales of cigarettes are declining in the United States due to the health hazards. To combat this decline, tobacco firms, besides diversifying into other businesses, are actively pursuing cigarette markets in the Third World. This effort has been encouraged by the United States through various programs to subsidize exports of "agricultural" products. Per-capita consumption of tobacco in the last decade increased 33 percent in Africa and 24 percent in South America. Egyptian workers now spend one fifth of their income on cigarettes.[20] People in poor countries have a dignity that must be respected, but their governments have not protected them with regulations. For a tobacco firm to advertise and to sell in such an environment is unethical.

The tobacco industry contributes more than $60 billion to the Gross National Product. Many jobs in farming and manufacturing also depend upon the sales of tobacco. Indeed the U.S. Federal Government still provides a series of price supports and subsidies to the tobacco industry, while another segment of government, the Surgeon General, requires health warnings.

Given the overwhelming evidence on the adverse effect of tobacco use on the life and health of its users, there is little moral justification for subsidizing tobacco or encouraging tobacco products. Advertising campaigns in magazines that are designed to induce young people to begin to use tobacco products are especially unethical. With present knowledge, if tobacco were discovered today, it would undoubtedly not obtain Food and Drug Administration approval. Tobacco products would probably be banned today, if it were not for the realization that trying to ban a product that is addictive and so widely used is a practical impossibility. But tobacco products are death dealing. Hence we believe it is unethical to advertise tobacco products that do so much damage to individuals and the community.

Targeting Youth and Alcoholics

Pervasive advertising for beer, wine, and liquor produces ad revenues of $1 billion per year. Spending for beer ads amounts to 7.3 percent of sales, for liquor 6.3 percent of sales; these are among the highest of any industry. Compare this with 1.8 percent of sales spent for bakery products, and 1.6 percent for shoes. Like cigarette advertising, advertising for alcohol products is ethically questionable. Alcohol industry executives generally protest, as do tobacco executives, that they are not trying to gain new users, but only trying to expand their own market share. Nevertheless, the data belies these protests. A glance at current beer, wine, and liquor ads shows that they most often picture happy groups of *young* people, their target audience. Directed to health-conscious youth, these ads present robust, athletic, and strong young people, always healthy and enjoying themselves. These ads encourage one to forget about the unhealthy side effects of alcohol, and "they project an unspoken promise that if you drink this product, you can be like the actors in the ads, attractive, popular, healthy winners."[21] Young people are particularly vulnerable to this type of advertising. When Seagrams found its market share declining, it developed an ad directed to youth. The ad showed a man and a woman in an embrace, with the caption: "Drink it with someone you know very, very well. . .or want to." Is this a suggestion that serving alcohol will lower the other person's inhibitions and defenses?[22]

Young people are particularly susceptible to alcohol advertising appeals. The exposure of adolescents to alcohol advertising and their attention to those same advertisements is greater than the population's as a whole. "Thus, there is ample opportunity for alcohol advertising to influence the cognitions, values, and behavior of the public, especially of young people."[23] In fact, adolescents' use of alcohol has increased dramatically over the last 20 years. While only 25 percent of youth in grades 9–12 reported using alcoholic beverages on 10 or more occasions during the year in 1968, that number jumped to 55 percent in 1977 and is still rising.[24] Budweiser, Miller, Pabst, and Coors all pitch their product to college students. They advertise in college newspapers, sponsor college events, sometimes even have campus representatives. They sponsor ads in college newspapers in states where the ordinary undergraduate college student cannot drink legally. A study of alcohol advertisements in college newspapers surveyed 32 colleges. It found that 10 had no alcohol ads (probably because the college did not take them), but in the rest more than one half of all the ads were for alcohol. Moreover, many of the ads urged students to play, and made studying look dismal and uninteresting.[25]

In the United States, problem drinkers and alcoholics consume between 50 and 70 percent of all alcoholic beverages. The shift of Miller's advertising strategy from "The Champagne of Beers" to "It's Miller Time" (with shots of working people enjoying a drink at the end of a work day) is an example of shifting to the more frequent drinker. Miller Lite ads encourage drinking while studying (for college students) and while working (for working people). Johnny Walker also encourages daily drinking in their ads.[26] Phillip Morris, the tobacco firm, now own Miller. Is this cavalier advertising strategy easier for Phillip Morris and Miller to undertake than it would be for firms in another industry? Are executives in these industries so accustomed to criticism that they have become unhearing and defensive? Would some people with an informed conscience not join such a firm? What sort of ethical norms would one then expect of the people left behind?

Targeting youth, large-usage consumers, and alcoholics makes good business sense, presuming that one's purpose is to increase sales. Youth can be induced to begin drinking early, and, if they begin with a particular brand, brand loyalty begins. The external, uncounted cost to society of alcohol is great. Early death from auto accidents and alcoholism, property damage, lost productivity, alcoholism treatment, and other costs are estimated to exceed $81 billion. Much of this cost is borne by innocent third parties.[27] In an attempt to lessen these costs, most states have raised the legal age at which one can drink alcohol to 21. Alcohol, unlike tobacco, when used in moderation can help bring people together. Nevertheless, advertising that is aimed at youth and heavy drinkers is unethical; it does not respect the dignity of the human person, and it harms society (common good). When too much alcohol is consumed, its effects violate the business values of individual responsibility.

One can readily see the ethical problems in targeting alcohol advertising to young people and to large-usage consumers. Young people are impressionable, and advertising people know that. Youth are more sensitive to alcohol-related injuries and damage to the body. A problem drinker already has a weakness: an addiction. Additional drinking may cause a total disruption of life in loss of family, job, and more. Although most advertising executives protest that neither group is the object of their advertising, an examination of their ads shows the contrary. Youth and alcoholics are especially vulnerable to alcohol. Given this vulnerability, plus the dangers, it appears ethically wrong to target them in advertisements.

Some claim that the government should not regulate alcohol or tobacco advertising, since that violates freedom and the habit affects only the individual. However, recall the huge loss to families, employers, and other third parties due to illnesses caused by tobacco and from alcohol abuse. We believe that the government not only has the right, but also the obligation, to try to moderate the use of tobacco and alcohol.

Breast Milk Substitutes in Developing Countries

For more than a decade, controversy has swirled around the issue of marketing breast milk substitutes in poor countries. There is, however, substantial agreement on a number of key issues. Industry spokespersons and critics alike agree that mother's milk is healthier and more nutritious for the child than substitute milk. They also agree that a minority of mothers are unable to provide all of their infant's nutritional needs through nursing, either because of illness, malnutrition, or some other disorder. In addition, all parties agree that, when properly used, breast milk substitutes do have nutritional value.

The number of infants born in developed countries, especially the United States and Europe, has been declining since the late 1960s. Manufacturers of infant formula realized that their best new markets would be the rapidly growing populations of Third World countries. The manufacturers then set out to sell their products in these poor countries. They used a mix of stand-ard and innovative marketing practices. They advertised on radio, billboards, and posters—especially around hospitals. Some posters pictured a healthy white child with a white-clad male, supposedly a medical doctor, with a caption indicating that infant formula was the way to feed your child. The implica-tion was that infant formula was the kind of food that educated, caring, and wealthy First World mothers would provide for their children. Like mothers everywhere, mothers in poor countries want to provide the very best for their newborns. So, they then sacrificed much to provide infant formula.

Meanwhile, hospital personnel gave free samples of infant formula to most new mothers while they were still in the hospital. Manufacturers pro-vided these samples to hospitals as a part of their marketing plan, along with free equipment. In turn, hospital personnel urged mothers to use a particular brand of substitute milk. In addition, manufacturers hired women to dress in white nurses' uniforms and go from door to door seeking women with new-ly born infants. They gave mothers free samples. Of course, if the mother used the substitute and did not nurse, her own milk would dry up and she would then be dependent on the substitute. These marketing techniques were effective, since new mothers are particularly susceptible to health personnel's suggestions for their newborn while they are still in the hospital or shortly thereafter.

The program of marketing breast milk substitutes in Third World countries was successful in the 1960s and 1970s. It was a rapidly expanding market for all of the manufacturers. Along with the increased use of the milk substitute, however, came serious problems. Many infants using formula con-tracted illnesses, and there were numerous deaths of infants who had been using infant formula. Why did this happen? Why did substitute breast milk prove to be dangerous to infants in poor countries?

Problems in Advertising Infant Formula to Poor Women

There are several problems associated with feeding manufactured milk to infants in poor countries. First, infant formula does not provide the anti-bodies to local diseases that breast milk does. A nursing mother communicates these immunities to her infant along with the milk, protecting the baby from local diseases.

Second, in poor countries infant formula is often mixed with water that is not pure. When infants drink contaminated stream and well water, sickness often follows. In order to purify the water, bottles, and nipples, scarce and expensive fuel is required; hence the required sterilization is often not done or not done sufficiently.

Third, as the child grows, it requires more infant formula before it can be weaned onto local and cheaper foods. This becomes expensive. Hence Third

World parents often dilute the formula, in order to make their money go further. The thick white liquid still looks the same.

Using infant formula is both costly and unhealthy for most Third World infants. Mass marketing practices, which imply that infant formula is good for all infants, are not truthful. Hence, the question: What sort of marketing practices are legitimate in Third World Countries? The various manufacturers of milk substitutes approached this problem differently.[28] Abbott Laboratories is one of the four American manufacturers that sold infant formula overseas in the 1970s. As early as 1974 Abbott published its own "Code of Marketing Ethics for Developing Countries".[29] This code prohibited mass marketing (posters, billboards, radio commericals, etc.) and emphasized the need for advice from health care professionals in deciding when to use infant formula. At that time American Home Products and Bristol-Myers, along with the Swiss-based Nestle, still used mass media promotions as described earlier. Borden realized that in good conscience it could not advertise in poor countries, and so it dropped out of the infant formula business.

Activist groups tried to discourage mass marketing by infant formula makers. During the 1970s the American firms, all publicly held, experienced a series of shareholder resolutions opposing mass marketing of infant formula in the Third World. In these resolutions, the firms were asked to curtail mass marketing of the breast milk substitute and/or to develop a code of marketing practices. While these shareholder resolutions attracted positive votes from only a small percentage of shareholders, they alerted the public and helped to raise social consciousness on the problem. Senator Edward Kennedy chaired Congressional hearings in 1978 on the issue. The hearings attracted even more attention. Industry representatives then asked Senator Kennedy to request that the World Health Organization (WHO) address the problem.

After several years of taking testimony, examining health data, and working with manufacturers, WHO proposed a code for marketing infant formula. In response to social pressures, all U.S. manufacturers had by this time agreed to restrict their mass marketing practices. They nevertheless all lobbied the Reagan administration to oppose the Code. The WHO vote was 118 to one with the United States casting the lone negative vote.[30] The U.S. vote was interpreted by peoples around the world as support for unfair and deceptive marketing tactics by U.S. firms, and it triggered much world criticism.[31] Swiss-based Nestle finally adopted a marketing code for infant formula in poor countries after it experienced an American boycott of its products.

When infant formula is mass marketed, it is almost impossible to include all the cautions and qualifying information that are necessary. Many poor parents can't read. Implying that infant formula is healthier and better for a child than mother's milk is false and deceitful. It is especially unfair to poor people, and does not respect their dignity as human persons. A better alternative to mass-marketing infant formula is to provide the product through responsible hospital personnel to mothers who need it.

There are other examples of products that are not needed or have some ill effects and which are still heavily marketed in poor countries. Coke, Pepsi, and other soft drinks are competing for customers in growing Third World markets. It is hard to present nutritional product information for sugared water with artificial coloring, flavoring, and often, preservatives. Ordinary water is healthier and much less expensive. The cost of Coke and other soft drinks is a luxury that people in Third World countries can little afford. Has advertising convinced them that soft drinks are modern and nutritious or drinks that go with success in the developed world? If so, this advertising is untruthful and unfair. The fact that these soft drinks have found a market does not make advertising them ethical.

IMAGES AFFECT ATTITUDES

Advertising projects images that have a profound influence on a person's attitudes; television affects attitudes in much the same way. Television advertising and programming directed to children are examples. The effects of children's immersion in television is a concern for parents, educators, and others. Two problem areas are: (1) advertisements aimed at uncritical children, and (2) the content of children's television programming. Children's television programming is largely cartoons. While cartoons can be legitimate entertainment, they dominate children's programming, and many are quite violent. Public broadcasting offers the widely acclaimed "Sesame Street" and other worthwhile programs, but the three commercial networks, ABC, CBS, and NBC have less educational programming now than they did 10 years ago.

Kid Vid: Trust to Cynicism

The National Institute of Mental Health has examined thousands of research projects that studied the effects of television. It provides some sobering data: television programming shows an average of five violent acts each hour and children's weekend programs portray 18 violent acts per hour. One researcher estimates that by the time a child is 15 years old, that child will have witnessed 13,000 homicides on television.[32] The report continues that "violence on television does lead to aggressive behavior by children and teenagers who watch the programs." Heavy viewers of television are more apt to think the world is violent, to trust other people less and to believe that the world is a mean and frightening place.[33]

There are other effects of heavy TV watching. Planned or not, sex education is also done by television. One researcher found that extramarital affairs are mentioned on TV shows five times more often than sexual activity by married couples.

A study of the social attitudes of TV and film makers may explain some of what we find on TV. Their attitudes are not typical of the population as a whole. Although this study was supported and published in a conservative journal and is trying to make a point, it illustrates a gap between the social attitudes of TV and film makers and the attitudes of the general American public. Ninety-six percent of the TV and film makers were in favor of abortion on demand. Only 16 percent strongly felt that adultery was wrong; and they were speaking of adultery, not fornication. Ninety-seven percent seldom or never attend a religious service. On the other hand, more than two thirds thought that TV should promote social reform, and only 12 percent thought that TV was too critical of traditional values.[34]

Thus one sees the roots of the attitudes, values, and ethics that are brought into our own homes on television. And attempting to change our traditional social values is an explicit goal of these TV-show writers and directors. In addition, there are some undesirable physical effects of TV watching. Reading and IQ scores decline as more TV is watched. In one town, reading scores of students fell sharply within two years after TV was introduced into the town.[35] In addition to the producers and script writers, advertisers have an ethical obligation to oversee the content of television programming. Merely drawing a large viewing audience is not enough. TV and advertising helps to form our values. Social values of community, solidarity, justice, and the dignity of each person, along with the business value of individual responsibility should be supported, and not undermined, if we expect our society to be healthy and humane.

Advertising and TV Make Money

Advertising, like television, is a business that is trying to sell itself and to sell its products. Each year children view an average of 20,000 television commercials. What is the effect of this barrage of television advertisements on children? Five- and six-year-old children confuse programs and commercials, and they tend to believe what is presented. From ages seven to ten, children experience great tension as they try to sort out what is exaggeration and what is not. By the time children are eleven and twelve years old, they tend to become cynical toward commercials and toward what they see on television: "By age 11. . .most children have already become cynical—ready to believe that, like advertising, business and other social institutions are riddled with hypocrisy."[36]

In most cultures adolescents must learn to cope with social hypocrisy and even with institutionalized lying. But today, "TV advertising is stimulating *preadolescent* children to think about socially accepted hypocrisy."[37] What the effects of this cynicism and expectation of hypocrisy will be, we do not yet know, since these children have not yet become parents or assumed the reins of authority in our institutions. However, most commentators point out that it brings on increased tolerance of shady deals, cutting corners, and being dishonest with other people.

Young children are particularly susceptible to advertising and television aimed at them. Some children actually believe that there are little people inside the TV set standing beside the products being advertised. Advertisers acknowledge this influence in the $700,000,000 that they spend annually on advertising aimed at children. Advertising revenues for children's Saturday morning TV total more than $100 million.[38]

About 60 percent of the products that are advertised on children's television—especially on weekends—are sugar products: candy, sugar-coated breakfast cereals, and other sweets. Research shows that younger children are particularly susceptible to damage to their teeth from excessive or regular consumption of sugar. The more sugar consumed, the more dental cavities that a child will have. Television advertising of sugar products works. At the supermarket young children have a significant influence on their parents' selection of cereals. Not surprisingly, the children tend to choose cereals not on the basis of nutrition, but on the basis of TV recognition.[39]

A group of mothers in Boston became concerned over the content of children's TV and its advertisements. Beginning in the 1970s, they tried to obtain better programming and more nutritional information on advertised products. Not one major broadcaster or advertiser offered to help this group of concerned mothers in their effort to seek improvements in children's television. The mothers then urged the Federal Trade Commission to impose regulations on the advertisers to protect children. Given the public nature of the problem and the fact that market forces tend to make the problem worse, this would have been an appropriate role for the FTC. It is a primary responsibility of programmers, advertisers, and the government (see Figure 2–2). At the hearings, of the major manufacturers of children's sugar-coated cereals, General Foods did not even show up.[40] Kellogg and General Mills defended their cereals and their advertising. Never once during the hearings did either manufacturer acknowledge that the quality of children's television or the advertisements directed to children could be improved. Alone among the manufacturers, Quaker Oats made proposals to improve the quality of children's television and to improve the advertisements directed to children.[41] The proposed FTC regulations were never enacted, and the quality of children's programming and advertising has not improved.

A carefully done ethical assessment of advertising directed to children begins by pointing out that children are not yet mature. Children, especially six years of age and under, do not understand exchange and what it means "to sell". Moreover, they are naturally very gullible. Hence, the basic ethical problem focuses on fairness and respect for children:

> The fact that children's advertising benefits advertisers while at the same time nourishing false beliefs, unreasonable expectations, and irresponsible consumer desires among children calls into play principles of fairness and respect. Critics have said that child-oriented advertising takes advantage of children's limited capacities and their suggestibility for the benefit of advertisers. As expressed by Michael Pertschuk, former chairman of the Federal Trade Commission, advertisers "seize on the child's trust and exploit it as weakness for their gain."[42]

Advertising on TV is effective in influencing children's values, and it induces them to want candy, soft drinks, sugar-coated cereals, and other items that are not only not nutritious, but often damaging to their health. Much of what children view in both programming and advertising encourages cynical and selfish attitudes and values. In taking advantage of a child's credibility, programmers and advertisers are not only unfair and unjust, but they fail to respect the human dignity of the child. In encouraging a child to be more acquisitive and materialistic, they encourage the child to be more self-centered. This makes ordinary maturity and moral growth more difficult.

We look to the family and schools to help a child grow in maturity. But many commentators maintain that television and advertising now have even more influence on the values of children. Therefore some basic questions arise. Does commercial television offer a net benefit to children or is it damaging to them? Is it then an important ethical priority to encourage children's television and advertising to be more helpful in inculcating social values? What alternatives do we have available to improve children's television and advertising?

We can do much better with children's television. We have the experience of positive, educational, and ethical children's programming. We know how to do it, and we know what good effects it has. Given the importance of children and their importance for the future of society, ethical considerations demand that we improve children's television and advertising directed at them. This could happen with the initiative of programmers and advertisers. Ken Mason, as president of Quaker Oats, made some excellent and workable suggestions on how to improve children's TV.[43] However, we must be realistic enough to acknowledge that market forces tend to discourage quality programming and good advertising. Hence, this may be an area where government regulation is appropriate. Either voluntary action or government regulation is called for on such an important issue.

Political Candidates Sold in 30 Seconds

Political candidates and parties have long looked to advertising people for slogans and paid advertisements. "Keep Cool With Coolidge" (1924) and "The Cross of Gold" (1896) were early contributions of advertising to politics. By the 1970s advertisers and public relations consultants were an essential part of every political campaign.[44] Today no serious candidate would attempt to run for office without engaging an advertising agency, and that agency is sure to propose a heavy TV and advertising program. Their efforts do bring votes; but they often have a negative effect on the understanding of issues. A 30-second TV commercial provides neither the time nor the atmosphere to discuss complex issues; it provides little or no new information. Even worse it suggests that the issues are really quite simple and afford easy solutions. Political ads appeal to image and the quick fix rather than to substance. It is important to remember that political issues are complex and not open to the ad or the slogan.[45]

The public is polled on their interests, and the successful candidate then tells citizens what they want to hear. This combination is becoming a proven method for getting elected. Hence, when serious problems face the country, if the solution requires some sacrifice, the politician will not mention the issue in the campaign. People want to hear good news, and will not vote for a candidate who tells them that there are problems that call for sacrifice on the voters' part. Yet many important difficulties facing us require short-term sacrifice; for example, the budget and trade deficit, toxic waste disposal, acid rain, race and sex discrimination, and debt in Third World countries.

Examinations of candidates in thoughtful articles and required debates on substantive issues are far more helpful in informing the voter. These are seldom forthcoming from public relations or advertising people. Advertising people shift our attention away from the complex issues to simplified images. Is this sort of descent to the simple image and slogan inevitable in a popular democracy? Obtaining wise and prudent national leaders requires that someone other than advertising and public-relations people be given pivotal roles in political campaigns.

Public relations and advertising campaigns are effective, but they make a mockery of the need for an informed electorate. They sell image more than substance. They make it more difficult to discuss common, long-term needs, and they do not encourage individual responsibility. Such campaigns make it even more difficult for democracy to work. The growing use of negative ads, which criticize opposing candidates, is even more debilitating. They are often unfair, fracture community, and, being sponsored by someone else, they undermine the personal responsibility of the benefiting candidate.

Denigrating the Working Person

The image of the working person that is presented on TV advertising is often degrading. While business firms are trying to encourage cooperation and participation at work, and greater dignity and self-esteem among all in the firm (see Chapter Three, "Work and Job Satisfaction"), a segment of the business community—TV and advertising—sometimes undermines these very efforts. From the rude mechanic in the auto parts ad to the inept and dumb female homemaker in Crisco or Dash detergent ads, individuals are not presented as competent people who enjoy work. Additional examples of the disparagement of the American working person in ads are slick and shady salespeople (Curtis Mathes TV), the bumbling executive (Federal Express), and dumb blue-collar workers (Budweiser), incompetent male homemakers (Pringles, Cheer, and Sucrets lozenges) and silly and shallow female homemakers (Downy fabric softener, Pampers, Bowl Guard toilet-bowl cleaner).[46] Happily, Ford, GM, and Chrysler are exceptions with their ads showing competent and able workers who produce quality products.

One third of all business people portrayed on television are corrupt or criminal; except for professional criminals, no one commits more crimes on prime-time television than the businessperson. Television says of business-people: "It's fun to be corrupt and almost everybody who's anybody is." Since television has an effect on attitudes and values, young people coming into business may become more self-centered and unscrupulous. In addition, respected media critic Pauline Kael points out that satisfaction at work is almost never portrayed in ads or TV. Rather, ordinary work is presented as dull, drain-ing, and sometimes stupid. People portrayed on TV work to make a lot of money; rarely because they enjoy their work. Therefore, Kael suggests that we should not be surprised at the paramount importance young people place on salary when seeking employment.[47] She goes on to cite a survey in which young people looked down on an accomplished and articulate artist, but ad-mired a lawyer-realtor who showed his wealth even though he was "astonishing-ly inarticulate—or inhibited—about his work." Business people on prime time TV are most often portrayed as selfish, grasping scoundrels. The business per-son on such TV shows as "Dallas," "Falcon Crest," and other series are not admirable people.

Note the irony: business firms try to encourage their people to take pride in their work, yet some pay for communications to those same workers that disparage working people and make light of their work. Moreover, executives and managers are presented as unfeeling, selfish people. In the vernacular we call this "shooting yourself in the foot."

Representing the Corporation to the Public

Many Americans' most immediate contact with, and impression of, business is obtained through advertising. Even though we all know individual storekeepers and managers, our image of business and the large corporation is less personal and obtained largely from advertising. If advertising is perceived as more manipulative than informative, more trivial than substantive, more rude than tasteful, Americans are likely to think of businesspersons also as slick and fast-talking, not to be fully trusted. Such advertising violates the dig-nity of the many businesspeople who strive to be fair and socially responsive.

Unfortunately, the level of confidence that Americans have in business leaders seems to support the self-made negative image. The leaders of American business firms have the confidence of less than 20 percent of the American people, and the leaders of advertising firms have the confidence of only 11 percent of Americans. Studies of Americans' perception of trust-worthiness toward the major U.S. institutional leaders find advertisers at the bottom of the list.[48] This severely negative attitude toward advertising affects attitudes toward business in general, and so violates fairness and justice. Adver-tisers are hired to communicate the benefits of the product and the firm. When they do this poorly, they do a serious disservice to the corporation. Adver-tisers are, of course, businesses selling their own services. This can lead them to overstate, use suggestive advertising, and subliminals (note the Virginia Slims ad with barely visible S-E-X in the ornate margin of the print ad). It is doubtful that subliminals are effective in selling goods and services, despite the attention they have received. Nonetheless, they are probably the results of attempts by the advertising agency to sell its own services. It is their "competitive edge" over other agencies, in spite of the negative long-term impact that such ads have on advertisers and on business in general.

Given the fact that advertisers touch consumers so intimately, one might expect that the firm paying for the advertising would exert special efforts to insure that its own advertising is truthful, substantive, tasteful, and ethical. This is not always the case. What could be an opportunity to build long-term trust and confidence is too often sacrificed in advertising campaigns that are overstated and shallow—an attempt to gain immediate sales. This is another instance of the corporation lacking social responsibility and even working against its own best interests.

Some firms deliberately set out to build a better corporate image through advertising. This is called *institutional* advertising. Several petroleum firms speak less of their products than of the good things their firms are doing for people or of their viewpoint on public policy issues. Mobil and EXXON have been in the forefront of such advertising. ITT and Gulf + Western tried to rebuild their tarnished images a few years ago through ads that told us the good things they were doing in research, for local communities—all for people.

Some advocacy ads provide useful information. They are able to counteract bias against an industry or a firm. They are able to counter public hostility to some corporations. While a firm's management has a right to present its point of view, it is not clear that a firm has a right to use corporate money to take a position on a controversial political issue. The financial resources of a firm are generally much greater than those of opposing citizen groups. Recall our more detailed discussion of lobbying and political contributions of business in Chapter Four.

The American Association of Advertising Agencies is responding to criticism in an expected fashion—by beginning an advertising campaign. It would be more fruitful if in an attractive way advertisers set out to "tell the reader or viewer of the ad what they want to know about the product in order to assess its usefulness in meeting the buyer's needs." Otherwise, the credibility of advertising will continue to decline and cynicism and a lack of trust will increase.[49] Truthfulness, fairness, and support of the community are involved here. Ultimately, freedom, growth, and productivity values also depend on these social values. Ethical conduct is essential for the health of our society; the stakes are high.

VALUES AND REMEDIES

We will now offer some reflections stemming from the traditional business values and the social values presented in Chapter Two on the effect of advertising and television on the attitudes and values of people. Moreover, we will again review the role of government in strengthening the common good, and will provide some recommendations for future actions.

Ethics and Values in Advertising and the Media

Two ethical issues loom immediately when one speaks of advertising. The first is that of truthfulness in advertising. Are ads that demonstrate only exaggeration and puffery legitimate? What sort of ads are deceptive and unfair? An advertising ethics check list is presented in Figure 5-2. This list will aid an individual in determining the ethics of a particular ad or advertising strategy. This issue is important to the advertisers themselves, also. Adver-

FIGURE 5-2 Advertising Ethics Checklist*

In judging whether a certain ad or advertising strategy is ethical, a large number of factors must be considered. The following questions cover many of these points and may serve as a preliminary checklist:

General
1. What does the advertiser intend to accomplish?
2. What are the actual effects of this advertising on the individual and on society as a whole?
3. Are these effects accidental, or do they result almost necessarily from the techniques used?

On Technique
1. Does the advertisement provide information, or does it appeal only to status and emotions?
2. If the latter is true, does the advertisement attempt to bypass the judgment of the person?

On Content
1. Is the information truthful?
2. Are the motives presented valid?

On Psychological Effects
1. Does the ad seriously disturb the psychic equilibrium of the individual without sufficient reason?
2. Does the ad present lewd, purely materialistic, or selfish values?

On the Product Being Advertised
1. Does the ad lead to the misallocation of individual resources relative to the real needs of an individual?
2. Does it encourage an abusive use of any particular product?

On Social Consumption
Does the ad and the product advertised lead to a waste of national resources for the nation under consideration?

Final Judgment
When the intent and technique are not evil in and of themselves, and where the harmful effects are not necessary, are there other effects that outweigh the harmful effects?

Adapted from the checklist in Thomas M. Garrett, S.J., *An Introduction to Some Ethical Problems of Modern Advertising* (Rome: Gregorian University Press, 1961), p. 180.

tisers want to have their claims believed, and do not want to develop a reputation for half truths or habitual exaggeration that cannot be trusted. The checklist enables a conscientious firm or advertising agency to examine the content and the effect of any particular ad.

The FTC is charged with overseeing truth in advertising. The government-imposed necessity to substantiate claims has helped to make advertisements and advertisers more truthful. Nevertheless, there still remain substantial questions, both theoretical and practical, as to what is unfair and deceptive. Putting it another way, how far can advertising go in touting the claims of a product or service before being considered untruthful?

The second issue is more far-reaching. Does advertising encourage shallow, materialistic, and selfish values or is it merely a reflection of the values that already exist in the American people? Such an important issue deserves careful consideration. Advertising, especially on TV and in popular magazines, very often intentionally appeals to acquisitiveness, social status, and fear of ridicule. Advertisers attempt to convince us that if we feel unattractive, unhappy, or ill, they have just the right product to fix us up. Critics have accused advertisers of being "creators of dissatisfaction." The picture they present of beautiful, immaculately groomed and dressed, often plastic men and women is an unreal picture of the world—both as it is and as it should be. Designer clothes, cosmetics, and "performance" autos promoted through advertising as the ideal are materialistic and shortsighted. It sets up shallow and generally unattainable expectations, especially in the minds of the young. Happiness is found in possessions; in having *things*. This leads to frustration later in life, when one discovers that money and possessions generally do not bring happiness.

Some claim that advertising merely holds up a mirror to our culture, and reflects the values and desires that it finds present.[50] According to this position, the public is essentially bored with advertising, ignores most of it, and hence it has very little influence on peoples' values. Since it is known as propaganda, people pay little attention to advertising. Even though advertising has grown and prospered, it has steadily lost influence over American life; its peak influence having been in the 1920s. These critics claim that anyone who is already poorly disposed to business will use advertising as a scapegoat. Being ominpresent and intrusive, it is the most convenient whipping boy for those who would criticize the free market system itself.

Advertising does have an influence on values, attitudes, and desires. This effect can be considerable even though it is not always what the advertiser intends. Business firms would not spend $60 billion every year on advertising if there were not evidence that it does affect preferences and attitudes. Note that the underlying message of image advertising is (1) your happiness lies in possessions; you are what you own, and (2) what you presently own is inadequate. So advertising not only teaches materialism but also the inadequacy of our own selves. This attempt to change our values is objectionable in that it attempts to have us turn in on ourselves, to make us more selfish; it fails to recognize the basic dignity of the human. Moreover, it can also undermine the business value of individual responsibility and freedom.

Advertising is an instrument of propaganda. Socialist countries use TV and ads not only to direct consumption but also to further their view of the national purpose and the common good. So, too, advertising in a free-market country conveys the focused message of the importance of material goods and dissatisfaction with present possessions, along with using sex, family, status, etc., to sell goods. Such an important vehicle for attitude change deserves careful examination by all of us.

Finally, looking to ethical criteria, we can say that good advertising does respect the freedom of the individual. It provides important information, and one is free to reject what one does not like. Moreover, good advertising also supports family values, caring, sharing, and the common good. We have seen examples of this sort of advertising from IBM, Gallo, and AT&T.

Nevertheless, some advertising does not respect the dignity of the person in a variety of ways. Moreover, it encourages shallowness, selfishness, and materialism—all of which tend to undermine the community. To that extent, such advertising is not ethical.

Government Regulation: Protection or Interference?

In Chapter Four we discussed the occasions in which government regulation impedes the free market and when regulation enables it to operate more efficiently and more justly. The market system can sometimes encourage individuals to cut corners. Being truthful in ads is one of those corners. The Federal Trade Commission (FTC) was established in 1914 to prohibit unfair and deceptive acts in commerce. Its hand was strengthened in 1938 when it was given explicit charge over advertising. The FTC has two important tools at its disposal. First, it can require any advertiser to submit on demand test data that will substantiate claims that are made in its advertising. Second, if advertising claims are found to be unfair or deceptive, the FTC can require the manufacturer to run "corrective" advertising, which sets the record straight.

The intention of corrective advertising is to correct false impressions, not to be punitive. Among products that were judged to be deceptively advertised, and were required to run counter advertisements, were STP motor oil, Listerine, Domino sugar, and Profile bread.[51] Listerine, for example, was required to run the following ad: "Contrary to prior advertising, Listerine will not help prevent colds or sore throats or lessen their severity."[52] Corrective ads are a powerful tool to encourage manufacturers and advertisers to be truthful in their claims for their products. However, in the current deregulatory climate, the FTC is understaffed and has not used this tool. Evidence also suggests that corrective ads are not very effective in correcting the impression that was originally created.[53] Corrective ads, however, do serve an ethical purpose in encouraging truthfulness.

The FTC sought to control advertising directed to children during the 1970s. Citing the evidence posed earlier in this chapter, they pointed out that we have long treated children differently from adults in everything from drinking alcohol to working for pay. Children need special protection. After months of preparation and hearings, the case for some sort of restraints, either voluntary or mandated, seemed very strong. Nevertheless, at that time the urge to deregulate swept the nation. The election of Ronald Reagan in 1980 and his appointment of James C. Miller as head of the FTC (1981–1985) further insured that no new regulations would be imposed. A glance at children's television on Saturday mornings indicates that much of the programming and advertising remains trivial, violent, and manipulative of children. One can agree that many regulations were not wise, and still argue that wholesale deregulation threatens important public policy goals and undermines the common good.[54] These goals include truthfulness, respect for the person, and encouraging mature, confident, cooperative, and self-confident people.

As to self-regulation, the American Association of Advertising Agencies (AAAA) has on several occasions tried to police its own members. An attempt in the 1940s to outlaw objectional ads collapsed in disinterest. A later attempt found only 10 objectional ads over a two-year period. And even in these cases there was no enforcement. In sum, self-regulation flounders because there is no ability among self-interested members to enforce decisions.[55] So far we have seen that advertisers are not about to change their way of doing things. This argues for additional government action to protect the basic business and social values of our society.

One of the principal arguments for regulation is that the air-waves belong to the public, and should not be the property of some private interests. While this argument still has weight, radio and television broadcasters no longer have the monopoly that they once had. Now cable TV, videocassette recorders, and other innovations have brought some additional market discipline to broadcasting. In fact, a current fear of advertisers and the media is that consumers will not watch advertising, since they no longer must. Any TV program or film can be recorded, and the commercial messages deleted or "fast forwarded." This is called "zapping," and advertisers and broadcasters are trying to determine how they can prevent it.[56]

There are important public policy objectives to be achieved by regulation. Deregulation stems from the ethical criteria of freedom, but it sometimes overlooks the reasons for government in the first place—encouraging honesty, solidarity, and community. Some regulation (for example, truth in advertising) is essential to insure honesty in the marketplace and respect for the dignity of the person.

Practical Recommendations

This chapter might lead the reader to conclude that advertising is often dishonest and manipulative. It is true that there is a tension between the goals of the seller and the potential purchaser. Nevertheless, advertising provides a vital service in our free-market system. It is important to distinguish also that several of the advertising programs discussed in this chapter can be unethical because of the effect of the product itself, in addition to the way it is advertised (tobacco, alcohol, and infant formula in poor countries). To help bring about good, and ultimately more effective advertising, we have several recommendations.

First, identify traditional business values and social values that you see in ads; note where they are present and where they are undermined. Educate yourselves and your children on the goals, techniques, and content of advertising. Recall that firms are trying to *sell* products, so *they* can make money. Hence, their goals are often in conflict with your own.

Second, encourage firms whose advertisements support social values. Some firms are far more conscientious in this; we have given examples in the chapter. We urge consumers to notice whether advertising is good or not, to purchase from firms that use good advertising, and to boycott firms that use unethical advertising. Thus, we can use market forces to support social values.

Third, reaffirm the role of the FTC in policing unfair and deceptive advertising. In this complex world, few of us are able to verify the exorbitant claims made by many advertisers. Moreover, it is vital for both seller and customer to have some confidence in advertising. The vigilance of the FTC helps both.

Fourth, examine ways in which we can eliminate advertising, especially from children's television. The availability of videocassette recorders makes this possible. We are now able to provide children with a whole set of recorded educational and informative programs, avoiding the commercial television networks altogether. The discipline of the market place might then bring good ads and better TV programming.

SUMMARY AND CONCLUSIONS

The values presented in television and magazine ads are generally not very generous or humane. The advertising campaign that emphasizes generosity or family life ("You can be a lifeline" or "Reach out and touch someone"— AT&T) stands out in its uniqueness and recognition of social values. The clear message presented by most advertising is that happiness consists in possessing commodities or services. Advertising values things over persons. It urges the "consume and discard" over the "use and maintain" ethic. The principles of competition and greed are more prominent in advertising than caring, stewardship, and sacrifice. Advertising not only reflects shallow, materialistic, and consumer-oriented values back to us, but it constantly repeats and reinforces them. We are independent human beings and have human dignity, so many choose to ignore or reject these values; yet the constant drumming and promotion of self-centered values has *some* influence on all and considerable influence on the more impressionable.

Commercial television is a business that must sell itself to advertisers who will pay for its programming. This leads to programs that appeal to the lowest common demoninator, and thus attract the largest audience. Hence we see violence, vulgarity, and shallowness on many popular programs. TV presents trivial stories, marital infidelity, and murder on prime time. Quality programming—and there is some of it on each network—stands out as the exception. Nevertheless, the overall effect of the violence, materialism, and sexual attitudes that we experience daily on television are having lasting effects on the attitudes of future generations.

If we educate ourselves and try to persuade advertisers and TV programmers to support social values, we may see a more constructive advertising and television industry. That would be a benefit to ourselves, individually and to society.

DISCUSSION QUESTIONS

5.1. In a free market, what is the purpose of advertising, from the standpoint of the seller? . . .from the standpoint of the buyer?

5.2. Is advertising to the consumers' advantage? When? When not?

5.3. Is deceptiveness in ads unethical (see Figure 2-1)? When? Is puffery unethical? When is the use of sex in ads unethical?

5.4. Indicate the various types of ads. What are their functions?

5.5. Does the media in which ads are placed influence their content? How so?

5.6. Ethically assess the arguments for advertising tobacco products (see Figure 2-1).
   a. What images do tobacco firms use in their advertising?
   b. Does the evidence indicate that cigarette advertising is aimed at obtaining new smokers or not?
   c. Ethically assess tobacco firms' attempts to expand sales in poor countries.

5.7. Describe a current liquor or beer ad campaign. Who is the target market? Are there beer ads in your local college newspaper?

5.8. Outline the dangers in the use of breast milk substitutes by poor mothers. How does this affect ethical advertising strategies?

5.9. What influence does TV have on children? What is the problem with advertising sugar products on TV?

5.10. In what ways is commercial television damaging to children? How can childrens' TV be improved?

5.11. Indicate the advantages and disadvantages of advertising political candidates.

5.12. What is the image of the working person that is presented on TV ads? . . .of the business person on TV programs? Would this affect the sort of person that is attracted to a business career?

5.13. Is the low level of esteem with which Americans view business a problem for business people? Does it affect the values of business people?

5.14. In your experience does advertising influence peoples' values? Does it encourage materialistic and self-seeking values?

5.15. Is it appropriate for the federal government to regulate advertising? What should government do?

NOTES

[1]Michael Belcher, et al., "Psychophysiological and Cognitive Responses to Sex in Advertising," *Advances in Consumer Research*, vol. 9, 1982, pp. 424–27.

[2]Stephen Fox, *The Mirror Makers: A History of American Advertising and Its Creators*, (New York: William Morrow, 1984), p. 328.

[3]See O. C. Ferrell, "Implementing and Monitoring Ethics in Advertising," *Marketing Ethics: Guidelines for Managers*, Gene Laczniak and Patrick E. Murphy, eds. (Lexington: Lexington Books, 1985), pp. 27–40; also "Why Children's TV Turns Off So Many Parents," *U.S. News & World Report*, Feb. 18, 1985, p. 65.

[4]"What Entertainers are Doing to Your Kids," *U.S. News & World Report*, Oct. 28, 1985, pp. 46–49.

[5]See an article outlining the classic arguments on both sides: Stephen A. Greyser, "Advertising: Attacks and Counters," *Harvard Business Review* (March–April, 1972), pp. 22–29; 140–46.

[6]Thomas M. Garrett, S.J., *An Introduction to Some Ethical Problems of Modern Advertising.* (Rome: Gregorian University Press, 1961), p. 18.

[7]C. H. Sandage, et al. *Advertising Theory and Practice* (Homewood, Il: Irwin, 1983), p. 459.

[8]Thomas Garrett, *An Introduction to Some Ethical Problems, op. cit.*, p. 47.

[9]Leo Burnett, *Communications of an Advertising Man* (Chicago: Leo Burnett & Company, Inc., 1961), p. 243.

[10]William J. Wilson, "Consumer Reality and Corporate Image," in *The Unstable Ground: Corporate Social Policy in a Dynamic Society*, S. Prakash Sethi, ed. (Los Angeles: Melville, 1974), pp. 490–91.

[11]Leonard N. Reid and Lawrence C. Soley, "Generalized and Personalized Attitudes Toward Advertising's Social and Economic Effects," *Journal of Advertising* (vol. 11, no. 3, 1982), pp. 3–7.

[12]James U. McNeal, "You Can Defend Advertising—But Not Every Advertisement," *Business Horizons* (September–October, 1981), pp. 33–37.

[13]George Moschis and Roy Moore, "A Longitudinal Study of Television Advertising Effects," *Journal of Consumer Research* (December, 1982), pp. 279–84.

[14]Jerome Marmorstein, M.D., "Tobacco Politics in the American Culture," *The Center Magazine* (July–August, 1986) pp. 27–33. See also, "Smoke Gets in Their Eyes," *Common Cause*, February, 1982, p. 8.

[15]*Mirror Makers, ibid.*, p. 303. See also Michael Schudson, *Advertising, The Uneasy Persuasion: Its Dubious Impact on American Society.* (New York: Basic Books, 1984), pp. 178–208, 239–43.

[16]"Sharpest Attack Yet on Passive Smoking," *Wall Street Journal*, Dec. 9, 1986, p. 22; also S. Prakash Sethi, "The Tobacco Industry and the Smoking Controversy," in *Up Against the Corporate Wall: Modern Corporations and Social Issues of the Eighties.* (Englewood Cliffs, N.J.: Prentice Hall, 1982), 4th ed. pp. 398–421.

[17]"Estimated Advertising Percentages in Selected Industries," *Sales and Marketing Management* (February 18, 1985) p. 112; Charles J. Dirksen, et al., *Advertising: Principles and Management Cases*, (Homewood, Il: Irwin, 1983), p. 609–11.

[18]"Tobacco Politics in the American Culture," *The Center Magazine*, Comments by Joe B. Tye (July–August, 1986), pp. 31–32; "Blacks in Debate on Tobacco Industry Influences," *New York Times*, January 17, 1986, p. 1.

[19]Jerome Marmorstein, M.D., "Tobacco Politics in the American Culture", *op. cit.*, pp. 28.

[20]For a discussion of the tobacco firm's strategies in the face of health evidence, see Robert H. Miles, *Coffin Nails and Corporate Strategies*, (Englewood Cliffs, N.J.: Prentice Hall, 1982). On blundering public policy and the efforts to sell in poor countries, see pp. 262–75. See also Michael D. Bernacchi, "A Study of the Marketing and Advertising of Cigarettes with an Addendum on Chewing Tobacco," University of Detroit Working Paper, February, 1986.

[21]Michael D. Bernacchi, "Alcoholic Beverage Advertising: Hindsight, Oversight and Insight," *Proceedings of American Council on Consumer Interests*, Spring, 1985; "Advertising-to-Sales Ratios, 1984," *Advertising Age*, July 15, 1985, p. 39; "Estimated Advertising Percentages in Selected Industries," *Sales and Marketing Management*, (February 18, 1985), p. 112.

[22]See *Advertising Age*, July 18, 1985, p. 14–17

[23]Charles Atkin and Martin Block, "The Effects of Alcohol Advertising," in *Advances in Consumer Research*, vol. XI, Thomas Kinnean, ed. (14th Annual Conference of Consumer Research, 1983), pp. 688–93.

[24]Michael Jacobson, et al., *The Booze Merchants*. (Washington, D.C.: Center for Science in the Public Interest, 1983), p. 48.

[25]James R. DeFoe and Warren Breed, "The Problem of Alcohol Advertisements in College Newspapers," Journal of the American College Health Association (February, 1979), pp. 195–99.

[26]Michael Jacobson, *The Booze Merchants*, p. 25.

[27]R. Fein, *Alcohol in America: The Price We Pay*. Care Institute, 1984, p. 27.

[28]For an excellent overview of the five largest manufacturers and a listing of their major markets and business strategies, see James E. Post, "The International Infant Formula Industry," in Post's book, *Corporate Behavior and Social Change*. (Reston, Va.: Reston Publishing, 1978), pp. 257–71. See also S. Prakash Sethi and James E. Post, "Public Consequences of Private Actions: Marketing of Infant Formula Food in Less Developed Countries," *California Management Review* 21 (Summer, 1979), pp. 35–48.

[29]"Abbott Laboratories Puts Restraints on Marketing Infant Formula in the Third World," in Earl A. Molander, *Responsive Capitalism: Case Studies in Corporate Social Conduct*. (New York: McGraw-Hill, 1980), 264–83.

[30]James E. Post, "Assessing the Nestle Boycott: Corporate Accountability and Human Rights," *California Management Review* 27 (Winter, 1985); pp. 113–31; also S. Prakash Sethi et al., "Impact of Socio-Political Environment on Corporate Strategy: The Many Faces of Infant Formula Controversy," *Journal of Business Strategy* (Winter, 1985).

[31]James Post, "Assessing the Nestle Boycott," and "The International Infant Formula Industry," p. 267.

[32]William S. Sachs, *Advertising Management* (Tulsa: PennWell, 1983), p. 499.

[33]"TV Bombs Out in New Federal Study," *U.S. News & World Report*, May 17, 1982, p. 17.

[34]Stanley Rothman and Robert S. Lichter, "Hollywood and America: The Odd Couple," *Public Opinion*, (December–January, 1983, pp. 54–58; also by the same authors, "What Are Moviemakers Made of?" *Public Opinion*, December–January, 1984), pp. 14–18.

[35]"TV Bombs Out.." *op. cit.*, p. 17.

[36]T. G. Bever et al., "Young Viewers' Troubling Response to TV Ads," *Harvard Business Review* (November–December, 1975), p. 109–20.

[37]*Ibid.*, p. 119.

[38]Kenneth Mason, "Responsibility for What's on the Tube," *Business Week*, August 13, 1979, p. 14.

[39]Charles K. Atkin, "Observation of Parent–Child Interaction in Supermarket Decision-Making," *Journal of Marketing*, October, 1978, pp. 41–45.

[40]At this time in the late 1970s, General Foods was also listed as sponsoring some of the most violent TV programs by the National Committee for Broadcasting. General Foods then changed its advertising policies and was later listed as one of the "Least Violent Sponsors" by the same group.

[41]Kenneth Mason, "Responsibility for What's on the Tube," p. 14.

[42]Lynda Sharp Paine, "Children as Consumers: An Ethical Evaluation of Children's Television Advertising," *Business and Professional Ethics Journal*. (Spring/Summer, 1984), p. 136. The entire double issue of this journal is devoted to the ethics of advertising.

[43]Kenneth Mason, "Revamping Saturday Morning Children's Television," *Vital Speeches*, Jan. 15, 1979. See also Mason's "The Multinational Corporation: Central Instituton of Our Age," *Corporations and the Common Good*, Robert Dickie and Leroy Rouner, eds. (Notre Dame: University of Notre Dame Press, 1986), pp. 78–90.

[44]Robert B. Westbrook, "Politics as Consumption: Managing the Modern Election," in *The Culture of Consumption: Critical Essays in American History*, Richard Wightman Fox and T.J. Jackson Lears, eds. (New York: Pantheon Books, 1983), p. 157.

[45]For the classic story of the media efforts behind the election of Richard Nixon, see Joe McGinniss, *The Selling of the President 1968* (New York: Trident, 1969).

[46]James U. McNeal, "Advertising's Disparagement of American Workers," *Business Horizons* (January–February, 1983), p. 7–12.

[47]Barbara Basler, " 'Bad Guys' Wear Pin Stripes," *New York Times*, January 29, 1987, pp. D1, D7; Pauline Kael in Studs Terkel, *Working.* (New York: Patheon Books, 1972), pp. 155–56.

[48]Louis Harris, "Public Confidence in Key Institutions is Down," *The Harris Survey*, November 25, 1982, pp. 2–3.

[49]See S. Prakash Sethi, "Advertising's Image Problem," *Advertising Age*, March 3, 1986. See also his "Advocacy Advertising in America," Keynote Address, Conference Board of Canada, Nov. 25, 1981.

[50]See, for example, Stephen Fox, *The Mirror Makers*, (New York: William Morrow, 1984), especially pp. 8, 328–330.

[51]William Sachs, *Advertising Management*, 488–96.

[52]C. Sandage, *Advertising Theory and Practice*, p. 480.

[53]George Belch, et al., "An Examination of Consumers' Perception of Purpose and Content of Corrective Advertising," in *Advances in Consumer Research*, Andrew Mitchell, ed., Vol. IX, 1981, pp. 327–32.

[54]See "Has the FCC Gone Too Far?," *Business Week*, August 5, 1985, pp. 48–54. While the Business Week article focuses on the FCC, which regulates television and radio, the same questions could also be asked of deregulation at the FTC.

[55]Stephen Fox, *The Mirror Makers*, p. 301–02.

[56]Barry M. Kaplan, "Zapping—The Real Issue in Communication," *Journal of Advertising Research*, (April–May, 1985), pp. 9–12. The same issue of this journal carried three articles on the cause of and the threat of zapping.

Chapter Six
LIVELIHOODS, NEIGHBORHOODS, AND THE CORPORATION*

Many people feel that corporations have little loyalty to their local communities. A firm, seemingly with no compunction, will move from one area to another, leaving a wasteland of dying neighborhoods, unemployed and unemployable citizens, and city treasuries dry from the lack of tax dollars. The same is true for companies that shut down totally, leaving a city or region impoverished. Often the closing comes without warning. Corporations, in hiring, firing, and locating in one city rather than another, affect us all. Social relations change; human lives are altered drastically.

Neighborhoods and cities depend upon local businesses; employees, neighbors, suppliers, and other dependent businesses are important stakeholders in a firm. When a firm disregards local community welfare in its actions, such disregard is ethically unacceptable.

On the other hand, the classic economist Joseph Schumpeter pointed out that the only way that innovation can continue in capitalist society is through the periodic purging of the useless, the decaying, and the dying, in this case companies whose day has come and gone.[1] He calls this a creative

*The principal author of this chapter is Michael J. Lavelle, S.J., Professor of Economics and Academic Vice President at John Carroll University, Cleveland, Ohio.

destruction that weeds out the garden so as to enable other, and presumably better, flowers to grow. Both the critics' and Schumpeter's positions have merit.

Plant closings and the influence of a firm on its neighborhood provide good vehicles for examining the way that a firm treats people. That is the major concern of this book: how the firm deals with the people with which it has contact. Plant closings, as difficult as they are, provide a good test of this. We will apply the norms we presented in Chapter Two to determine the ethical responsibilities of a corporation to its local community.

In 1977, the Lykes Company closed a major steelmaking plant in Campbell, Ohio, near Youngstown. The closing came despite the fact that the plant was still profitable, earning $19.1 million in 1976.[2] The closing had dramatic consequences. Five thousand workers in Youngstown and the Mahoning Valley lost jobs; the ripple effect eliminated an estimated additional 11,000 jobs. An analyst predicted that the Youngstown area population of 543,000 would drop by 8 percent.[3] The picture in Youngstown became bleak. Disbelief, anger, frustration, and stress ran through the local community. A local coalition tried to purchase the plant, but they did not succeed. To understand the closing, let us examine the background.

Lykes Company, based in New Orleans, was formed in 1969 with the merger of Youngstown Sheet and Tube (YST) and Lykes Steamship. In 1968 YST had a good cash position.[4] It dropped an invitation to merge by stating it wanted to move its operations beyond that of steelmaking. At the same time, the Lykes Steamship Company was interested in corporate expansion or merger. Lykes also had a good cash position, but was in the shipping industry, in which it anticipated little growth.[5] In 1967, Lykes had earnings of $18.9 million; YST had net earnings of $39.8 million, so both at that time were healthy.[6]

THE ILL-FATED MATCH: LYKES AND YOUNGSTOWN

After negotiations between the two companies, a merger was effected in May, 1969.[7] The new Lykes immediately experienced difficulties; they had borrowed $100 million to buy out YST. Lykes then had to use the cash reserves of YST, which YST management had earmarked for aggressive modernization, to pay off the debts that were incurred at the time of the merger.[8] It was not until 1972 that the new company was able to turn a profit, but in 1975 and 1976 the United States economy softened. Lykes' steelmaking operations had been significantly weakened by the failure to invest in updated equipment and techniques. Lykes Company announced in September, 1977, that it was closing the Campbell plant of the Youngstown Sheet and Tube Company, effective January 1, 1978.[9] Lykes cited costly EPA requirements, Japanese dumping, and the deterioration of the plant in a declining market.

As a positive alternative, an Ecumenical Coalition of the Mahoning Valley was formed; it wanted to buy the now-closed YST plant in hopes of reopening it.[10] In retrospect, this group had little or no chance of success, but it did mobilize the affected community in an effort to protect the existing plant and jobs.[11] The periods leading to the decision to close the plant were (1) the time immediately before the Lykes-Youngstown Sheet and Tube merger (2) life during the merger and (3) the closing of Youngstown Sheet and Tube and its aftermath. To complete the story we will examine Lykes merger with LTV, and LTV's bankruptcy.

For each of these periods, we will try to answer the following: Was justice done in this most difficult decision? Were the actions in the best interests of all those involved? Was the dignity of each person and the community respected? Were the actions of the executives involved ethical?

High Stakes for Stakeholders

In order to make an ethical judgment on the plant closure, it is essential to identify all people that were affected by it. Stakeholder analysis aids that assessment, since it identifies those parties.[12] A stakeholder is someone who has "a stake" in the firm and in the decisions of its management (see Chapter One, Figure 1–2). This stake is more than the passing interest of the newspaper reader or occasional observer. Corporate decisions touch each stakeholder, and it is desirable that the best interests of each be balanced and served in keeping with the norms of Chapter Two.

The stakeholders of the original YST include the legal owners, the stockholders, along with the workers, the union, and the managers of the company. Customers, suppliers, the local neighborhood, the city, and state and federal government were also stakeholders.

The responsibility that YST and Lykes-Youngstown has to each stakeholder varies. Where the stake is larger, there is a larger, more binding responsibility to take into account that party's interests. There is a duty to inform, consult, and perhaps to gain consensus to carry out a proposed business decision. The norm is: the greater the stake, the greater the claim on a share in decision making.

Stakeholder analysis parallels and supports ethical analysis. We urge that individual responsibility, dignity of the human person, community, and justice be respected by all parties that are touched by the decision or action. To maintain one's dignity, a person should be a participant in economic life. Here stakeholder analysis and social values intermesh. The more one is touched by an act, the more one should be a part of those decisions. Moreover, note that such participation encourages the traditional business values of freedom and individual responsibility, also (see Chapter Two).

YST has a primary responsibility to their customers. However, where there are many other potential suppliers and the possibility of moving from one to another is relatively easy, the moral responsibility—in this case of informing or consulting customers—seems to be minimal. As the possibility of substitution becomes less likely, the stake of the customer becomes greater, and so the company has a greater obligation to consider the needs of the customer stakeholder in its decision.

Prior to the merger of YST and Lykes, both were companies with large cash reserves operating in declining industries. YST might have used its cash reserves for modernization and possibly overcome the decline in the steel industry. But they chose to use these reserves not in steel, but in other lines of business. Whose interests did YST president Williams serve when he told *The Wall Street Journal* that his company was looking toward diversification?[13]

Stockholders were adversely affected by the merger; for five years the new company did not pay dividends even on its preferred stock. Perhaps management had originally perceived the merger to be in the stockholders' interest, but stockholders lost severely with the eventual bankruptcy of the new parent company, LTV, in 1986.

Workers and their Stake

Those who worked in the plants were probably the most severely affected by the plant closing. Economic theory maintains that workers can move to obtain other jobs when their company closes, but experience shows that this mobility is likely only for the second generation, the children of the displaced workers. When the textile mills of New England closed, it was the children of the mill workers who either moved or were incorporated into the new high-tech electronics industry that grew up outside Boston. The laid-off mill workers remained on the fringe of economic activity in New England.[14] While mobility of workers keeps our economy flexible, there is a serious trade-off cost because families and communities suffer. Simply presuming that people should move, and failing to provide counseling, training, and other help, does not respect their years spent with the firm.

When a plant closes, the affected workers lose much; income may be lost for the rest of their working lives. If the worker remains unemployed, he or she moves onto the welfare rolls with the accompanying discouragement, despair, anxiety, and detrimental effect on the family. The workers are the ones who are the most disadvantaged stakeholders, so justice and their dignity as persons demand that they be considered when making a decision to close a plant. Justice even demands that these people be brought into the decision-making process.

Workers have a moral claim on the company, because of an implicit (and sometimes explicit) "contract" between the workers and the company. All have worked to make the company what it is, and have thus formed a relationship. Managers, workers, and owners are now much more; building the company was a process of working together. This formed relationships that brought obligations of each party toward the others.[15]

Obligations also arise from a firm's position in its community. Just as individuals living in a community have built a network of interdependencies with others in the community, so too has the firm.[16] We live as individuals, yet we are also dependent upon others.[17] Without jeopardizing the tradition of individual rights, we stress here the communal nature of all human life. Freedom and productivity cannot be achieved at the cost of disrupting community. No individual may exercise freedom in ways that harm others without sufficient reason and without corresponding benefit.

Application of these principles presents some difficult moral problems, yet the claims of the various stakeholders must be translated into practice. Various models exist. Germany has a type of codetermination where, in the steel and coal industries, there is a tripartite division on governing boards; management, workers, and the government each have a third of the representation. In Spain, the Mondragon cooperative is another example of sharing decision-making power. ESOPs are an American method of employee ownership (for additional discussion of the Mondragon Cooperatives, ESOPs and other participative methods, see Chapter Three). The American Catholic Bishops have called for a new model of cooperation.[18] Those whose stake is large should have something to say about what happens to their lives and livelihoods.

Many people were affected by the YST plant closing. Cities and towns surrounding the plant had a varying stake in the plant's remaining productive and in its original location. The closing brought many problems: families breaking up and leaving the area, tax losses, welfare increases, rising alcoholism, suicide, violence, and other social ills associated with unemployment. This is a serious impact, and violates justice and community. The corporation had a responsibility to the community to provide some warning, to consult, and to help see that the attending social evils be mitigated insofar as possible.[19]

In closing the Campbell plant, management did not listen to stakeholders, and it hampered efforts of workers and others to buy the plant in order to try to keep it operating. In this it violated justice and disrupted community. Perhaps the plan to purchase the plant was not viable, but Lykes owed it to the stakeholders to at least hear and discuss their proposal.

A more positive example of workers' participation in decision making is provided by another steel firm, the Weirton Steel Division of the National Steel Corporation in Weirton, West Virginia.[20] In 1983, Weirton employees, after considerable consultation and bargaining with management, bought the Weirton facilities for $386 million, after the workers had agreed to a 32 percent pay cut.[21] This participation plan has proven successful. In 1985, the employee–owners picked up their first bonuses, thus demonstrating that recognizing human dignity, community, and solidarity can be practical and profitable. In 1986, the Weirton CEO was included among the "best" CEOs in the United States. He was recognized for "turning in a second-straight profit year at a successful employee-owned company in a depressed industry."[22]

We have tried to show that a company has a moral obligation to its stakeholders. The closer the bonds a company has to a stakeholder and the more intimate the ties of dependency, the greater that obligation is. In any decisions affecting their future, justice and the human dignity of all stakeholders must be considered. One way of implementing these obligations is to have the most seriously affected stakeholders enter the decision-making process, or at least be informed of the impending decision well in advance. In the case of a plant closing, some sort of compensation is required from the company, assuming it can pay. This is required for justice. When workers have given a portion of their lives to the past success of a firm, they deserve some help in becoming reestablished.[23] Lykes-Youngstown management acted unethically in announcing the YST Campbell plant closing without prior consultation with workers and the municipality; they failed to take into account the decades of work and the stake that workers had in the firm.

The right of stakeholders to a voice in decision making at the time of a plant closing is consistent with our comments in Chapter Three about the rights of workers within the plant. YST's problems should have been addressed long before the time of the plant closing. YST's final decision to close was the culmination of many decisions made earlier, starting at least from the time Mr. Williams said he wanted YST to diversify. When YST was still profitable and had a good cash position, there was an opportunity for a participative decision on whether to use the money available to reinvest in the steel industry, or to use the funds to diversify. Steel was YST's basic business, yet the decision made by YST's board was one based on greater earnings possibilities outside the steel industry. Unfortunately, this lack of responsibility is not YST's alone. The president of US Steel (now USX) took a similar position when he stated publicly that US Steel's goal was not to make steel, but to make money.

Investing YST's cash elsewhere injured people who had a major stake in the company, and it injured affected communities in the Mahoning Valley. Ethical considerations demand that the purpose of a company be not solely to make money but to live as a citizen in an environment with fellow citizens.

Limitations of Shared Decision Making

A major difficulty with shared decision making is that most stakeholders have an undesirable bias toward conservatism. In this case, the workers and the city undoubtedly wanted to avoid closure. They were biased toward the status quo even when evidence was clear that the company was in poor shape in spite of the best efforts of management. Other conditions enter into decision making: proximity to raw materials, migration of customers to other areas, and a plant that is not competitive in the world market. Local decision making tends to be conservative, and would have defended the Campbell plant from cheaper, more efficient operations elsewhere.

Each case must be examined individually. The closing of the Campbell plant was the result of poor management decisions that contributed to making it inefficient. Exclusively financial decisions led to using scarce capital to diversify. Then the decline in the market for steel brought the company to where closure seemed the only viable solution.

Soon after the Campbell plant closed in 1978, Lykes, and what remained of YST, merged with LTV. In July, 1986, LTV filed for bankruptcy in Federal Court. Bankruptcy meant that thousands of white- and blue-collar workers would not only lose their jobs, but also their pensions. In 1985, the year prior to bankruptcy, LTV had lost $724 million; yet in that same year, top management received "performance awards" of almost $1 million. Even in that year of poor financial performance, the company paid $135,000 for nine country club memberships, $5000 for box seats for the Kentucky Derby and similar lavish expenses. Such largess to management is unjust when company performance is so poor and the workers are about to be left with no job and no pensions.[24]

Mergers, which move firms from their primary areas of expertise, often fail.[25] Lykes had no experience in steel. LTV was a conglomerate, and its managers were financial, not operating, people. These managers were distant from local plants and communities. Knowing people face to face makes it harder to err on local conditions, and harder to neglect them as persons.

EFFECT ON NEIGHBORHOODS

In September 1980, the Atlantic Richfield Company (ARCO) announced it was closing its Anaconda, Montana copper smelter.[26] In the future, Anaconda would process ore in Japan. The reasons cited are familiar. Costs of meeting federal pollution and safety regulations were said to be $400 million when sales hovered around $1 billion over the previous five years.[27] The EPA disputed this estimate, saying that costs would be lower and could have been spread over a two-and-one-half-year period.

Petroleum and Copper Did Not Mix

The Anaconda plant had been closed since July, 1980 due to an industry-wide strike. Reports circulated that the firm had no great desire to negotiate an end to the strike, since prices in the copper industry were flat.[28] ARCO had acquired Anaconda Copper, the third largest copper producer in the United States, in 1976 for $700 million. It then added $500 million to modernize the company, which had lost $38 million in the year before the purchase. ARCO was at least moving into an allied field.[29] Even before the purchase, Anaconda had moved its corporate headquarters to New York City; when

ARCO acquired the firm, management became even more distant. On the other hand, ARCO had a reputation for being a leader in their concern for corporate social responsibility. ARCO prided itself on its leadership in environmental protection and community involvement.[30]

Anaconda dominated the local economy. Anaconda, Montana, with a population of 12,500, was a company town; 1085 people worked for Anaconda and an estimated 80 percent of the economy was tied to the smelter. The firm built the local high-school football stadium, helped maintain the local golf club, and constructed a company club with bowling alleys.[31]

Given a small town like Anaconda, the effects of the closing were immense. Anxieties, heart disease, family stress and breakup, loss of most of the tax base—all followed the closing. A Chevrolet dealer cut his staff from 29 to 12.[32] Ancillary services went with the smelter. By 1985, five of nine local schools had closed, unemployment was 16 percent, and population had declined from 12,500 to 8500.[33] Many of those who were working were forced to accept lower-paying jobs.[34]

The Anaconda closing was somewhat different from the YST closing. YST was not the only employer in Youngstown. People could get work elsewhere without incurring the monetary and psychological costs of moving. This was not true in Anaconda. The townspeople of Anaconda tried to create jobs, but for many workers the only solution was to relocate.

Three major stakeholder groups in the Anaconda closing were management, the workers and their union, and the town itself. Management's claims that EPA requirements cost $400 million and would make the plant unprofitable were contested by the EPA.[35] The smelter was old and obsolete in addition to being a major polluter, the cost of copper had dropped dramatically, and the cost of the workforce had increased. To build a new smelter would be unwise, because it would be too far from new sources of copper—the Anaconda copper was running out. ARCO's management may also have been inclined to close the plant as a means to be rid of the bothersome union and the strike.[36] The company gave early retirement to those over 55, and provided generous severance pay to others. The actions of executives situated a long way from Anaconda had drastic results for 12,500 people.

Anaconda's workers were unionized and the union's activities had great impact on the local population in the small company town. The threat of a strike has great impact, and this requires more responsible behavior on the part of the union. Given the small, one-employer town, both company and union had greater responsibilities in their negotiations.

A third major stakeholder is the city of Anaconda. In good times, Anaconda enjoyed the benefits of the smelter's relatively benevolent and paternal management.[37] The local people were dependent on the smelter. In a town as small as Anaconda, managers and workers knew each other and had to develop ties of friendship or at least mutual respect. Unfortunately, neither the face to face relationships, nor ARCO's attempt to be socially responsible, saved the smelter. The town itself tried to help the region bring in other business firms, but the efforts have not been very successful.

Anaconda was alone in feeding economic life to the area, and therefore its responsibility to stakeholders was much greater. Yet note the lack of responsibility shown by all three major stakeholders. The common good calls for collaboration. Respect for the dignity of the people involved required that those parties have some input into the final decision. Justice to those who had a stake in Anaconda demanded that the firm, union, and city work to settle the strike and to broaden the economic base of the area.

Both the Lykes and the Anaconda cases illustrate the stress, illness, and anxiety left in the wake of a plant closing. Moreover, neither closing involved a discussion of options with the major stakeholders. There may be a greater tendency to leave stakeholders out of planning when ownership and management are located a thousand miles away. People can more easily be thought of as statistics. One can make an economic case for the closings, thus satisfying the ethical norm of growth and productivity. However, the lack of discussion with stakeholders violates the social norms of community, justice, and the dignity of the individual.

Control Data and Teaching Machines

Control Data, under the leadership of CEO William Norris, has had, at least until recently, a happier outcome. William Norris began Control Data Corporation (CDC) in 1957 after experiencing frustration at IBM. The new company was to produce large-scale computers for engineering and scientific application. Norris' purpose was to identify unmet computer needs and make filling them profitable to his company.[38]

In 1967, Norris had attended a seminar at which Whitney Young, of the Urban League, spoke. Young told a group of executives about the social and economic injustices that blacks were suffering in the United States. The next year the United States experienced a series of shattering race riots. Minneapolis–St. Paul, the company's corporate-headquarter cities, were not spared.[39] These experiences left Norris with the conviction that his company had a responsibility to help remedy the social ills that were the root of the riots. Norris was convinced that job creation was a socially responsible answer to the problem.

CDC built a plant in the inner city, where many blacks lived. Norris stressed that the plant had to be new, and it had to produce goods that were essential to the life of CDC. This was to show that the company was sincere and committed, since they could not bail out if problems arose.[40] The new Northside plant took three years to come up to other plants in the Control Data system in productivity, quality, and cost performance, but William Norris had the patience to wait for the social good to be achieved.

Support systems were necessary to make the inner city plant a success. A major portion of the workforce for the Northside plant were women with small children and students who needed part-time jobs. Therefore, Norris allowed part-time employees; they fashioned their workday around their other needs.[41] Ex-convicts wanted to work, but most needed automobiles to get to work; they found it very difficult to get a loan for buying second hand cars. Norris set up a program, Wheels, to help finance the purchase of these cars. In the beginning, the company lost 37 cars and $137,000. However, CDC continued the program, tightened it up, and it became a success.[42]

People in the inner city often have personal problems that erode their ability to be productive workers. So, Norris started EAR (Employee Advisory Resource), a counseling service that helped with personal finance, marriage, and family difficulties. Then came a health advice system.

Norris also developed a computerized learning program that had as one of its applications the teaching of language and math skills to prisoners and other disadvantaged people.[43] The company then branched out into computerized city planning and farm planning. Moreover, CDC eventually made money on these learning programs.

CDC is a corporation that acted in a moral manner, perhaps even in a virtuous way. Norris may have been paternalistic in not encouraging participation in the company's decision making, but this does not detract from his basic ethical actions and policies. Without William Norris' conversion in 1967, most likely there would have been few socially responsible actions undertaken by Control Data. This was possible because Norris was CEO; he formed the climate and culture of his company. While CDC has not done as well financially since William Norris retired as chief executive officer, Norris' and CDC's record stands to the credit of both.

This is a brief description of William Norris' efforts in the area of social responsibility. The company grew dramatically under his leadership. In 1977, it had revenues of $2.3 billion and profits of $63 million.[44] The company and Norris profited by the socially responsible activities outlined here. Some claim that CDC would have done better financially if it had not been concerned with the inner city. However, those who had jobs and those who had a new chance to learn will readily testify to the long-term value of CDC's policies. Recall the point made in Chapter One that profit maximization is not, in fact, the objective of most CEOs. This is another instance in which sacrificing short-term profits achieved considerable social benefits—jobs for the disadvantaged and valuable new products for those who need them most.

Conditions for Participation

Decisions that touch the lives of many people are in the hands of a very few corporate executives. Moreover, the *large* corporation is less likely to be sensitive to the needs of a local community, and hence is more apt to close a facility abruptly. When management is not on the scene, but in a distant headquarter city, the people directly affected by such a move are only numbers, not flesh and blood.

An investigation of plant closings showed that firms that close plants are more often diversified companies that use diversification as an investment strategy.[45] Also more likely to close plants are firms that are unionized, have foreign investments, or that license technology to foreign firms. Larger firms are also more likely to shut down a plant than smaller firms.[46]

Another examination of plant closings highlighted situations where companies did inform their stakeholders, discussed with them ways of avoiding a shutdown, and tried to relocate them when the facility did move. The study found that the likelihood of remaining in a present location increased where there was more commitment to the current site, a smaller firm with a single site, a greater level of organizational tolerance, and more organizational flexibility.[47] In these situations executives are better able to recognize the stature and human dignity of all the workers and to take them into the planning process.

GM and Ford Close California Plants

Northern California provides us with contrasting examples of how two auto assembly plant closings were handled. General Motors and Ford both had plants in California to supply the West Coast, but by the early 1980s Californians were purchasing about one half of their autos from Japanese manufacturers. This left excess capacity, and forced a decision to close several plants. Both GM and Ford had plants in the San Jose area, south of San Francisco. The closing processes show how GM "created an environment of uncertainty and anxiety, which caused inordinate suffering among workers and sharp public criticism", while Ford "was able to generate a smooth shutdown transition because its policies elicited understanding and cooperation from its employees and the community."[48]

General Motors decided to close its plant before Ford did. By March 1982, the entire GM facility in Fremont was closed, idling more than 5000 GM workers. The Fremont plant had suffered poor labor relations, the highest rates of absenteeism of any GM facility, and alcohol and drug problems among its workers. After the plant was initially closed, it was 13 months before GM finally announced that it would not reopen. With the possibility of a joint GM–Toyota venture, workers were left in a state of doubt as to the future of their jobs. Because of generous unemployment benefits, the possibility of the plant reopening, and the unwillingness to relocate families to communities around other GM plants, many of the unemployed workers remained without work for more than a year. This uncertainty led to anxiety, illness, abuse of families and eight suicides.

A GM–Toyota joint venture did eventually utilize the Fremont plant. The new venture, with Japanese management principles, used the same physical facility and many of the same workers. In contrast to the former GM operation, it has good labor relations, low absenteeism, and is very efficient. It is now a model from which GM is learning.

The Ford plant was closed for the same major reason as the GM plant, the demand for Ford cars on the West Coast had declined. The Ford plant, however, enjoyed an exceptionally good labor-management record. The Ford Employee Involvement (EI) program, in which groups of 20 to 25 workers made suggestions for improvement of quality, safety, and efficiency, had been very successful. The assembly line would stop each Thursday morning at 9 am, and workers would gather on company time in their EI groups to make suggestions.

Ford's EI program rested on the principle that "people have more to offer than the strength of their bodies—that when given the opportunity, the time and the training, they can and will contribute mightily in terms of positive ideas that solve work related problems, improve the work environment, and enhance work relationships."[49] GM has a similar program, which they call Quality of Work Life (QWL) (see Chapter Three).

The San Jose Ford plant was closed in May 1983, 14 months after the GM plant. Local newspapers and TV had given considerable attention to the apparently insensitive way that GM handled their closure, and Ford management benefited from GM's mistakes. Ford announced the closure six months before it took place, giving workers a chance to adjust themselves. They thus had the opportunity to seek new work or to retrain during this period. Ford was more generous than GM in providing financial and professional help to its laid-off workers. Moreover, all of Ford's planning for retraining programs was done jointly with the union, the United Auto Workers. Since labor and management at the Ford plant had a history of cooperation, they worked together in planning the shutdown to lessen the negative impact on the workers. Of the Ford employees, 63 percent obtained jobs after 15 months, while only 46 percent of the GM employees obtained work within two years of GM's closure. Most of this cooperation and the programs for retraining had been a part of negotiations one year earlier with the United Auto Workers Union.[50]

Note the effects on the health of the two groups of workers. Eight GM workers committed suicide, while no Ford workers did so. "Numerous other deaths were reported from heart attacks and cirrhosis of the liver among GM employees. Child abuse incidents reported to local police increased 240 percent in the first four months after the plant closed."[51] The stress of the sudden announcement, coupled with uncertainty as to the future, caused great anxiety and much illness among the GM workers. Former Ford workers did not suffer the same health problems.

Ford began a series of educational and training programs for their newly laid-off workers (see Figure 6–1). Both at the plant and off-site a number of adult basic education courses (basic math, reading, English as a second language, and other courses) helped to build skills. Vocational exploration and

FIGURE 6-1   Comparison of General Motors and Ford Plant Closures

	GM	FORD
Plant setting		
Type of plant	Assembly	Assembly
Union representation	UAW	UAW
Number of workers affected	5836	2300
Notice given to workers	3 weeks	36 weeks
Classroom and remedial training		
Percent of workers entering	22	70
Percent of entrants finishing	89	99
Percent of workers who found new work	46 (in 24 mos)	63 (in 15 mos)
Climate in plant before closure		
Participation	____	Employee involvement
Labor relations	Poor	Good
Absenteeism	High	Low

Source: Dale Yoder and Paul D. Staudohar, "Management and Public Policy in Plant Closure," *Sloan Management Review,* Summer, 1985, p. 45–57.

specific vocational retraining courses were also offered. More than 2100 workers took advantage of these courses.[52]

The two plant closings showed dramatic differences in policies toward workers. During the layoffs, GM–Fremont management seemed to feel little obligation toward its employees, seemingly anticipating that the state and federal government would take care of the newly unemployed. Local news media portrayed the plight of suddenly laid-off workers, noting that GM seemed to lack a social conscience. Then, perhaps in reaction to the negative publicity, "the company shifted its policy toward greater commitment of its resources."[53] Ford, in preparing for its closure, learned from GM's experience, and set out to do a better job helping its terminated workers obtain training and new employment.

Most American workers caught in plant closings or layoffs get less than two weeks' notice, making it virtually impossible to provide them with adequate help in finding new jobs or retraining for other jobs.[54] Of the major industrialized countries, only the United States does not have legislation requiring some advance warning to workers; Germany, France, Japan, Sweden, the Netherlands, and Great Britain all require advance warning. If firms do not respect the implicit contract they have with their workers by providing early warning and discussion in the case of plant closings, the public will probably call for legislation; voluntary action would mean that legislation would not be needed.

An early announcement of a plant closing could mean that morale would suffer and key employees would leave, but that did not happen at Ford. Moreover, a 1960s study of U.S. plant closings showed that advance notice rarely led to higher quit rates or lower productivity.[55] Even if good employees were lost and low morale were realized, justice and the dignity of the individual worker require that early warning of a plant closing be given to workers.

ETHICS AND ALTERNATIVES TO PLANT CLOSINGS

Nearly 35 million jobs were lost during the 1970s. About 55 million new jobs were added during this same period, bringing a net increase of about 20 million new jobs during the 1970s.[56] Most of these new jobs were service-related; most of these were lower paying than the jobs lost, and a majority went to women. New jobs continue to be added during the 1980s, but at a slower rate. The relative impact of job loss and job creation is illustrated in a study of both. From 1972–76, major metropolitan areas lost between 25 to 40 percent of their jobs, while *new* jobs accounted for 25 to 62 percent of jobs. For example, two of the areas with the lowest number of jobs lost, Worcester, Mass., and New Haven, Conn., had an even lower number of new jobs created, so there was thus a net loss of jobs in each city.[57] The total number of jobs in a given area is more the result of the new jobs created than of the jobs lost.

In most cities of the United States, the average loss of jobs is high. What makes the difference in employment opportunities is having a larger number of new jobs created. David Birch, who gathered these data, concludes ". . .one of our greatest strengths as a nation is our capacity for failure—the grace and even enthusiasm with which we accept those who try and fail and come back to try again." He makes the point: "The reality is that our most successful areas are those with the highest rates of innovation and failure, not the lowest."[58] The basic business values of Chapter Two, freedom, individual responsibility, productivity, and growth, provide the foundation for job generation. The social values of the dignity of the individual and community also support job creation so that the individual may have work.

For looking at the economy as a whole, Birch's comments are undoubtedly valid. However, Americans prefer "winners," those successful in their endeavors, whether it be corporate or personal life. To be known as a "loser" brings loss of self-esteem. People do not tolerate failure very well. The 35 million people who did lose their jobs faced a physical and psychological cost, suffering anxieties and adjustment problems. The dignity of the individual worker was injured. While growth and flexibility are vital to job creation, those who lose their jobs must not be disposed of as obsolete plant and equipment. It is not just to expect terminated workers to bear this cost alone. When necessary, they must be aided in building skills and smoothing the transition to new work.

There are alternatives available to abrupt plant shutdowns, and corporate executives have an ethical obligation to carefully review these options. One alternative is to sell the entire facility, thus maintaining it as an economic unit.

New management may do better; they may be able to reorganize the work, negotiate new wage rates, or utilize other means of lowering costs. And jobs would be saved. Another alternative is to sell the plant to the employees themselves, through an ESOP (see Chapter Three). General Motors, National Steel, Sperry Rand, and other firms have sold units to employees.[59] Although some of these new firms have had difficulties, in part because of the financing that was necessary in the purchase, most are now success stories.

Ford Motor in San Jose serves as an example of what can be done for workers. Corporations considering plant closings have an ethical obligation to inform workers in ample time of the upcoming closure. Three months would seem to be a minimum, so that workers can prepare themselves; YST provided this much time. Ford's six months is preferable. Responsible management will work with the local government to provide worker education, training, and help in finding other jobs.[60]

Federal legislation regarding plant closings will be demanded if corporations do not voluntarily provide notice and help terminated workers. Several states have laws that demand prior notice to workers. New laws tend to restrict the private sector and create additional red tape. The red tape and restrictions could be lessened if the laws embodied "people policies" that stress helping the workers affected to retrain and relocate.[61] Legislation could be avoided entirely if corporate executives recognized ethical obligations toward their workers. Responsible, voluntary action can meet the demands of justice and also forestall additional legislation.

When considering closing a facility, corporate executives must take into account the people who will be affected. To assess the morality of the act, we must (1) examine the seriousness of the economic impact of the act, and (2) allow participation of the stakeholders in the decision.

If the economic impact of a closing is not great, the ethical obligations involved are correspondingly fewer. Closing a small plant or a section of five workers would not carry the same ethical responsibilities that closing a large plant would. Although consultation is appropriate and good, the demand for participation of stakeholders in the decision-making process is less urgent if fewer are affected. If the economic impact of a plant closing is great, as in the Youngstown case, the responsibility for consulting with stakeholders becomes greater. Consultation with stakeholders might lead to an agreement on the necessity of closing the plant. Consulting is an ethical responsibility if the impact on workers and the locale is great. Unfortunately, in the vast majority of closings, mergers, or moves, we observe unethical and socially irresponsible behavior.

GM's New Poletown Plant: A Plant Opening

In 1980, General Motors determined that its old Cadillac and Fisher Body plant operations in Detroit were too costly. GM decided to build a modern new plant that would require almost 500 acres of land. GM Chairman Thomas

Murphy informed Detroit Mayor Coleman Young of GM's decision. Closing the old plants would mean a loss of about 6100 GM jobs in Detroit. Unemployment in Detroit was high, and the city wanted to preserve the jobs. So, Mayor Young and the city set about to find a site where a new GM plant could be built.

GM found a good site that included 165 acres of what had been the old Dodge Main auto assembly plant, plus an adjacent 300 acres of commercial and residential properties. The neighborhood was called "Poletown" because part of it housed first- and second-generation Polish families, many of whom were elderly.

Poletown was not the most economical location for GM. It would have been cheaper and easier to build a new plant in a rural area, perhaps in Michigan or in the South. Detroit helped to acquire the Poletown property by using its power of eminent domain to condemn the old buildings and residences. To provide the site for the new GM plant, 1176 houses were destroyed and 3438 people were displaced.[62] The homeowners were compensated and aided in finding new homes. Nevertheless, a neighborhood was destroyed. The use of eminent domain produced "intangible losses, such as the severance of personal attachments to one's domicile and neighborhood and the destruction of an organic community of a most unique and irreplaceable character."[63] We must weigh this evil against the good of having a new plant in the City of Detroit.

General Motors was willing to place the long-term welfare of the people of Detroit, vitally interested stakeholders, ahead of its own short-term benefits. It would have been cheaper to move out of the city and avoid the onus of destroying a neighborhood. GM and city officials judged that the jobs, income, and welfare provided to the thousands of people who would be employed at the new plant outweighed the loss of the neighborhood. There was little time for the City of Detroit to consult with the people, but they should have involved the leaders of the Poletown community. The final outcome might not have been different, but the dignity of the residents would have been better respected.

The dignity of the person and social justice required that GM address the needs of the 6000 people who would be laid off from the two plants to be closed. GM offered to build its new plant within the city, providing additional jobs in a city that needed them. Few complex decisions that involve so many people, however beneficial, are without criticism. The residents of Poletown, affected stakeholders also, could have been better heard. Nevertheless, on balance this was an ethical and praiseworthy decision, and can serve as a model of social responsibility for other large firms.

Contributions to the Local Community

When a corporation decides to help a local community, the easiest method is to contribute dollars to community organizations. An examination of firms in a Western high-tech metropolitan area found three popular methods of contributing:

1. Donation of funds;
2. Donation of goods or services to nonprofit organizations;
3. Encouraging employees to volunteer their time to non-profit and civic organizations.[64]

The 46 firms that were examined in this study averaged contributions of between one and two percent of pretax profits to non-profit organizations, with older and larger firms more generous in their contributions. Younger firms and their executives were not as involved in outside activities. When they were, these executives contributed to more directly business-related activities; for example, a donation of computer equipment where they could obtain a tax write-off, or a grant to a computer education facility. The difference in execution (and perhaps perception) of responsibility for outside activities was especially apparent between the CEOs of the older established firms and the CEOs of the newer entrepreneurial firms. Many of these community activities required cooperation with other firms and other CEOs, yet their interests diverged so much that there was not much communication or understanding between the two groups of CEOs.[65] The new entrepreneurs were largely in high-tech startup firms that were developing computer software and hardware. For example, the two brilliant founders of Apple Computers did not have the skills to enable the firm to grow and mature. Entrepreneurs, while essential to job creation, generally have a narrow vision; their contributions to the community are often small. As a firm matures, statesmanship emerges. In both cases, there is a need for formal attention to ethics and social responsibility.

Institutionalizing Corporate Ethics

In this chapter we have discussed the ethical responsibilities of firms with respect to stakeholders in a given locale. We would like, before concluding the chapter, to raise a larger issue that could be included in any of the chapters of this book. To what extent have U.S. firms made ethics an integral part of the fabric of their daily life? The evidence is mixed. Some firms have made serious efforts, while others have done little. In some way, however, most firms have tried to institutionalize an ethical climate. About three-quarters of large American corporations now have a code of ethics.[66] More than 100 boards of directors of large firms have established an ethics, social responsibility, or public-policy committee of the board.[67] If one watches the concerns of CEOs and of business journals, one can witness their renewed interest in ethical issues. Some firms, such as Allied, McDonnell-Douglas, General Dynamics and E.F. Hutton, have educational and training programs on ethics for their managers. Most of these firms had a specific crisis that brought about their interest in ethics.

The Norton Company of Worcester, Mass. has a long-standing tradition of striving to create an ethical environment. The Norton effort is not the result of ethical lapses, but stems from a respect for justice and human dignity. Norton manufactures grinding wheels and abrasives, with plants in 28 nations. Disappointed at ITT's attempt to help topple the elected government of Chile, Norton drew up a code of ethics for its own world-wide operations in 1973. With multi-cultural operations, it is difficult to develop a code that respects all the host cultures. Yet differences in culture only underscore the need for a code of ethics. The Norton code is practical and realistic. After the first draft was written, it was circulated to managers throughout the world in order to get their suggestions and feedback.

To help implement the *Policy on Business Ethics,* Norton began The Corporate Ethics Committee. This group, made up of top management and outside directors, helps to interpret the *Policy* to managers and others at Norton. It clarifies hazy items and updates the *Policy* where it is necessary. For decades Norton has had a remarkable record on emphasizing ethical behavior.[68] The current CEO, Robert Melville, is also genuinely committed to strengthening the ethical environment at Norton.[69]

Eighty percent of large American firms have a code of ethics. One of the models for these codes is that of Caterpillar Tractor Company. Some ask why a code of ethics is necessary, since we have laws to guide our actions. Caterpillar addresses this issue: "The law is the floor. Ethical business conduct should normally exist at a level well above the minimum required by law."[70] The Ethics Resource Center of Washington, D.C. helps corporations in designing their codes of ethics.

The Investor Responsibility Resource Center (IRRC), also in Washington, D.C., helps institutional investors make informed judgments when voting their stock on social questions. Whether the issue is withdrawal from South Africa or publishing a report on the firm's record on toxic waste disposal, the IRRC investigates, outlining the major issues and questions. The investor can thus make an intelligent judgment when voting shares at the shareholder's meeting.

Business schools are bringing ethics into the university curriculum. Business schools in the United States are required by their accrediting association to teach ethics in the course curriculum. Many of America's most respected educators have regularly and loudly called for ethics in the university and the business school curriculum. Among them are the dean of Stanford's Graduate School of Business and the president of Harvard University. Russell Palmer, dean at Pennsylvania's Wharton School, says: "We who run America's business schools are concerned about how people behave in business, and our responsibility to influence positive ethical behavior is considerable and urgent.

We must teach not only the skills of management but also the principles of right and wrong."[71] This book is an attempt to aid that effort.

Practical Recommendations

The corporation has many stakeholders, and those who have a stake in the firm should be involved in major decisions that affect their future. Within the organization, a climate of openness and communication is a good foundation for such participation. Again, allow some practical recommendations.

First, encourage communication and participation at every level of the organization. When major decisions are being considered, obtain the input of those parties who will be affected.

Second, encourage consultation in any group of which one is a member. Whether it be neighborhood, work group, or office, encourage a discussion of mutually important issues.

Third, encourage cooperation between a business facility and the local government.

Fourth, help those who are without work to make the transition to new work.

SUMMARY AND CONCLUSIONS

Workers generally have a larger stake in a firm than anyone else. Most firms recognize this; it is in their long-term self-interest to acknowledge this, and it is also socially responsible. A test comes when a facility is no longer profitable and management considers closing it. A plant closing has a major impact on workers, municipalities, and stockholders. With Lykes and Anaconda, entire regions were affected.

The stake that workers have developed in the firm over the years demands that they be notified of a potential plant closing, and be encouraged to provide their suggestions. Lykes and GM did not consult their workers. Ford notified their workers in advance and helped them obtain new jobs.

Control Data and GM Poletown both provide models of responsible and statesmanlike corporate behavior; each opened plants and provided job opportunities where there was high unemployment. Norton and Caterpillar provide models of institutionalizing ethics into the very fabric of the company.

The principle that runs through a firm's relations to its workers and the local community is that of treating all stakeholders as human beings. Providing information and listening to the ideas and suggestions of employees, neighbors, and other stakeholders respects the dignity of these individuals. The success that Ford had with its plant shutdown in California rested largely on the trust and communication between the managers and the workers at that plant. While we would not urge additional government restrictions on plant movements or closings (beyond perhaps mandatory notification of workers, say 90 days ahead of time), it is nevertheless the responsibility of management to recognize the immense efforts of their workers over the previous decades. Whatever successes the firm has had in the past depended on the efforts of its workers; they should be involved when a plant closing is being considered.

We do find that over the past 20 years, corporations have become more aware of their stakeholders—workers, cities, regions, and others. In this, we see a positive sign for the future. We see a move from the narrow view of the corporation as merely a generator of growth and profits to the view of the corporation as a citizen with responsibilities in society.

DISCUSSION QUESTIONS

6.1. How can a stakeholder analysis provide one with a framework for making an ethical judgement as to whether Lykes' decision to close their Youngstown plant was correct?

6.2. Assess the workers as stakeholders using traditional business values and social values (Figure 2-1).

6.3. What are a company's obligations to its stakeholders? Do these duties change depending on the situation? Think of examples from recent history.

6.4. The right of stakeholders to some input into major decisions derives from which values (Figure 2-1)? What are the limitations of shared decision making?

6.5. Why did Arco and the Anaconda worker's union have a greater responsibility to their stakeholders than might be the case if the operation had been in a larger city? (Use the norms presented in Figure 1-2.)

6.6. In what manner did Control Data benefit from their socially responsible behavior? How can one defend William Norris' decisions?

6.7. Contrast the General Motors and the Ford plant closings in Northern California, using the values in Chapter Two. Is some warning required in justice? Explain your answer.

6.8. What are the alternatives to plant closings? Evaluate these alternatives, using traditional business values and social values (Figure 2-1).

6.9. What values and norms would you suggest to GM to help them in balancing the contradictory claims concerning their Poletown plant? Was it an ethical decision? Explain.

6.10. In what way are ethics being made a part of the fabric of many firms? How do corporate ethical codes help employees? Is there any evidence that codes are more than window dressing?

NOTES

[1]Joseph A. Shumpeter, *Capitalism, Socialism, and Democracy* (New York: Harper and Row, 1950), Chapter III, especially pp. 82–84.

[2]"Lykes to Slash Steel Operations at Youngstown," *Wall Street Journal*, Sept. 20, 1977, p. 2.

[3]"A Year-End Closing of Youngstown Steel Plant," *Wall Street Journal*, Oct. 18, 1978, p. 48.

[4]U.S. Congress, House Committee on Small Business, *Conglomerate Mergers—Their Effects on Small Businesses and Local Communities,* Hearings before Subcommittee, Jan. 31–Feb. 28, 1980, p. 21.

[5]"Digest of Earnings Report," *Wall Street Journal,* Feb. 20, 1968, p. 24.

[6]"Digest of Earnings Report," *Wall Street Journal,* Jan. 31, 1968, p. 20; *Wall Street Journal,* Feb. 8, 1968, p. 11.

[7]"Latest Lykes' Bid for Sheet and Tube Backed by Boards," *Wall Street Journal,* Feb. 3, 1969, p. 5.

[8]*Conglomerate Mergers,* pp. 21, 24.

[9]National Center for Economic Alternatives, *Youngstown Demonstration Planning Project,* (Washington, D.C., 1978), p. 3.

[10]*Youngstown Demonstration Planning Project,* p. 4.

[11]*Ibid.,* p. 33.

[12]R. Edward Freeman, *Strategic Management: Stakeholder Approach* (Boston: Pitman, 1984), pp. 31–48, *passim.*

[13]"Sheet and Tube Plans Major Reorganization in Move to Diversify," *Wall Street Journal,* March 13, 1968, p. 10.

[14]Barry Bluestone and Bennett Harrison, *The Deindustrialization of America* (New York: Basic Books, 1982) p. 98.

[15]Judith Lichtenberg, "Workers, Owners, and Factory Closings," *Report from the Center for Philosophy and Public Policy,* vol. 4, no. 3 (Fall, 1984), 9–10.

[16]John P. Kavanagh, "Ethical Issues in Plant Relocation," *Business and Professional Ethics Journal* 1, (Winter, 1982), p. 21.

[17]United States Catholic Bishops, *Economic Justice for All: Catholic Social Teaching and the U.S. Economy.* (Washington: Origins, Nov. 27, 1986), nn. 41–47.

[18]*Ibid,* nn. 295–325.

[19]John P. Kavanagh, *op. cit.* pp. 22–28.

[20]Eileen P. Kelly and Joseph A. Zoric, "Corporate Social Responsibility in the Steel Industry—The Case of Weirton Steel," *Academy of Management Proceedings,* 1984, pp. 343–45.

[21]*Ibid,* p. 245.

[22]"Weirton CEO in 'Best' of '85; Carbide's is Not," *Industry Week,* Feb. 17, 1986, p. 28.

[23]Kavanagh, *op. cit.,* p. 22.

[24]See, for example, the account in *The Cleveland Plain Dealer,* "Executives Got $1 Million in Bonuses," July 26, 1986; and "Perks of LTV Brass Irk Ex-Staffers," Aug. 19, 1986.

[25]Richard P. Rumelt, *Strategy, Structure and Economic Performance* (Boston: Harvard University Press, 1974), pp. 79–128, 146–62.

[26]"Closing the Anaconda Smelter (A)" by Kirk O. Hanson and Cynthia M. Ulman. Graduate School of Business case, Stanford University, 1982. Also "Anaconda to Close Two Montana Units Over Pollution Rules," *Wall Street Journal,* Sept. 30, 1980, p. 22.

[27]Bill Curry, "Town Loses its Payroll, Keeps its Hope," *Los Angeles Times,* April 5, 1981, p. 1.

[28]"Asarco and ARCO Unit Are Only Copper Firms Left to Settle Strike," *Wall Street Journal,* Nov. 19, 1980, p. 38.

[29]"Tale of Two Mergers: One Success, One Failure," *U.S. News and World Report,* July 22, 1985, pp. 53–54.

[30]*Atlantic-Richfield 1979 Annual Report,* p. 30.

[31]Bill Curry, *Los Angeles Times,* April 5, 1981, pp. 1, 12.

[32]Bill Curry, "Anaconda Montana Weighs a Bleak Future," *Los Angeles Times,* Jan. 11, 1981, p. 10.

[33]"Closing the Anaconda Smelter: Teaching Note" by Kirk O. Hanson and Cynthia M. Ulman. Graduate School of Business case, Stanford University, 1982. p. 7. Also, *Industry Week,* Oct. 28, 1985, p. 44.

[34]*Ibid.*, pp. 45–48.

[35]*Role of Clean Air Act Requirements in Anaconda Copper Company's Closure of Its Montana Smelter and Refinery.*

[36]"Copper Firms Don't Seem Anxious to Settle Strikes in Face of Soft Market for Metal," *Wall Street Journal,* October 20, 1980, p. 40.

[37]Bill Curry, *Los Angeles Times,* April 5, 1981, p. 12.

[38]William Norris, *New Frontiers for Business Leadership* (Minneapolis: Dorn Books, 1983), pp. 9–19.

[39]*Ibid.*, pp. 16–17.

[40]*Ibid.*, p. 25.

[41]"Firms and Job Seekers Discover Benefits from Part Time Positions," *Wall Street Journal,* Oct. 4, 1978, p. 1.

[42]"How Control Data Turns a Profit On Its Good Works," *New York Times,* III, Jan. 7, 1979, p. 3 and "Seeking to Aid Society, Control Data Takes on Many Novel Ventures," *Wall Street Journal,* Dec. 22, 1982, p. 1.

[43]*New York Times,* III, Jan. 7, 1979, p. 4.

[44]*Ibid.*

[45]James J. Chrisman and Archie B. Carroll, "A Survey on Plant Closings: Testing Propositions from The Deindustrialization of America," Institute for Business, the University of Georgia, pp. 4–7.

[46]*Ibid.*, pp. 10–12.

[47]Rajeswararao S. Chaganti and Robert D. Hamilton, "Corporate Plant Closing and Relocation Decisions," *Research in Corporate Social Performance and Policy,* vol. 6, Lee E. Preston, ed. (Greenwich, Conn.: JAI Press, 1984), pp. 141–67.

[48]Dale Yoder and Paul D. Staudohar, "Management and Public Policy in Plant Closure," *Sloan Management Review,* (Summer, 1985), p. 45.

[49]Statement of Ernest J. Savoie, Director, Labor Relations Planning and Employment Staff, Ford Motor Co. Cited by Gary B. Hansen in "Ford and the UAW Have a Better Idea: A Joint Labor-Management Approach to Plant Closings and Worker Retraining," *Annals,* AAPSS, 475, (September, 1984) p. 160.

[50]"Management and Public Policy in Plant Closure," *op. cit.*, p. 51; also see "1982 Ford-UAW National Agreements," (Dearborn, MI.: Labor Relations Staff, Ford Motor Co., 1982) pp. 3–4.

[51]*Ibid*, p. 52.

[52]"Ford and the UAW Have a Better Idea," pp. 163–69.

[53]"Management and Public Policy in Plant Closure," p. 53.

[54]The Congressional Office of Technology Assessment did the report. See "Study Critical on Layoffs," *New York Times,* Business Section, p. D4, Sept. 18, 1986.

[55]For an examination of 32 plant closings in the 1960s, see Arnold R. Weber and D. P. Taylor, "Procedure for Employee Displacement: Advance Notice of Plant Shutdown," *Journal of Business,* (July, 1963) 302–15.

[56]David L. Birch, *The Job Generation Process* (Cambridge: MIT Program on Neighborhood and Regional Change, 1979).

[57]David L. Birch, "Who Creates Jobs?," *The Public Interest,* vol. 65 (Fall, 1981) pp. 3–14.

[58]*Ibid*, p. 7.

[59]Archie B. Carroll, "When Business Closes Down: Social Responsibilities and Management Actions," California Management Review, (Winter, 1984) pp. 130–32.

[60]*Ibid.*, pp. 132–37.

[61]James Fallows, "America's Changing Economic Landscape," *Atlantic,* March, 1985, pp. 47–68.

[62]Joseph Auerbach, "The Poletown Dilemma," *Harvard Business Review,* (May–June, 1985) p. 95.

[63]*Ibid.*

[64]Lee Burke, Jeanne M. Logsdon, Will Mitchell, Martha Reiner, and David Vogel, "Corporate Community Involvement in the San Francisco Bay Area," *California Management Review*, vol. 28 (Spring, 1986), pp. 122–141.

[65]*Ibid.*

[66]See *Chronicle of Higher Education*, August 6, 1979, p. 2.

[67]"Business Strategies for the 1960s," in *Business and Society: Strategies for the 1980's* (Washington, D.C.: U.S. Department of Commerce, 1980), pp. 33–34.

[68]See the detailed account of Norton's efforts by Theodore V. Purcell, S.J. and James Weber, *Institutionalizing Corporate Ethics: A Case History*, (New York: The American Management Association, 1979); see also the earlier account by the then Norton CEO, Robert Cushman, "The Norton Company Faces the Payoff Problem," *Harvard Business Review*, (September–October, 1976) pp. 6–7.

[69]For a brief description of Melville and his statesmanlike leadership, see Gerald Cavanagh, *American Business Values*, (Englewood Cliffs, N.J.: Prentice Hall, 1984), pp. 175–76.

[70]*A Code of Worldwide Business Conduct and Operating Procedures*, Caterpillar Tractor Co., revised May 1, 1985, p. 4.

[71]Russell E. Palmer, "Let's Be Bullish on Ethics," *New York Times*, June 20, 1986, p. 23. For additional data on the institutionalizing of ethics into the firm, see Gerald F. Cavanagh, *American Business Values* (Englewood Cliffs N.J.: Prentice Hall, 1984), pp. 151–160.

Chapter Seven

THE ENVIRONMENT: CLEAN AIR, WATER, AND THE CORPORATION

Until recently, we have taken the air and water around us for granted. Yet without air and water we cannot live. With growth in civilization and population, air, water, and even the earth itself are threatened by pollution. This pollution is a result of our own activities—especially of people. Modern society, with its mining, chemical, and power production, which demand many resources, vastly increases the amount of pollution that is generated.

Our environment is essential for human life to exist, and yet it is also fragile. The ethical challenge is to balance (1) using the earth's resources to provide a decent standard of living for billions of people, and (2) keeping the earth liveable now and for generations to come. Each nation and generation has a right to their fair share of the world's resources, whether that be air, water, copper, or petroleum; and this limits the rights of others. We also have a responsibility to decrease pollution, and we do this out of the social values of community and respect for other people. No one has the right to excessively pollute the environment. This chapter will outline some challenges to the environment, especially those that stem from the operations of the business corporation. We will use norms from the business and social values of Chapter Two in order to better decide the complex trade-offs between growth, life styles, and protecting the environment.

LIFE-THREATENING POLLUTION

More than 20 percent of all deaths in the United States are due to cancer.[1] Nine out of ten cases of cancer stem from compounds that we have introduced into the environment. These cancer-related deaths could be avoided.[2] In some of these cases the compounds were known to be carcinogenic (cancer causing), and many more were only found to be so later. Foreign intrusions into the environment include cigarette smoke, food additives, toxic materials at work, and pollutants in air and water, many of which have been identified as carcinogenic. Air and water contaminated with carcinogens seem to be beyond the control of the individual. Yet, almost all U.S. citizens are willing to pay a significant price for clean air and water; they support government efforts to clean up pollution.

The majority of Americans want even cleaner water and air than they now have.[3] On the other hand, most Americans also want a new auto, a larger home, plastics, and more electricity. We judge our success by our increased income and the ability to buy more material goods. Hence the dilemma: Is it possible to have the goods and not pay the hidden costs? The demand for more material goods presents two problems: (1) We use increasing amounts of finite, irreplaceable resources (for example, copper, petroleum, and bauxite), and (2) Increased consumption of material goods results in more pollution. Plastics, steel, and electricity cannot be produced without toxic by-products. Autos cannot be driven without producing toxic exhaust. We choose a lifestyle that values material things, yet we do not want to suffer the consequences of polluted air, water, or land.

It is expensive for chemical and metal processing firms to dispose of toxic chemicals in a safe manner. It is much cheaper to dump contaminated materials into the ground without safeguards. This is a case where the free market encourages irresponsible behavior that can have devastating effects on people. Protecting public health demands outside intervention, and this is a legitimate function of government. The considerable costs of safe disposal of toxic materials must be borne equally by *all* competitors. Otherwise, an unscrupulous firm that disposes of pollutants in an irresponsible manner will gain a cost advantage over the honest firm. The polluting firm does not pay the full cost of its operations, but rather places those costs on innocent bystanders who breathe the polluted air and drink the contaminated water, and hence have months or even years taken off their lives. Therefore, dumping toxic waste or large quantities of pollutants into the air, water, or ground is unjust.

Polluted Localities and Industries

Environmental pollutants that cause cancer come from a wide variety of sources. Some cities suffer a higher incidence of cancer. Los Angeles has more smog and air pollution than nearly any other city in the United States. But following closely behind are New York City, Pittsburgh, and the region of San Bernardino–Riverside–Ontario (adjacent to Los Angeles).[4] The higher incidence of cancer in these localities has been traced to airborne pollutants. Industrial areas of Contra Costa County, east of San Francisco, count lung cancer rates 40 percent higher than the average. Five oil refineries and 37 chemical plants are located in this county.[5]

Each year 100,000 Americans die from occupational illnesses and almost 400,000 new cases are recognized.[6] Asbestos fibers carried home from work on clothes and bodies have caused cancer among the families of asbestos workers. Toxic lead and mercury are carried to families in the same way as asbestos. Residents of areas where copper, lead, or zinc smelters are located get lung cancer more often than the average person, most likely because they inhale the airborne pollutants. There are higher lung cancer rates among males living in counties where paper, chemical, petroleum, and transportation industries are located. Twenty percent of the bladder cancers occurring in males in the Boston area stem from exposure to toxic materials at work. People in several counties of New Jersey experience a higher incidence of cancer because of their proximity to chemical industries.[7] For the major sources of pollution, along with an overview of the issues, see Figure 7-1.

Plastics workers exposed to the chemical vinyl chloride have a 200 times greater risk of developing lung cancer than the general population.[8] More pointed studies found that workers at a Shell Oil Company refinery experienced cancer at four times the national average, while workers at Firestone and at Goodrich synthetic rubber plants suffered leukemia at three times the national average.[9] The United States Surgeon General stated that "if the full consequences of both current and recent past occupational exposures are taken

FIGURE 7-1 Pollution of the Environment: Sources, Carriers, and Solutions

SOURCE	CONTAMINATED CARRIER	SOLUTIONS
Major Producers		Care during production
Mobile Sources		Careful waste disposal
Automobiles and trucks		Limiting use of
	Air	carcinogenic materials
Stationary Sources		Product stewardship
Chemical production		
Petroleum refining		Clean-up (after poor
Nuclear and coal electrical-	Water	disposal):
power generation		1. Superfund
Weapons production		Government
Other Producers		program
Manufacturing and service firms	Soil	2. Clean Sites
Households, especially waste		Private sector
disposal		program
		By means of:
		government regulation
		and/or voluntary actions

into account, perhaps 20–40 percent of all cancers may be related to carcinogens encountered in the workplace."[10]

The worst single tragedy caused by industrial pollution occurred at the Union Carbide plant in Bhopal, India. In one accident 2100 people were killed, and 86,000 more were blinded or permanently injured by the highly toxic gas that escaped from the plant. Hundreds of thousands who lived close to the plant were engulfed in the gas and treated in hospitals. Few familes escaped without someone being killed or seriously injured. Inadequate safety precautions, faulty equipment, and a series of errors allowed the gas to escape. Could such an event happen again? It would be foolish to think that it could not. The Bhopal incident underscores the importance of safety features in the design and maintenance of a chemical plant, and the immense moral and ethical responsibilities that corporations assume when they deal with toxic and carcinogenic materials.

Preservatives and additives are put into the food we eat. They have helped efforts to wipe out scurvy, botulism, rickets, and goiter, and they also supply needed vitamins and minerals. Preservatives help keep food prices lower by adding a longer shelf life. Nevertheless, some fear that a number of chemical additives (preservatives, coloring, taste enhancers) are more dangerous than helpful. A widely used additive was Red Dye No. 2, which was found to cause cancer in laboratory animals in 1971. Nevertheless, as late as 1975, about 1.3 million pounds of Red Dye No. 2 was still used in the United States—in ice cream, processed cheese, cookies, pie crusts, cake mixes, mayonnaise, jam, lipsticks, and pill coatings. The dye was finally banned in 1976.[11] Many other suspicious dyes are still used in foods. The U.S. Food and Drug Administration estimates that more than 95 percent of American children eat food containing coal tar or petroleum-based dyes. After a normal diet of thousands of soda pops, candies, and sweet baked goods, a child may eat as much as three pounds of artificial color additives. Moreover, ten common food dyes still used in food, drugs, and cosmetics, have caused cancer in laboratory animals.[12] Medical personnel find that substances that cause cancer in laboratory animals are likely to cause cancer in humans; hence our concern.

Determining the ethics of food additives requires that one balance the relative benefits of the additive against the relative cost. In the case of preservatives that prevent spoilage and serious diseases, most would be willing to run some risk. In the case of taste enhancers and colorings, it is more difficult to justify them ethically, since the actual benefit to the person using them is so small. Rather, the benefit is to the firm that markets the food. When a product is made more "attractive" in color or taste through additives, it sells better. Yet those very additives imperil a person's health, so it is difficult to understand how the individual's health, safety, and dignity are respected. It is hardly freedom to choose when I am not aware of the potential dangers. If the actions of competitors dictate that I must do the same or lose sales, then the market does not work toward the health and safety of people. For a food processor to be ethical might mean that the food producer would lose sales. Outside intervention has been found to be necessary in the United States; regulations are imposed to maintain public health and safety by the FDA and the FTC. Justice and respect for the health of people require government intervention, and responsible companies also want it. As we saw in Chapter Four, government action is ethical and socially responsible when producers either cannot or will not take the initiative.

Disposal of Toxic Wastes

Petrochemicals and plastics are generally not biodegradable. One desirable feature of plastics is that they do not stain or corrode. Formica tabletops and plastic parts also will not decompose in a landfill. Plastic packaging, styrofoam cups, and cellophane will remain for generations. Some by-products and wastes generated during the production of plastics, pesticides, and thousands of other chemical products have been discovered to be highly toxic. Many are now known to be carcinogenic, and not biodegradable. If these wastes are carcinogenic now, they will likely remain so for generations. The human cost of toxic waste has been demonstrated by the Love Canal and Times Beach cases.

Love Canal, a suburban neighborhood of Niagara Falls, was built on the site of an abandoned chemical waste dump. When surface water accumulated in this old clay-lined dump, it acted like an overfilled bathtub. The toxic materials slopped over the sides of the clay walls and into the ground and groundwater. Residents found toxic chemicals in their backyards, streets, and even their basements due to seepage. The dump had belonged to Hooker Chemical. Under duress, Hooker had given the dump to the school board to build a school. Eventually a housing subdivision was also built in the area. More than 1000 families lost their homes and tens of thousands have been exposed to what were found to be highly toxic and carcinogenic chemicals.[13] Who is responsible for this damage to human lives and property? Hooker had advised against building the school and the homes, but transferred land ownership. They sold the dump for a nominal sum, and the dump became someone else's problem. Yet the toxic chemicals were buried by them; they had been produced in Hooker's plants. Hooker Chemical's present owner, Occidental Chemical, has acknowledged some responsibility, and agreed to spend between $40 and 50 million cleaning up the Love Canal toxic dump. They agreed to put in a better drain system, and will monitor the disposal site for 35 years.[14] Monitoring will tell officials when seepage occurs, to enable them to take steps to limit further contamination.

The Times Beach, Missouri, tragedy is also the result of mistakes and poor information. The dirt roads of Times Beach, as well as many other rural roads in Missouri, were sprayed with oil to keep the dust down. The oil contained dioxins—small amounts of which cause death to laboratory animals.[15]

Russell Bliss, who had been paid to dispose of the contaminated oil in an environmentally acceptable manner, found a way to double his money. He sprayed the contaminated oil on the dirt roads, and he was paid for that, too. The town's soil and homes thus became laden with dioxin from the oil. All the people of Times Beach were forced to abandon their homes and their town. It was cheaper for the government to buy out the homeowners than to clean up the dioxins. Times Beach remains a ghost town.

Short-term thinking and possibly profit-seeking caused immense damage at Love Canal. Greed and ignorance brought about the tragedy of Times Beach. The cost of reclaiming or replacing the damaged physical property is many times the cost of careful initial management. The cost in deaths, disease, and ailments is impossible to accurately quantify, but it is great. Ignorance can lessen personal guilt. Carelessness and short-term thinking are not excusable, especially when there is so much at stake.

Chemical manufacturers have an ethical responsibility to oversee the safe use and disposal of toxic chemicals. Our evaluation rests on some basic ethical principles. The possession of a livable environment is something to which we all have a right.[16] Our current lifestyles enable us to do serious, and perhaps irreparable, damage to the environment. Such damange limits other basic rights; a livable environment is essential if people are to achieve their rights to life, health, freedom, and dignity. This position might seem to call for an absolute ban on pollution. On the other hand, absolute bans on pollution are unrealistic, and the cost of eliminating all existing pollution would be inordinate. It is then necessary to determine the extent of pollution that is acceptable, and to effectively enforce the regulations that are agreed to.

One method used to deal with such dilemmas is the utilitarian cost/benefit methodology.[17] Air, water, and earth are easy and cheap places to dump refuse. When there are few people in the area, and the refuse is not toxic, dumping might be acceptable; the environment has the ability to cleanse itself over time. However, when population increases, when the amount of refuse per person increases, and when that refuse is carcinogenic, random dumping is no longer acceptable. In economic terms, the external costs to society are not borne by the polluters. It is unjust because, when toxic refuse is dumped in the earth, the producer (and so the owner/shareholder and the purchaser, too) gains the benefits in lower costs, while innocent third parties pay in poor health.

Superfund and Clean Sites

Thousands of tons of nonbiodegradable toxic wastes have been produced annually in the last four decades. The typical method of disposal was to place the wastes in used 55-gallon steel drums and bury them. These steel drums can and do rust through. The toxic materials then flow into the ground and pollute the groundwater. Burying toxic waste in this fashion has proved to be unacceptable since it places health and lives in danger.

More than half of the population of the United States depends on wells and groundwater for its drinking water. When that water becomes contaminated, it places huge social and financial burdens on local communites. Even if a source of contamination is contained, it can take the aquifer or the groundwater generations to purify itself—if it is *ever* able to become as clean as it was originally.

Toxic waste dumps must be cleaned up, because of their long-term danger to health and life. The national dimensions of the necessary cleanup emerged in the 1970s. A private contractor hired by the EPA estimated that there are 32,000 to 50,000 disposal sites scattered throughout the country. Of these, 1000 to 2000 are very dangerous.[18] It has proven far more expensive to clean up an old waste site than to dispose safely of the toxic materials in the first place. Such shortsighted, cost-cutting behavior results in costs many times greater at a later date.

In order to clean up old toxic waste dumps, the United States Congress proposed a tax that resulted in Superfund. The chemical manufacturing firms became active in the legislative process. Dow, Allied, and Hooker opposed any federal intervention, as did the Chemical Manufacturers Association. Monsanto, Olin, and Rohm & Haas supported some form of legislation. DuPont changed its position and gave its support midway in the legislative battle. Superfund became law in December, 1980. One final note: the practical result of the negative stance of Dow, Allied, and Hooker, coupled with their previous hard-line position on other issues, was that they lost credibility with both Congress and the Executive branch of the government for many years to come.[19]

By 1985, after the EPA had spent more than $1 billion (the total amount collected by the Superfund taxes), only six of 1000 priority sites were cleaned. Much of that money, in true American fashion, was spent on legal fees, trying to determine who bore responsibility for the costs of the cleanup. By the EPA's own count there are 1800 additional sites yet to be cleaned up.[20] In the early years of the Reagan administration, some businesspeople complained that regulations were too stringent and costly. Consequently, the EPA removed its restrictions on the disposal of hazardous liquid wastes for three months.[21]

Clean Sites Inc. was set up by the chemical manufacturers as a not-for-profit corporation that would take the initiative in cleaning up some of the EPA's priority toxic dump sites. The organization is a coalition of leaders of chemical companies, conservation groups, and other private organizations, led by the Chairman of the Board of Monsanto. It was set up to expedite toxic waste cleanup and to bypass bickering and costly legal disputes. Thus the chemical industry's full efforts could be put into cleaning up toxic sites. The goal for the first few years was to clean up a dozen waste sites a year, eventually rising to an average of 60 per year.[22]

Unfortunately, most toxic waste cleanup efforts do not prove permanent. The toxic materials will remain toxic for thousands of years. Refuse dump landfills now receive most of the waste taken from Superfund and Clean Sites dumps. The beter-designed dumps have clay-lined or cement walls that allow only slight permeation of the toxic materials each year. Nevertheless, in time cracks are likely to develop and the toxic materials will seep through the clay or cement liners. The contents of many of the dumps will have to be moved again, perhaps several times, over the next dozen generations. Monitoring and rebuilding toxic dumps are very expensive tasks. They place immense costs on future generations. It is not just to ask future generations to deal with the toxic garbage that we have produced. At some future date they may not have the resources to deal with it, even though the waste endangers their health and lives. Chemical treatment can detoxify some toxic waste and burning could destroy most of it. While more expensive, these treatments are permanent. Pumping toxic waste into deep wells or burying it costs less, at least in the short run.[23]

Most toxic waste dumps have not been safely constructed or monitored. The firms that produced the waste are now being called back to pay for yet another disposal, and the costs are in the hundreds of millions of dollars. So, after being asked to share the costs of disposal of toxic wastes that had been mismanaged for a second time, some firms are turning to more long-term solutions. If a toxic waste is neutralized or destroyed it will not come back to haunt future generations. Dow Chemical in Louisiana has a huge rotating furnace that "reduces toxic organic waste—steel drums and all—to steam and ash that can be safely buried." Allied Corporation and 3M are able to process some toxic materials into harmless, or even useful, products. Allied generates a gas used in air conditioners and refrigerators from a caustic sludge waste. And 3M sells its ammonium sulfate, a corrosive by-product of videotape manufacture, for conversion into fertilizer.[24] Such efforts are more responsible and often cheaper in the long term. People should pay the full cost of the goods and services they use. A parallel issue is the case of nuclear power.

NUCLEAR PROMISE

Electricity is essential for any modern civilization. It lights, heats, and powers motors of every sort. Yet there are few sources of electricity that are free of pollution. Hydroelectric (waterfalls), geothermal (from steam in earth) and solar generation are relatively free of pollution; but these sources generate a small fraction of the world's electric power. Most electric power is generated from petroleum, coal, gas, and nuclear power sources.

In order to meet the increasing demand for electricity, utilities throughout the world face difficult decisions in planning new power-generating facilities. Should these plants be powered by nuclear, fossil fuel, or some other source? Two decades ago nuclear power promised low costs and seemingly pollution-free energy. The development of nuclear power and much of the nuclear industry was and is heavily subsidized by the federal government. Yet in spite of great promise and billions of dollars of subsidies, the nuclear power industry today is in trouble.

Environmental Impact of Electric Power

Both nuclear and fossil fuel power plants have serious environmental and personal costs. Since the United States has hundreds of years of coal reserves (far more than its petroleum and natural gas reserves), coal would seem to be a good fuel source. Yet coal must be mined beneath the earth's surface, and mining it exposes workers to black lung disease and the dangers of mine accidents.

Moreover, the burning of coal by electric utilities is a major producer of acid rain. Acid rain threatens not only lakes and fish, but entire forest areas in the Northeast, West, and Canada. The rapid deterioration of trees in West Germany's Black Forest has brought far-reaching regulations aimed at reducing air pollutants.[25] Sulfuric acid from high-sulfur coal and nitric acid from automobile exhaust pour into the atmosphere and then come back to earth in rain and snow. The accumulation of these acidic compounds disrupts the delicate balance in lakes and soil, leading to the death of trees, fish, and other aquatic life.[26]

Acid rain is a short-term result of fossil fuel combustion. The amount of carbon dioxide produced by such combustion has more long-range effects. It contributes to a "greenhouse effect," creating a shield that does not permit heat to escape out of the atmosphere. When carbon dioxide levels rise, the forests and oceans are unable to continue to buffer it, global temperatures rise. A small increase in temperature will flood some coastal areas, and could turn some temperate zones into deserts.[27]

Nuclear power does not generate acid rain, nor does it contribute to the greenhouse effect. It was once seen as a clean and low-cost producer of electrical energy; however, electricity generated from nuclear sources has other costs:

1. The huge dollar cost of building a nuclear power plant;
2. The danger of an accident (such as that which occurred at Three Mile Island, Pa., or Chernobyl, USSR);
3. The possibility that materials could be obtained by irresponsible governments or terrorists, and used to produce nuclear bombs;
4. Exposure of uranium miners to cancer due to radioactivity, and the continued radioactivity of mine tailings;
5. The unsolved problem of what to do with the high-level radioactive wastes, some of which will remain dangerous for up to 250,000 years.

The cost of building a nuclear plant has been rising steadily during the last two decades. Most nuclear facilities cost more than $1 billion to construct. Because of these immense costs, few nuclear power plants have been finished in the United States in the last decade. Moreover, nuclear power plants are usable for only a few decades. Since it is then too expensive to dismantle the old power plant because of its radioactivity, utilities merely close them down. After several hundred years of using fission reactors, the landscape would be dotted with old nuclear power plants that continue to be highly radioactive.

The Faustian Bargain: Is It Worth It?

The nuclear plant accidents at Three Mile Island and at Chernobyl made worldwide headlines. Citizens today are aware of the extraordinary costs of a major nuclear accident. Costs include lost lives and property, adverse effects on health for many decades to come, and agricultural crops destroyed by exposure to radiation or too dangerous to eat. A member of the United States Nuclear Regulatory Commission pointed out that U.S. reactors are not designed to contain a major meltdown. He notes that the Commission estimates a 50 percent chance of a major meltdown in an American reactor over the next 20 years. That meltdown could be more serious than Chernobyl.[28]

Wherever there is a nuclear power plant, there is material that could be fashioned into a bomb. As more nations of the world build nuclear reactors for electric power, more nations will also be able to build nuclear weapons. For decades the United States and the Soviet Union have signaled to the world by their actions that a nation can not be a world power if it does not possess nuclear weapons. Other nations have followed the example of the superpowers. As more nuclear power plants proliferate, it becomes easier to obtain the fissionable materials to make a bomb. The United States, France, the Soviet Union, and Israel have all sold nuclear technology to poorer nations. Terrorist groups thus find it easier to obtain the uranium or plutonium necessary to put together a primitive atomic bomb. The Nuclear Regulatory Commission is charged with keeping track of all fissionable materials. About four tons of radioactive material, most of it highly enriched uranium and plutonium, are lost or "unaccounted for." A firm in Pennsylvania reported a loss of over 200 pounds of bomb-grade uranium.[29] It takes only about eleven pounds of uranium to make a Hiroshima-type atomic bomb. The technology for making bombs is available.

After more than four decades of producing tons of radioactive and highly toxic nuclear waste annually, the United States still does not have a long-term plan of what to do with the high-level wastes. There are serious problems associated with any permanent disposal plan: (1) some high-level waste will be toxic for up to 250,000 years; (2) the lack of disposal methods to prevent the release of the radioactive materials into groundwater; (3) the cost of replacing rusted or corroded containers many times during the life of the waste; (4) the cost of guarding the nuclear waste that might be made into nuclear weapons; and finally, (5) people who do not want the waste disposed of in the area in which they live.[30]

The world needs electricity. People in poor countries use much less electricity than we do, yet they have a great need for it. Four presidents of the United States urged Americans not to use more energy and electricity than was necessary. Not overheating or overcooling buildings saves millions of barrels of petroleum and lessens pollution. Because of the long-term trade-offs associated with energy use, justice requires us to be conservative in using electricity and fossil fuels.

An alternative to nuclear and fossil fuel power plants is electric power generated from hydroelectric, solar, and geothermal sources. These sources do not have the external costs of pollution or the danger of serious accidents. Solar and geothermal energy sources, even though they have many advantages, are both in the early stages of development, and presently generate a small fraction of our electrical power. Better solar cells and batteries are necessary before abundant solar energy can be harnessed. This is an area of technical challenge and great business possibilities.

WEAPONS AND POLLUTION

Military use of nuclear materials, from nuclear weapons to power plants for submarines and aircraft carriers, adds to the problems just cited. In volume, military waste is more than four times that of commercial waste, and there is no plan for its disposal either.

Plutonium and the Cost of Waste

The Rocky Flats Nuclear Weapons Facility of Rockwell International illustrates many of these problems. The Rocky Flats plant is a fabricator of nuclear warhead components. It also reconditions and recycles plutonium taken from older warheads. The plant covers 350 acres and is only 20 miles northwest of Denver.[31]

Concentrations of plutonium, a highly toxic element, have been found in the water supplies of communities adjacent to Rocky Flats. Plutonium and other toxic materials have also been released into the air, especially when accidents occurred at the facility. Rockwell took over the management of the plant in 1975, and improved the safety record of the earlier manager, Dow Chemical. Under Dow there were several major accidents: fires in 1957 and 1969 and an accidental release of plutonium into the air in 1974. As early as 1974, the governor of Colorado recognized the danger of the plant, and appointed a citizen watchdog committee, the Rocky Flats Monitoring Committee. The Committee has suggested moving the plant, since an accident could endanger many people in the heavily populated Denver metropolitan area. Rockwell shareholders have also raised the question of plant safety at shareholder meetings.

An ethical assessment of both civilian and military use of nuclear materials can begin with justice and community norms. Those defended by nuclear weapons and those who use electrical power generated from a nuclear reactor are obliged to pay the costs of disposing of nuclear wastes, including building and maintaining waste dumps and an estimate of the costs of future nuclear waste accidents. Opinion polls, hearings, and local legislation have shown that most people do not want a nuclear or a toxic waste dump near their home. Social costs are not accepted voluntarily, but must be *imposed* on some people. This imposition may be unjust.

It is not just for us to use nuclear power and to manufacture nuclear weapons, and to leave our debris for future generations to manage. If we placed ourselves in the position of people 100 years from now, how would we react to the nuclear and toxic waste dumps that dot the land—each of which requires continual monitoring and frequent rebuilding? Future generations may look on us as being interested in ourselves and our own comfort and having little concern for others. Our present actions seem shortsighted and unjust. Some may counter this by saying that technology may be developed in the future to neutralize nuclear wastes. This *may* be so. But until we are certain that we are not passing on an environmentally damaged world, our ethical obligation is to pay the full costs and dispose of our own wastes safely and permanently.

Dow's Hard Line

Dow Chemical, one of the largest chemical manufacturing firms in the United Staes, is headquartered and has its major manufacturing and research facilities in a remote area of the Great Lakes region: Midland, Michigan. Jane Fonda was invited to speak at neighboring Central Michigan University some years ago, and she criticized Dow Chemical for exploiting poor countries and for discharging pollutants into the air and water. Dow president Paul Oreffice, after reading press reports of the speech, wrote to the president of Central Michigan notifying him that Dow would suspend all support of the school "until we are convinced our dollars are not expended in supporting those who would destroy us."[32] The incident set off what became a national discussion of the free expression of ideas on university campuses versus corporate support of universities, and the relationship between universities and corporations in general. In characteristic fashion, Dow met its critics head on. Oreffice insisted on being allowed to address the students at Central Michigan in order to present Dow's case, and he did so.

As noted earlier, Dow resisted government Superfund efforts to clean up toxic waste. Yet at the same time Dow has been a leader in voluntarily cleaning up pollution. As early as 1972, Dow earned a *Business Week* award for corporate responsibility for its pollution-control programs.[33] Dow also instituted product stewardship by accepting complete responsibility for the environmental impact of products from the mining (through manufacturing, packaging, distribution, and us as waste or recyclable material.[34] The original manufactu: tion to know the toxicity of a chemical. The user often l label on the package announces. This puts the manufact responsible position. Prior to this, manufacturers had no the mining or manufacture of raw materials, nor had they felt responsible once the product was sold and left their hands. Dow and other manufacturers' "Product Stewardship" policies reverse that. Moreover, to bolster its stewardship image, Dow began a $50 million five-year ad campaign featuring idealistic students and recent graduates working at Dow to make the world a better place.[35]

Dow's record on issues of social responsibility does not lend itself to any simple moral judgment of good or bad. Dow opposed Superfund legislation and in 1986 was charged with polluting a river that runs by its Michigan industrial complex. Dow has produced weapons, napalm, and agent orange, which was used in the Vietnam War to defoliate the environment, and poisoned many innocent people in the process. These cases also illustrate the organizational and ethical climate at Dow. Reflecting its chief executives' attitudes, Dow is paternalistic and strong-willed, demands loyalty, and is not about to cave in to external demands. At the same time Dow has shown that it can exercise effective responsibility, as evidenced by its pollution control and product stewardship programs.

PRODUCT STEWARDSHIP

Many large chemical firms, following the example set by Monsanto and Dow, are now taking responsibility for all the social and environmental effects of their products during the products' entire life cycle. This stewardship is a policy that respects the health, safety, and human dignity of all who may have any contact with these products. Moreover, justice and fairness require the manufacturer and users to bear the full costs associated with those products. Some argue that this policy is merely self-defense for chemical firms; otherwise government would enforce more stringent and costly regulations. This may be part of the motivation for the new policy. But, in any case, product stewardship is ethical and is policy at many chemical manufacturing firms.

A major source of air pollution are petroleum refineries. Petroleum firms that have refineries in Texas and Los Angeles were examined on their response to citizen demands to reduce air pollution.[36] The extent to which firms resisted or cooperated with efforts to reduce air pollution was measured; firms varied in their reactions over a period of several decades. Some executives recognized the importance of the health, and thus the dignity, of people in the neighborhood of their refineries. Others were more callous to the people

thing their refinery's fumes. Mobil, Shell, Exxon, Atlantic Richfield, and
un took the lead in voluntarily investing in pollution controls. On the other
hand, Texaco, Gulf, Chevron, Phillips, and Union were not sensitive to the
air pollution that their refineries generated, and resisted air pollution controls
until legislation forced change on them.

Another group of businesses less likely to be concerned with pollution
are smaller firms, or firms on the verge of failing or being taken over. It is
expensive to reduce pollution. When any manager is careless or incompetent,
the damage can be great as pollutants enter the air, ground, and groundwater.
There is even evidence of organized crime getting into the toxic-waste disposal
business. Toxic waste disposal is an easy way for an unscrupulous person to
make a lot of money fast. Then they can go out of business, disappear, re-
appear in a new location and begin anew.

The manufacture, use, and disposal of pesticides often reflect a lack of
product stewardship. Pesticides have enabled farmers to raise yields on their
land. More people can be fed as the productivity of land increases, and food
means much to a hungry people. Pesticides, of course, kill insects that would
ruin the crop. However, the same poison that kills insects often can seriously
harm and kill people. Dozens of pesticides that are banned in the United States
because they are too dangerous are still manufactured here and sold for use
in Third World countries. If a certain chemical is considered too toxic for use
in the United States, its use in poorer countries must be carefully assessed.
The extent to which yield is raised and more food is provided must be balanced against the negative health effects of the pesticides. These evaluations
are difficult, especially when long-term health effects are not fully known. The
firm that manufactures the product has a special responsibility to oversee its
safe use, because of the company's technical ability and unique competency.
The health, safety, and dignity of citizens in poor countries must be respected
as much as that of citizens in wealthier countries.

Returnable Bottles and Reynolds Aluminum

The increase in solid litter in recent years presents problems of collec-
tion, trucking to a landfill, and final disposal. Beverage bottles and cans are
not toxic waste, but aluminum and glass do not quickly decompose. The problems and costs of disposal are not of the same dimensions as we found with
cancer-causing petrochemicals. The sheer volume, however, is greater. Landfills are becoming filled, especially near crowded metropolitan areas; the costs
of disposal of solid waste and the cost of virgin raw materials are constantly
increasing. Roughly 70 percent of the waste in landfills could be recovered,
recycled, and converted into reusable materials and energy.[37]

One way to lessen the problem of excessive solid waste and lost resources
is to place a significant deposit on beverage cans and containers. Thus a market

force is created with an incentive for consumers to return the cans and bot-tles for a deposit, rather than to throw them in the trash—or worse yet, out of their car onto someone's front lawn.

In response to citizen pressures, Oregon passed the first mandatory deposit legislation in 1972. Most were pleased with the results of the bill: there was less litter.[38] The EPA estimated that the year after the Oregon bill was enacted, 90 percent of all bottles had been refilled and 80 percent of all cans had been recycled. As a result, more than five million tons of raw materials had been recycled. This recycling represents about four million tons of glass, one million tons of steel, and more than 300,000 tons of aluminum that were saved.[39] There are six states with returnable bottle legislation, including heavily populated New York and Michigan. Savings in energy, aluminum, and glass—much of which is non renewable—are immense.

CEO David P. Reynolds made Reynolds Metals Company a leader in low-cost aluminum recycling. The aluminum can is a superb candidate for recycling, because it does not rust. It takes only one twentieth of the electrici-ty to recycle aluminum as it does to produce aluminum from bauxite ore, so recycling also saves electrical energy. Even the mining and use of aluminum, along with the refining and use of petroleum, take energy and generate pollu-tion. So Reynolds Metals pioneered in recycling, even when it was not yet profitable for the company to do so. In 1981, Reynolds completed a multi-million dollar expansion of its aluminum reclamation plant in Sheffield, Alabama. When reclaiming materials in automobile scrap, Reynolds found that the non-ferrous residue contains about 30–40 percent aluminum and 40–50 percent zinc.[40] To David Reynolds, recycling was a long-term investment.[41]

Finite and non-renewable resources, such as petroleum and copper, that are used and not recovered, are lost to future generations. The market does not protect people in the future, since they are not able to bid on the price of these resources. Therefore, in justice each generation has an obligation to protect the interests of future generations.[42] Community and solidarity with future generations argue that we conserve resources for future generations. Conserving resources is not new and also stems from traditional business values.

Reynolds Metals, through the stewardship of David Reynolds, stands out as a leader in recycling and conservation. Given the long-term advantage to society, the effort and success of Reynolds and his firm constitute ethically superior performance. Enlightened self-interest is not the only motivator for businesspeople. Reynolds judged that recycling was good for the community. In addition, he was trying to overcome the negative image of aluminum lit-ter, and also hoped that the recycling program would be profitable in the long run. Recycling reduces the use of raw materials, energy, and pollution, and helps to leave the world in a better state for future generations. Such sustained, informed, and ultimately successful efforts at recycling are eminently ethical.

Silicon Valley's High-Tech Pollution

High tech firms are perceived to be relatively free of pollution. Yet Silicon Valley in California suffers serious air pollution from autos. An even more serious source of pollution surfaced in 1981, when Fairchild Camera and Instrument found leaks of toxic materials from a tank at its San Jose plant. Since then more than 400 neighbors of the Fairchild plant have filed suits claiming brain damage, cancer, birth defects, and other injuries.[43]

Scores of additional toxic dumping sites at electronics firms have since been found. These are now added to the thousands to be decontaminated already on the Superfund list. National Semiconductor, Hewlett-Packard, IBM, Advanced Micro Devices, located in Santa Cara, Palo Alto, Sunnyvale and Mountain View, respectively, all have toxic waste dump sites. These firms bear special responsibility in justice to clean up their own dump sites.

Santa Clara Valley, or Silicon Valley as it is popularly known, has little rainfall, and thus depends upon an underground aquifer for drinking water. If the aquifer is polluted, it affects the drinking water of hundreds of thousands of people, and can take centuries to purify itself. Some of these sites have begun to leak toxic waste into the groundwater. The need to protect groundwater from pollution is a deadly serious matter. Southwestern states have too little rainfall or groundwater to support their populations. The Ogallala Aquifer, which provides drinking water and irrigation to portions of South Dakota, Wyoming, Colorado, Nebraska, Kansas, Oklahoma, New Mexico, and Texas, is being rapidly depleted. It has dropped from a functional depth of 20 meters in 1930 to less than two meters in two generations.[44] Once that water is depleted, the agricultural capability of the great plains states, the present breadbasket of the United States will be severely limited. The future of cities like Phoenix and Los Angeles is also questionable.

We have taken water for granted throughout most of our history. However, it is becoming increasingly precious. The largest body of fresh water in the world, The Great Lakes, is becoming more valuable. Not depleting vital groundwater and maintaining its purity are urgent ethical priorities. They are long-term national economic priorities. On the other hand, individual financial goals urge the use of more water. Irrigation can increase the value of land's output many times. The aquifer is then used at a much greater rate than it can be replenished. Most forms of irrigation, such as flooding and spraying, are wasteful of water. Watering lawns and washing autos in the dry southwest is generally not a conscientious use of water. Allowing toxic substances to seep into groundwater is extremely damaging.

Ethics demand that we do better. The business values of freedom and growth conflict with the social values of justice and community. In deciding priorities, drinking water should come first. Yet without irrigation, far less food can be grown on that land. To increase return on investment, we sometimes recklessly use and pollute water that is vital to people today and for the future. Once again, others will pay the bill for our carelessness. Beyond these basic judgments, difficult trade-offs must be made. Wise, ethical policies for the use of water are demanded; at present we lack these principles and policies.

Auto Makers and Waste Disposal

Heavy manufacturing remains one of the major sources of air, water, and solid waste pollution. Autos, trucks, and tractors manufactured by auto firms contribute a substantial portion of the existing air pollution. Nevertheless, General Motors is making enlightened efforts to reduce air, water, and solid waste pollution. A source of pollution is the disposal of old 55-gallon drums that had contained toxic substances. GM is phasing out these drums, and replacing them with 300 or 500 gallon drums that are refillable. This then eliminates the disposal problem.[45] GM has identified hazardous wastes and auto emissions needing special attention.[46]

General Motors' actions and policies receive more attention than those of smaller firms, because of its size, visibility, and influence. GM executives realize that this also gives the firm greater responsibilities. GM presents a varied picture, partially because like other large firms, it has many people speaking and acting in its name. GM stands out as an exemplar of good ethical behavior on several counts. It was one of the first firms to have a black on its Board of Directors (Rev. Leon Sullivan); it took a strong stand opposing apartheid and, under public pressure, finally withdrew from South Africa; it has published a report on its social responsibility accomplishments each year for the last 15 years; it has a Public Policy Committee of its Board of directors, and a high-level internal committee that recommends actions on social responsibility issues. In each of these cases, GM has determined long-term community needs and has acted ethically, even in situations where there are some trade-off costs to the firm.[47]

GM does not always act in the long-term best interests of society. Less pollution is generated and petroleum is saved when vehicles are more fuel-efficient. But General Motors, along with Ford, successfully lobbied the U.S. Congress to roll back the federal fuel-economy standards that had been imposed on auto manufacturers in 1975. The fuel-economy standards had urged the automakers to design and manufacture lighter and fuel-efficient autos, resulting in less use of metals. Thanks to the fact that the government won out over automaker objections, we now have less pollution. The gasoline required to drive a given distance is now less than half of what it was in 1974. When an auto uses less gasoline, it therefore pollutes less.[48] The resulting rollback of the fuel-economy standards will now cost us millions of tons of auto pollution and millions of barrels of petroleum. Since much of this petroleum is imported, this is the largest item adding to our international imbalance of payments.

Some customers prefer large autos, and automakers can make more money selling large autos. Automakers claimed that if they could not make large autos, thousands of layoffs would be necessary. However, if GM and

Ford again fall behind in the ability to design and manufacture small cars, in the future even more jobs will be lost when the public again wants small cars.

This debate over large versus small cars represents a conflict between the traditional business values of freedom and prosperity and the social values of personal health and preserving resources and environment for others. The latter values are more long-range. GM did not act as ethically as it might have when it lobbied to roll back the fuel-efficiency standards. Executives at GM did not sufficiently weigh the importance of (1) people's health (more pollution from larger autos) and (2) future generations (using more petroleum now). Moreover, given the influence GM has, both their beneficial and their detrimental actions have a greater impact.

Practical Recommendations

Preserving the environment, so that it can be handed on to future generations, is ethically essential. Individual responsibility, justice, and community call on each of us to be conservative. The individual, especially in a developed country, has many opportunities to help. At the risk of oversimplifying, we offer some suggestions.

First, in whatever capacity one has in the organization, be aware of the importance of conservation. Where one has responsibility for the use of electricity, heat, metals, or other resources, be conservative.

Second, exercise personal self-restraint on environmental issues. Try not to litter or use tobacco. Drive a fuel-efficient auto. Try to lessen the materials used and the refuse generated by packaging. Recycle cans, bottles, paper, and other materials. Work for deposit legislation requiring a significant deposit to make returning containers worthwhile.

Third, be aware of the toxicity of materials at home and at work. Make sure that they are disposed of properly, especially where you have primary responsibility.

Fourth, follow and aid the work of an environmental group, such as the National Resources Defense Fund, Nature Conservancy, Sierra Club or the Environmental Defense Fund. Stay informed on environmental legislation, and write to your congressperson to express your views.

Fifth, keep these issues in mind when choosing a career and a job. Consider a career and a position in which you can work on solutions to such problems as toxic waste disposal, alternate energy sources, energy efficient engines, acid rain, or nuclear waste disposal.

Sixth, choose a lifestyle, or a way of living (personal habits, size and location of home) that will enable you to use only as much electricity, petroleum, and other resources as is necessary. This will not only save resources, but will also help to keep their prices down and to reduce the United States trade deficit. Similar efforts on the part of many will have a significant positive impact.

SUMMARY AND CONCLUSIONS

The issues and values discussed in this chapter show that there are often trade-offs of short-term prosperity and growth versus justice, health, the good of others, and prosperity in the future. Opting for immediate growth and prosperity sometimes generates secondary, often unintended, social costs. We are already paying some of these costs; Love Canal, Times Beach and the huge costs of digging up and again disposing of toxic wastes. These immediate social costs have been recognized only in the last two decades. The long-term social costs are even greater. Note the financial costs and the ongoing threat to health of polluting drinking water, depleting the ozone layer and thus increasing the risk of skin cancer, and monitoring and periodically moving millions of gallons of toxic waste. These are social bills that are being run up now to be paid by others later.

When those costs are uncertain, as is often the case with environmental, health, and safety issues, do they then not carry obligation? On the contrary, even though the risks cannot be exactly measured, if the danger is probable and serious, ethics demands that one be conservative. The stakes are too high to conclude otherwise. It is ethically difficult to justify one group living comfortably while forcing another group to bear a significant portion of the cost of that lifestyle. It is unjust and shortsighted for one group to derive benefits and to place the costs on others.

Americans highly value the physical environment; this partially stems from our social values. We desire (1) to preserve the purity of our air and water, and (2) to pass on the world in at least as good condition as the world into which we were born. We sometimes compromise these values for the sake of small and short-term gains. A better understanding and application of the social values of community, justice, and respect for the dignity of the individual will enable us to achieve what we desire: a world in which both we and coming generations can live out a healthy, full life.

DISCUSSION QUESTIONS

7.1. List the sources known to cause cancer. How much cancer in the United States stems from these sources?

7.2. Are artificial colorings and flavorings for food, which bear some risk, worth it?

7.3. What lessons for the future do we learn from Love Canal?. . .from Times Beach?

7.4. What does Superfund's slow rate of cleaning up old toxic waste dumps tell us? Is Clean Sites a solution? Are there any other solutions?

7.5. What sources of electrical power are relatively safe and free of pollution? What are the environmental difficulties with nuclear and fossil fuel electrical-power plants? Assess these dilemmas, using traditional business values and social values (see Figure 2-1).

7.6. Is the military a greater producer of nuclear waste than electric utility firms? Ethically assess this use.

7.7. What is the ethical problem in leaving behind long-lived results of military use and electrical power production, nuclear waste? Who bears these hidden costs?

7.8. Assess product stewardship, using the values of individual responsibility and justice (see Figure 2-1).

7.9. Assess the issues of pesticides and returnable bottles using traditional business values and social values.

7.10. Though high-tech industry is a growth sector of the U.S. economy, should it not also be held to the same pollution standards as heavy industry? Use Figure 2–1 to assess.

7.11. Use the values of Chapter Two (Figure 2-1) to assess the ethics of our increasing use of water.

7.12. How has GM dealt with its problem of disposing of old 55-gallon steel drums that contained toxic materials? Give some other examples of GM's proactive ethical and social responsibility efforts.

7.13. Using the ethical values of Chapter Two, assess the U.S. auto makers' stance regarding the production of automobiles that use more fuel.

NOTES

[1]*Monthly Vital Statistics Report.* vol 32, no. 13. Hyattsville, Md.: U.S. Public Health Service, Sept. 21, 1984.

[2]Ernst L. Wynder, M.D. and Gio B. Gori, Ph.D., "Contribution of the Environment to Cancer Incidence," *Journal of the National Cancer Institute,* vol. 58 (April, 1977) pp. 825–32.

[3]See "Environmentalism Will Be Born Again," *U.S. News & World Report,* Jan. 5., 1987, p. 45; also Harris Poll, "A Call for Tougher—Not Weaker—Antipollution Laws," *Business Week,* January, 24, 1983. p. 87.

[4]Ranking of Cities, 1976–78 on Pollution Standards Index, *Environment and Health.* Washington: Congressional Quarterly, 1981. See also "Los Angeles's Setback In Smog Battle Raises Doubts on Other Cities," *Wall Street Journal,* Nov. 20, 1979, pp. 1, 39.

[5]"High Cancer Rate is Causing Anxiety in Industrial Area Near San Francisco," *New York Times,* May 28, 1982, Sect. I, p. 15.

[6]*Environment and Health, op. cit.,* p. 93.

[7]"Contribution of the Environment to Cancer Incidence", *op. cit.*

[8]*Environment and Health, op. cit.,* p. 3.

[9]"Doctor Cites Benzene Exposure as Likely Cause of High Cancer Death Rate at a Shell Refinery," *Wall Street Journal,* Feb. 14, 1985, p. 4; also "The Leukemia Link to Synthetic Rubber," *Business Week,* May 17, 1976, p. 40.

[10]*Ibid.,* p. 94.

[11]"Food: Is It Safe to Eat?," *Environment and Health,* p. 88.

[12]Joan Claybrook, "Public Citizen Newsletter," Spring, 1986.

[13]"The Unhealthy Environment," *Environment and Health,* p. 1–2.

[14]"Cleanup Agreed on for Niagra Landfill," *Chemical and Engineering News,* December 16, 1985, p. 14. For a good summary of the scientific studies and the ethics of Love Canal, see James Brummer, "Love Canal and The Ethics of Environmental Health," *Business and Professional Ethics Journal,* (Summer, 1983), pp. 1–25.

[15]For a good review article on the conflicting evidence on the toxic effects of dioxin on humans, see Fred H. Tschirley, "Dioxin," *Scientific American,* 254 (February, 1986), pp. 29–35.

[16]See William T. Blackstone, "Ethics and Ecology," in his *Philosophy and Environmental Crisis*, (Athens, Ga.: University of Georgia, 1974), pp. 16–43.

[17]For an excellent summary of these issues, see Manuel G. Velasquez, *Business Ethics: Concepts and Cases*, (Englewood Cliffs N.J.: Prentice Hall, 1982), pp. 170–223.

[18]*Ibid.*, p. 29.

[19]John Mahon, "Corporate Political Strategies: An Empirical Study of Chemical Firm Responses to Superfund Legislation," in *Research in Corporate Social Performance and Policy*, vol. 5, Lee E. Preston, ed. (Greenwich, Conn.: JAI Press, 1983), pp. 143–82.

[20]"$1 Billion Later, Toxic Cleanup Barely Begun," *U.S. News & World Report*, April 22, 1985, pp. 57–58; also "A New Wave of Environmental Laws Looms," *Wall Street Journal*, Dec. 17, 1986, p. 22.

[21]"EPA Lifts Ban on Burial of Toxic Liquids for 3 Months Pending Eased Restrictions," *Wall Street Journal*, March 2, 1982, p. 12.

[22]"Chemical and Conservation Groups Form Toxic Cleanup Unit," *New York Times*, June 1, 1984, p. 11; and "Conciliation: Charting a Future Without Rancor," *Conservation Exchange* (National Wildlife Federation), July, 1985, p. 1.

[23]Allen A. Boraiko, "Hazardous Waste," *National Geographic*, (March, 1985) 326.

[24]*Ibid.*, p. 330.

[25]See Fred Pearce, "The Acid Rain Threat," *World Press Review*, vol. 29 (October, 1982), pp. 26–28.

[26]Cass Peterson, "Acid Rain Wars: Civil at Last," *Sierra*, November/December, 1986, pp. 35–36. Also Lois R. Ember, "Acid Rain Implicated in Forest Dieback," *Chemical & Engineering News*, Nov. 22, 1982, pp. 25–26.

[27]For a report on an international conference that found evidence of rising world temperatures due to this problem, see "Facing Life in a Greenhouse," *U.S. News & World Report*, Sept. 29, 1986, pp. 73–74. Also Roger Revelle, "Carbon Dioxide and World Climate," *Scientific American*, August, 1982, pp. 35–43.

[28]"How Chernobyl Alters the Nuclear Equation," *New York Times*, Sunday, May 25, 1986, Sec. 4, p. 1.

[29]David Burnham, "The Case of the Missing Uranium," *Atlantic*, April, 1979, pp. 78–82.

[30]"Nuclear Waste War Cry: 'Not Here, You Don't'," *U.S. News & World Report*, Aug. 15, 1983, p. 23.

[31]Much of this information is taken from *Proxy Issues Report*, Investor Responsibility Research Center, Jan. 21, 1986, Analysis A.

[32]See the account, "Jane Fonda Speech Angers Dow President," in George Steiner and John Steiner, *Casebook for Business, Government & Society* (New York: Random House, 1980), pp. 27–35.

[33]See "Dow Cleans Up Pollution at No Net Cost," *Business Week*, Jan. 1, 1972, p. 32.

[34]See "Product Stewardship at Dow Chemical Company," in Earl A. Molander, *Responsible Capitalism: Case Studies in Corporate Social Conduct* (New York: McGraw-Hill, 1980), pp. 38–47.

[35]"Dow Chemical's Drive to Change Its Market—And Its Image," *Business Week*, June 9, 1986, p. 96.

[36]Jeanne M. Logsdon, "Organizational Responses to Environmental Issues: Oil Refining Companies and Air Pollution," *Research in Corporate Social Performance and Policy*, vol. 7. Lee E. Preston, ed. (Greenwich, Conn.: JAI Press, 1985), pp. 47–71.

[37]Robbe DiPietro, "Time to Stop Burying Solid Waste," *Natural Resources Register*, June, 1985, pp. 4–5.

[38]See Peter T. Chokola, "Pennsylvania Needs a Bottle Bill," *Beverage World*, February, 1986; also "After Three Years, Oregon's 'Bottle Bill' Gets Residents Cheers, Many Businessmen's Boos," *Wall Street Journal*, Jan. 9, 1976, p. 28.

[39]"Changing Public Opinion: The Bottle Bill Campaign," in James Post, *Corporate Behavior and Social Change*. (Reston, VA.: Reston Publishing, 1978), p. 155.

[40]"Reynolds Completes Recycling Plant Expansion," *Beverage Industry*, May 22, 1981, p. 2.

⁴¹"David Reynolds, The Aluminum King Who Refuses to be Dethroned," *Business Week,* January 13, 1986, p. 127–28, and "The Alchemy in the Reynolds Metals Recycling Program," in Earl A. Molander, *Responsive Capitalism: Case Studies in Corporate Social Conduct,* pp. 167–77.

⁴²Manuel G. Velazquez, *Business Ethics, op. cit.,* pp. 202–23.

⁴³"A 'Tough on Toxics' Bill has Silicon Valley Quaking," *Business Week,* Oct. 27, 1986, p. 122; Also "Finding of Toxin Leakage in Silicon Valley Hurt Chip Makers' Reputation for Safety," by Michael W. Miller. *Wall Street Journal,* August, 29, 1984, p. 25.

⁴⁴Ronald Taylor, "Water: The Nation's Next Resource Crisis?", *U.S. News & World Report,* March 18, 1985, p. 64; also "Massive Groundwater Fix Studied," *Engineering News-Record,* Nov. 20, 1986, pp. 28–29; and Wayland R. Swain, "Water: 'Thirst Belt' Eyes Turn Toward the Great Lakes," *Detroit Free Press,* March 15, 1983, p. 7A.

⁴⁵See *1984 General Motors Public Interest Report.* (Detroit: General Motors, 1984). GM has issued these excellent reports on their own public-interest activities every year for the past 15 years.

⁴⁶Elmer W. Johnson, "How Corporations Balance Economic and Social Concerns," *Business and Society Review,* (Summer, 1985), p. 13.

⁴⁷*Ibid.,* p. 11.

⁴⁸*1985 GM Public Interest Report,* p. 31.

Chapter Eight
MULTINATIONALS
AND THE THIRD WORLD

Solving ethical dilemmas takes time, especially when issues are interwoven and complicated by significant disagreements about their causes. This certainly applies to relations between multinationals and the Third World, where economic issues frequently have strong political overtones and where cultural and ideological differences abound. We have therefore approached this chapter somewhat differently, devoting more time to gaining an understanding of the problems involved with greater attention to past histories.

The history of U.S. multinationals (companies with headquarters in the United States and operations in other countries) and their relation to the Third World (countries with underdeveloped economies) reflects also the extent to which political "moods" at a given time shape attitudes toward a problem. The United States emerged from World War II as the most powerful nation in the world. Most Americans were confident about America's role as protector of the free world and about the benefits of American business at home and abroad. The late 1960s saw a shift in mood. Strident criticism was voiced initially about civil rights and the war in Vietnam; in the 1970s social critics often focused on large corporations.

Storm Over the Multinationals, by Raymond Vernon, was an apt title for controversies about the power and impact of multinational corporations.[1] Senator Frank Church, prompted especially by charges that ITT had sought CIA and

U.S. government support to undermine Salvador Allende's regime in Chile, conducted a series of senate hearings (1973–1975) on multinationals. Richard Barnet and Ronald Muller, in *Global Reach,* sent out a cry of alarm about multinationals to a wider public. They saw multinationals as a threat to the very structure of nation-states and as a detriment to both home and host countries. They cited a disturbing prediction (which proved to be rather exaggerated) that by 1985 eighty percent of all productive assets outside of Communist countries would be controlled by the leading 200–300 multinationals.[2] This would give enormous power to the less than 1000 corporate executives who, they believed, controlled decision making in the top corporations and banks.[3] The political mood has shifted again and the "storm" has generally subsided, though multinational investment in South Africa has kept at least that specific issue prominent in the public eye. These shifts in political moods are mirrored strikingly in the changing theories about multinationals that we will discuss, and in the case histories.

This book began with a chapter on ethical values and norms. Ethical questions that apply these values and norms need certainly to be raised about the impact of multinational operations on Third World (developing) countries. Ethical issues are present whatever the political mood of the moment may be. Do multinationals—or the actions of a particular firm—respect the dignity not only of individuals but of the nations in which they locate? Do they promote or harm the welfare of the peoples in host counties? Do they allow countries greater participation in the world economy or do they make them dependent?

Answers to these ethical questions, however, are often difficult because of the number and complexity of factors involved. The literature on multinationals is vast[4]; the amount of literature on problems of development and the Third World is greater still. Views on the relation of multinationals to Third World development range from lofty praise to caustic condemnation. Some see multinationals as instruments of salvation; Daniel Patrick Moynihan called them "the single most creative institution of the 20th century."[5] Others castigate them as ruthless exploiters of poor nations. Most would judge that the truth, needed for any discussion of ethical responsibility, lies somewhere between these two positions.

Ethical judgments call first for understanding. Since the issues discussed in this chapter are complex, most of our effort will be directed toward explaining problems and differing views as clearly as possible, to establish a basis for ethical discussion and appropriate judgments. We begin with an overall perspective, noting the claims made in behalf of multinationals and the charges raised against them, and linking these arguments to three models or conceptual frameworks: modernization, dependency, and bargaining. We then investigate three different periods of multinational operations in Guatemala, Chile, and South Africa, respectively, to illustrate how and why conflicts arise. The final third of the chapter includes a section "in defense of multinationals," a section on the "appropriateness" of multinational products and technology, and some concluding reflections about the ethical issues involved. We place greater stress in this chapter on theoretical models and we offer longer case histories because the issues are more complex and the evidence presented by critics and defenders of multinationals is often highly selective. Understanding the different "paradigms" that follow is essential for evaluating conflicting arguments in light of business and social values (see Chapter Two).

AN OVERALL PERSPECTIVE: THREE PARADIGMS

Those who write or speak about the impact of multinationals on developing countries have some implicit, if not explicit, assumptions about how development can and should occur. The paradigms that follow contain conflicting assumptions about development and different attitudes toward multinationals. The *modernization* theory views development as best achieved through the technology, skills, and business values used in the development of the United States and Europe; it tends to stress the positive contributions of multinationals to developing countries. *Dependency* theories argue that foreign investments, including those of modern multinationals, have impeded or distorted development in poor countries. The *bargaining* school of thought looks beyond conflicting theories of development to study the process by which multinationals and host countries reach agreements; the stronger the bargaining power of a Third World country, the more likely it is to benefit from multinational investment.

Modernization

The modernization model is based chiefly on the successful path already taken by Western Europe and the United States. If poor nations wish to develop, they need to confront and overcome the same sort of problems that nations which are now advanced encountered in ages past. W.W. Rostow, in *The Stages of Economic Development,* indicated the stages that all countries have passed through, or still need to pass through, to become truly modern developed nations.[6] Advanced industrial countries had to reach and then go beyond a necessary "take-off" stage; so too must currently underdeveloped nations. They must break out of traditional cultural methods of production and become modernized. Traditional, pre-capitalist economies were generally satisfied with providing subsistence. The breakthrough toward economic growth occurred when savings were accumulated and reinvested to produce more wealth. The profit incentive was an essential motivator toward growth. It led to more efficient ways of producing, to cutting costs, and to new technologies.

Multinationals, from the persepective of the modernization model, serve a beneficial role in breaking through the constraints and obstacles that impede development. They spur new and expanded production. They bring needed capital or help to mobilize local capital. They create new jobs. They possess the technology and managerial skills needed to stimulate development. They put poor nations in contact with new markets. In short, they supply many of the missing components needed to "prime the pump" of development.

When corporate executives praise the benefits of multinationals to developing nations, they implicitly embrace the modernization paradigm. A.W. Clausen, president of the Bank of America, praised the blessing of multinationals in glowing terms:

> I believe the multinational corporation, more than any other institution, promises a global order in keeping with the age-old yearnings of mankind. . . No other institution, public or private, has the motivation, the resources and the power to tackle global inequities as effectively as multinational corporations. . . Multinational corporations have a powerful self-interest in the prevention of war, and a clear stake in the development of a harmonious and non-coercive world order. That multinationals have the ability to enhance the quality of life in the underdeveloped world is no longer debatable. The continuing transfer of capital, technology, and managerial and entrepreneurial skills from the rich northern to the poorer southern countries has become the classic justification of global multinational acitivity.[7]

Other chief executive officers have spoken in similar tones: Harry Heltzer, as president of 3M, "How else but through the distribution of technology can a growing world population achieve economic progress?";[8] D.M. Kendall, as president of PepsiCo, "Since multinationals stimulate world trade, everyone benefits,";[9] and Thomas A. Murphy as chair of the board of GM, "Our continued growth as a worldwide company depends upon the raising of living standards in the developing countries of the world."[10] These comments clearly reflect a conviction that multinationals are not just self-serving but help to achieve the *social* values we presented in Chapter Two: multinationals enhance quality of life for all; they help to meet basic human needs; everyone benefits.

Dependency

Dependency theorists do not share the views of these executives; they argue that foreign investment impedes or distorts the development of Third World countries. Other critics of multinationals agree with this negative assessment of foreign investment, and so we have included them under this general heading of "dependency." Writers like Barnet and Muller, in *Global Reach*, say little about theories of development and focus on data and examples to demonstrate the negative consequences of multinational operations. Writers like Paul Baran, Paul Sweezy and Harry Magdoff fit their criticisms into Marxist theories of capitalist "imperialism." Even those who are classified as dependency theorists, like Andre Gunder Frank and Fernando Henrique Cardoso, often differ sharply in their explanations of dependency.[11] But all of these writers agree with the view that multinationals hinder, rather than help,

underdeveloped nations. Hence all have been sharply critical of the modernization paradigm adopted by most conventional, main stream economists.

In its strongest version, the dependency theory claims that Third World
underdevelopment was *caused* by, and maintained at the expense of, the
development of capitalist countries. The theory sees development and
underdevelopment as simply "two sides of the same coin." This strong version of dependency borrows from the Leninist theory of imperialism that claims
that capitalism overcomes domestic economic crises by developing new
markets and exploiting cheap labor in developing countries. Karl Marx, ironically, seemed to espouse the modernization model; he believed colonialism was
a brutal but historically necessary step to jar undeveloped nations out of their
backwardness by introducing capitalist modes of production. A more nuanced
version of dependency recognizes that economic growth can occur in dependent nations. But it sees growth as "distorted" by inequities and class divi-
sions within the developing countries, and by inequities of power between
nations.[12]

Dependency theorists and Marxists agree in viewing the history of
capitalist foreign investment as exploitative. First, gold and silver in South
America were plundered to finance the industrial revolution in Europe. Second, developing nations concentrated on one or two primary export products
(coffee, copper, bananas) that served the needs of rich nations and made Third
World nations dependent on supplying these exports. Finally, major revenues
were controlled and drained off once the industrialization process began.

But what of the specific charges directed at multinationals? The charges
can be grouped under two main headings: (1) exploitation—draining off capital
from the host country through excess profits, transfer pricing, overpricing,
use of local capital, and cheap labor, and (2) distortions—impeding the kind
of development that would benefit all levels of society. Multinationals distort
development by introducing inappropriate technology and products, by impeding the development of local enterprises, by creating benefits only for the
"elite" in Third World countries, and by reinforcing right-wing, undemocratic
political rule. Countless studies have been made to evaluate these charges
against multinationals.[13] We note briefly some of the specific charges of exploitation and return, in a later section, to the issue of distortions (under the
section of appropriate products and technology). The case histories of
Guatemala and Chile deal explicitly with the questions of political influence
and intervention. Examine Figure 8-1 for a summary of the conflicting
arguments used to support the modernization model and the dependency
model.

Global Reach brought to a broader audience many of the arguments
presented in more technical journals and books. In sharp disagreement with
business leaders cited earlier, who believe that "everyone benefits" from
multinational investments, Barnet and Muller argued that one person's profit
usually means another's loss: "The profits of the global corporations derived

FIGURE 8-1   **Multinational Corporations (Conflicting Views and Arguments)**

I. Modernization Theory
Development is best achieved through the technology, skills and business values used by now-advanced industrial nations. Multinationals contribute positively to developing nations. Multinationals:
  1. Bring technology, management, and capital to poorer countries;
  2. Develop leadership and provide training for local peoples;
  3. Reinvest at least some of the profits in the local economy;
  4. Provide orders, and hence business and jobs for local firms, both for suppliers and through workers' purchases;
  5. Provide mechanization, fertilizers, and other aids to local agriculture;
  6. Aid the host nation's development plans;
  7. Encourage the development of engineering and other professional skills among local people;
  8. Work with local and shared ownership projects.
II. Dependency Theory
Foreign investment has impeded or distorted development in Third World countries. Multinationals:
  1. Send profits from operations in poorer countries back to richer home nations;
  2. Support right-wing dictatorships over democracies because they are stable, predictable, pro-business regimes;
  3. Widen the gap between the rich and the masses of the poor in the host country;
  4. Intrude on and threaten the sovereignty of host countries;
  5. Close plants abruptly when wage rates rise or regulations become burdensome;
  6. Use local capital for its own purposes;
  7. Undermine local business initiative and leadership;
  8. Encourage the use of expensive and unnecessary consumer goods;
  9. Promote inappropriate technology transfer and capital-intensive operations.
III. Bargaining School of Thought
How much a poor, developing country benefits or loses from multinational operations may depend on its level of bargaining power.

from poor countries, it must be said, are made at the expense of the people of those countries."[14] To substantiate this point they cited the excess profit rates of many multinationals in developing countries: Exxon with a 52.5 percent profit rate; the rubber industry averaging 43 percent; pharmaceuticals in Latin America with profit rates of 79.1 percent (this latter rate fed by mark ups on drugs averaging 155 percent.[15] They noted also that for every dollar invested nearly four dollars was repatriated in profits.[16] *Global Reach* also challenged the practice of "transfer pricing" to conceal real profits. The cost of imports from subsidiaries are over priced or the cost of exports from host countries are underpriced.[17] In addition to transfer pricing, multinationals also profited by cheap labor, paying hourly wages that were only $\frac{1}{10}$ to $\frac{1}{5}$ of wages in the home country. Each of these criticisms could be restated in terms of the ethical social values we presented in Chapter Two; for example, injustice in overpricing and transfer pricing and harm to the common good of poor countries when considerably more money is taken out in profits than is invested.

While newer studies continue to press the same charges, others have countered these arguments. Raymond Vernon, one of the most prominent writers on multinationals, found the kind of criticisms noted here to be greatly exaggerated. The profit rates of the pharmaceuticals, he argued, were not typical, and even their overpricing was based on a need to avoid unusual restrictions placed on them.[18] For multinationals engaged in manufacturing in Third World countries, he found profit rates after taxes to be generally less than 15 percent of book investment.[19] While acknowledging the continued problems caused by transfer pricing, Vernon believed that it would become less of an issue as host countries gained more control in dealing with multinationals.[20] Others also have argued that rates of profit and inflow versus outflow of capital do not necessarily signify losses for host countries; what counts is not how much the foreign investor gained, but whether the host country gained. On the question of exploiting cheap labor, many business leaders reply that they generally pay higher wages than local rates, and then are accused of creating an "elite labor class."

Bargaining Power

Recognizing the complexity of evaluating the positive and negative effects of multinational operations, a new school has emerged concerned with analyzing the respective bargaining power of multinationals and host countries. The bargaining school of thought does not present a new theory of development, but offers a method of studying the conflict of interest that arise between multinationals and host countries. Raymond Vernon used the expression "obsolescing bargain" to indicate that initial agreements, which tended to favor the multinationals, often shifted in time to give greater advantages to host countries.

Theodore Moran, in various works, has studied in detail the process by which contracts are made and then changed, and the factors that may tend to give host countries more equal bargaining power. We will draw upon his studies. He analyzes the process of bargaining according to these main points: (1) most contracts have some mutual benefits for the contracting groups; (2) in the initial bargaining process the bargaining strength will generally lie on the side of the foreign investor; and (3) with fixed investments in place, greater power will accrue to the host country.[21] A host country would usually not invite multinationals to invest unless it perceived some clear benefits; for example, the host country lacks the capital and technological skills to build copper mines. The multinational, for its part, will not risk investment unless the investment promises a significant payoff. The terms of the initial concessions are heavily weighted in favor of the foreign investor, usually in the form of land grants and low taxes. Thus, "extreme disparity of bargaining power will exist at the initiation of any concession agreement."[22]

Without major concessions the investor will not take the risk; the host country must compensate for this risk by its concessions. In the years following the intital investment the bargaining power of the host country may improve significantly. The multinational has invested much; pulling out would be costly. The host country can now take advantage of this and demand that the original contract be changed, that higher taxes be paid, that more local executives be employed, and so on. These new demands do not simply reflect new-found power. They can also be made in terms of fairness, though foreign companies may see the host country as reneging on the original contract. Large concessions may have been both necessary and fair initially to compensate for the risk in the original investment, but to continue to offer the same concessions when the same risk is no longer present would not be fair.

Four factors, which are not always present, tend to give host countries more bargaining power.[23] Large fixed investments limit the bargaining power of foreign investors; an auto company cannot easily "pull out" its plants. Stable technology can be copied by host countries; but in industries with constantly changing technology, like the computer industry, the multinational will usually retain its advantage. Standardized marketing favors the host country; product differentiation (customers wanting *this* brand) favors the company. Competition among multinationals gives host countries a bargaining power they lacked when faced with the oligopolistic power that initial investors may have exercised. The bargaining model applies best to the more developed, newly industrialized countries such as Taiwan and Brazil. It may be less applicable to countries with weak development and less bargaining forces at their disposal. Where bargaining power is more equal, social norms of justice and the common good are more likely to be realized.

Comments about the Models

Each of these models contains some truth but, like all models, stresses some aspects to the neglect of others. The modernization model tends to view all contracts as mutually beneficial but often ignores disparities in bargaining power and social effects, such as loss of national autonomy and unequal income distribution. Dependency theories focus almost entirely on the disparities of power and the negative social effects while ignoring the benefits. The bargaining model appears more balanced and more credible, but it does not measure whether the bargaining power of host countries translates into benefits for the common good of the country as a whole. Ferdinand Marcos in the Philippines and Mobutu Seko in Zaire may have gained more bargaining power in dealing with multinationals. But the benefits—wealth estimated as high as

$10 billion for Marcos and hundreds of millions for Mobutu[24]—accrued to them personally, not to their people. Brazil actively courted multinationals and was hailed for its "miracle growth" in the late 1960s and early 1970s. But dependency theorist A. Gunder Frank argued that even during this period the poorest sectors of society suffered, in both relative and absolute terms. By 1975 minimum wages had been cut to 45 percent of the 1964 level. In 1960 it had taken 5.7 hours of work, for an average worker, to obtain a minimum daily diet for his family; by 1970 it took the same worker 8.5 hours.[25]

The exaggerated claim of dependency theory—that investment by multinationals always causes underdevelopment—has been rightly challenged by most analysts. Some countries where multinationals operate have clearly experienced economic growth. But economic growth does not tell the whole story. The growth may only benefit a wealthy elite or a relatively small percent of the people, neglecting the human needs and dignity of the majority. It also does not assure national pride and autonomy. In two of the cases that follow, national pride and concerns about autonomy were strong factors. In Guatemala, earlier in this century, United Fruit did in many ways spur economic growth and build up the infrastructure (railways, ports, roads) that served the nation. But the company so dominated the economy, and so affected many national policies, that strong resentment developed. The same drive for national autonomy became evident in the conflicts between Chile and American copper companies in the decades after World War II.

The United States once fought its own war of independence because it resented taxation without representation. Reactions to the incursions of the Japanese auto industry give some indication of what Americans would feel if foreign companies dominated our whole economy. We can understand, then, that nations as well as individuals want to experience the social value of dignity that comes from autonomy and independence.[26]

If Americans need to be aware of the aspirations of other nations, they need also to be aware that the conditions that aided economic development in the United States do not necessarily apply in Third World countries. The United States had a remarkable resource base, a young immigrant population, relatively free and strong social institutions, and an absence of feudal entanglements as a basis for its development. Four of five white Americans owned their own farms or trade prior to the Civil War (slavery and the takeover of native American Indian lands, however, show that the United States provided this opportunity to whites at the cost of injustice to others). By way of contrast, most countries in Latin America never had widely dispersed private property. Property was viewed rather as a "patrimony" bequeathed by the queen or the state. This Latin American cultural heritage continues to affect the present, with 1.3 percent of landowners controlling 71 percent of all land under cultivation.[27] This concentration of land ownership, in countries still primarily agricultural, has created great inequities in distribution of income and almost precludes broad participation in free enterprise.

Current multinational investors are not responsible for creating these conditions, nor for creating apartheid in South Africa. But they often do go along with situations in which their size and wealth reinforce inequity, and their desire for stable order is viewed as opposition to change. These comments, we hope, will be helpful in considering the case histories that follow. These histories are admittedly dramatic cases. They are not proposed as typical of multinational operations but they do demonstrate a lack of concern for the social values that we have stressed: the dignity of persons and nations, their common good, and justice.

GUATEMALA AND UNITED FRUIT

In 1954 the Guatemalan government of Jacobo Arbenz was overthrown. Though U.S. hostility toward Arbenz was clear at that time, his overthrow at first appeared to be a domestic affair. Later it became evident that the CIA and the U.S. Department of State had initiated and organized the overthrow, and that officials from the United Fruit Company (now United Brands) had significantly influenced U.S. attitudes toward Arbenz.[28] The overthrow was an event with significant moral implications. The United States justified its actions on different counts: the threat of Communism—both to the U.S. and to Guatemala—was its primary reason; but protection of the property rights of a U.S. company was also a factor. A strong case, however, can be made against the morality of the U.S. action and United Fruit's involvement. Guatemala's right to freedom and self-determination was involved. Arbenz had been democratically elected; after decades of military dictatorships, Guatemala had finally achieved democracy a decade before (in 1944). International law, and the United States' own agreement with the OAS not to intervene in the affairs of another state, appeared violated. Guatemala's attempt to meet basic human needs and to create more just participation in the economy were also at stake. Arbenz' reforms were viewed by many as a real attempt to improve the lot of the majority in Guatemala, a majority that lived in often-desperate poverty. The per-capita income in rural areas was $87 a year, while only 2 percent of the population owned 72 percent of the land, most of it uncultivated.[29]

Conflict with the United States

Arbenz' conflict with the United States arose on two counts: his expropriation of land owned by United Fruit along with denial of concessions previously granted the company, and his recognition of the Communist Party as legal, together with the alleged influence of Communist labor leaders on Arbenz' policies. Arbenz angered United Fruit by enacting new labor and tax laws. These changes could be analyzed in the light of Moran's theories on shifting bargaining power. A number of concessions had been made to United Fruit in the 1930s: no internal taxes, duty-free imports, and guarantee of low wages. Benefits had come to Guatemala in the form of development of the banana industry and the building of railways, ports, and roads. Now the agreements were changed; in particular, higher minimum wages were called for. But Arbenz also expropriated huge tracts of land owned by United Fruit: 240,000 acres at first, then 172,000 acres later.

Arbenz justified the takeover on the grounds that only uncultivated land was expropriated and that just compensation was offered, based on the evaluation of $630,000 which United Fruit itself had made for tax purposes. United Fruit countered by saying that it needed uncultivated land to replace depleted soil and that the true value of the expropriated land was $16 million. While the higher figure was closer to the true value, United Fruit was trapped by what Thomas McCann, a later vice-president of United Fruit, admitted as a common practice among multinationals: using "every tax and bookkeeping gimmick they can get away with to minimize their obligations to the nations in which they operate."[30] But the overthrow would have been highly unlikely based on the expropriation alone. The threat of communist influence in the government became crucial and United Fruit did all in its power to dramatize this threat.

The political mood of the United States in the 1950s made anti-communism a natural appeal. It was the era of Joe McCarthy, and the State Department's John Foster Dulles had made "rolling back communism" a major goal. It did not require much evidence to gain support for actions to stop communism. The very promotion of land reform was cited by the U.S. Ambassador to Guatemala as a sign of communism. The United States criticized Arbenz for legalizing the Communist Party, for accepting its support, and for including young communist leaders as friends and advisors on land and labor issues. Later studies that tried to substantiate the threat of communism uncovered no evidence of direct support by the Soviet Union, but argued guilt by association. Young Guatemalan communists had traveled to the Soviet Union and had modeled their party on other international communist parties.[31] A shipment of arms from Czechoslovakia was later also used as proof of communism, though the overthrow of Arbenz's government had already been decided upon before the shipment was discovered.

United Fruit in Action

The threat of communism in Guatemala might not have arisen, or at least not been judged serious by the United States, were it not for the influence of United Fruit on U.S. public opinion. United Fruit hired public relations advisors, who intentionally focused on the threat of communism, to rouse U.S. opinion against Arbenz. They retained a journalist who wrote a *Report on Guatemala* which depicted changes in that country as due to a "Moscow-directed Communist conspiracy." While the report, Thomas McCann acknowledged, was so distorted that no publisher would accept responsibility for it, it was distributed to all members of Congress and to 800 other important opinion-molders.[32] Reports about the "growing threat" of communism, including some fabricated incidents, were submitted regularly to journalists and government officials. Many of the top government officials who advised the overthrow of Arbenz had close connection with United Fruit: John Foster Dulles (Secretary of State) and Allen Dulles (C.I.A. Director) had been partners in the law firm representing United Fruit; Henry Cabot Lodge (U.S. Representative to the UN) and John Moors Cabot (Asst. Secretary of State for Latin America) were prominent stockholders in United Fruit.

Most Americans are quite aware of the evils of communism, but they often overlook the tragic consequences of our own country's actions. When then Vice President Richard Nixon visited Guatemala after the overthrow of Arbenz, he proclaimed: "This is the first instance in history where a Communist government has been replaced by a free one. The whole world is watching to see which does the better job."[33] United Fruit got its land back after the overthrow. Agrarian reform was reversed and less than one percent of the peasants retained the land gained under Arbenz. Voting rights were denied to all who were illiterate—70 percent of the population. The Catholic bishops of Guatemala, who had staunchy opposed communism, recognized a few years later that peasants were working for salaries "that hardly permit them to avoid death by starvation" and that plantation workers were living "in situations closely resembling concentration camps."[34] Their human dignity was violated.

Guerilla opposition formed in the 1960s. The government forces, trained in part by U.S. Green Berets, struck out at all who sympathized with the opposition. Amnesty International estimated that more than 30,000 people were abducted, tortured or assassinated between 1961–1981.[35] Thousands more were killed under the government of Rios Montt in the early 1980s. Hundreds of thousands of Indians became refugees. The overthrow of Arbenz contributed significantly to the whole direction U.S. foreign policy would take in Latin America, including U.S. relations with Cuba in 1959. On the basis of the Guatemala experience, Castro was convinced that the U.S. would not permit any far-reaching reforms that affected U.S. property holdings, and the Eisenhower government believed it could bring down Castro as it did Arbenz.[36]

This story of United Fruit's self-centered involvement represents an extreme end of the spectrum in terms of multinational power. Rarely is one company so dominant in the life of another nation or so influential in affecting its history. At times U.S. foreign policy has run counter to the desires of a particular multinational firm. But the ethical implications of the use of multinational corporate power are clear. United Fruit gained many concessions from Guatemala in the 1930s; through the power of its influence, it promoted the downfall of a democratically elected government in the 1950s. United Fruit, under its new name United Brands, also gave a $1,250,000 bribe to a Honduran official in 1974. This violation of integrity only added to its violations of the dignity, freedom, and common good of the Guatemalan people.

CHILE AND THE COPPER MULTINATIONALS

The story of multinational corporate involvement in Chile's government followed the script of Guatemala in some respects, leading to the overthrow of Chile's president, Salvador Allende, in 1973. The history leading up to the overthrow, however, provides a more interesting illustration of conflicts in bargaining power. Copper mining has played a central role in the history of modern Chile. Copper is Chile's greatest natural resource and the major source of its export income. Thus Chile's relations with multinationals involved not only issues of economic growth, but of national autonomy and dignity. The history of the conflicts between Chile and the U.S. copper companies illustrates how bargaining power changes[37], but it also shows how a host nation perceives its freedom, its dignity, and the good of its people to be undermined by multinationals.

Anaconda and Kennecott were invited into Chile in the first decades of this century, when sufficient capital was unavailable locally to expand Chile's copper mining, and local business lacked the technology to tap the richest veins of copper. The multinationals were given generous concessions at first: no taxes at the outset and low tax rates during their first decade or more of operations. Their net profit rates were high, 20–40 percent, remaining as high as 40 percent through World War II. The copper companies contended that the profit rates were not unfair since they had taken a significant business risk and been successful. They accepted massive increases in tax rates, up to 70 percent by 1952; they argued that Chile itself was gaining far more than they were. From 1945–1955 Anaconda and Kennecott together recorded profits of $275 million and from 1955–1965, profits of $465 million. But Chile had gained $328 million and $909 million in tax revenues during these same periods.[38] From this perspective alone, Chile may have had little complaint about justice. But other related social issues did trouble many in Chile, issues related to external controls over copper prices leading to losses in terms of trade.

An International Monetary Fund report in 1947 showed Chile to have the worst terms of trade of all the Latin American countries except Bolivia. For Chile the reason appeared clear. Despite great copper shortages during World War II, the United States insisted on keeping copper prices low, and prices were kept low after the war, although prices of imports into Chile grew rapidly. The low prices had meant a loss of somewhere between $100–500 million for Chile. Artificially low prices after the war, Chilean officials argued, meant that Chile was, in effect, funding the U.S. Marshall Plan. National dignity was also involved. In 1950, the United States set a low price on copper without even inviting any Chilean representative to discuss it.[39]

Chile was not in a free market; its copper sales were tied to prices and trading partners determined by its agreements with the United States. But it did gain one concession in 1952; it could sell 20 percent of its copper supply on the free market, setting its own prices. Through this concession it gained $70 million, but this did not compensate for Chile's declining share in the world market, which was down from 22 percent in 1945 to 14 percent in 1954.[40] Chile then adopted a new tactic in 1955. It gave the multinational copper companies substantial new concessions and freedoms: lower taxes, higher profits, fewer controls, and preferential import rights. Kennecott's profits doubled; their profit rates were two to three times higher than from their other operations. But this strategy likewise backfired on Chile. With no obligations corresponding to the concessions granted, the copper companies used increased profits for other long-range goals that looked to the multinationals' whole system rather than to the host country's interests. They invested in aluminum and coal; Kennecott increased its copper refining in the United States, and sought *not* to rely as much on Chilean operations.[41]

Growing Resentment in Chile

Resentment grew in Chile and with it a strong sense of Chilean dependency on foreign multinationals. Chileans viewed the multinationals' decisions and the policies of their home countries as detrimental to Chile's own patriotic interests. Demands for nationalization became strong in the 1960s; the first moves were made by Chilean President Eduardo Frei in the second half of that decade. Popular support for such a move was strong. Right-wing conservatives, incensed by the U.S. "Alliance for Progress" and its call for land reforms, joined in the outcry against the multinational copper companies. Conservatives wanted to shift the blame for Chile's problems from internal factors (concentration of land ownership) to external causes (the copper companies). Frei called on the companies to sell 51 percent of their shares to his government and to improve their profits by increased production. Kennecott agreed; Anaconda refused. By the 1970 election, won by Salvador Allende, every major candidate called for nationalizaiton. In July 1971, legislation nationalizing the copper companies passed *unanimously*. Chile felt it had gained its sovereignty and control over its economy. The New Chile Copper Company raised again the issues of how profits had been divided. It claimed that the largest U.S. copper companies had taken out of Chile wealth estimated at $10.8 billion over a sixty-year period, an amount greater than all the rest of the wealth produced in Chile during its entire history.[42] It refused compensation to the multinationals for the nationalization on the grounds that the copper companies had already been compensated by exorbitant profit rates. Kennecott, Allende argued, had an average annual profit rate of 52.8 percent from its Chilean operations during 1955–1970; Annaconda averaged 21.5 percent in profits from Chile during the same period, as opposed to 3.5 percent from their investments elsewhere.[43] The ethical issue was not the right to make profits, but fairness and justice in their distribution.

As in Guatemala, once nationalization became a threat, U.S. multinationals demonstrated the political influence they could exert. The copper companies retaliated against Chile by attempting to block payment for Chilean copper sold in Western Europe, and they called on United States officials to thwart Allende's efforts. But it was ITT, trying to protect its $153 million telephone enterprise, that took the most active role in undermining Allende. As later U.S. Senate hearings would confirm, ITT first met with the CIA and with U.S. government officials to block Allende's election in 1970. After Allende's election and after ITT's telephone property was expropriated, a new plan was developed by ITT to assure the collapse of Allende's regime. The White House denied acceptance of the ITT plan, but the plan's suggestions were in fact pursued: the fostering of discontent in the Chilean military, cutting off bank loans, withholding the shipment of spare machine parts, and slowing trade between the United States and Chile.[44]

Allende was overthrown in 1973 and Chile has lived under a military dictatorship since that time. U.S. multinationals played a significant, though hardly decisive, role in this change. The ethical question on this last point is whether the multinationals' self-interests justified interfering in another country's right to self-determination and establishing its own common good. We believe they were not justified.

SOUTH AFRICA AND MULTINATIONALS

As public attention focused on corporations in the 1970s, many groups turned to a new form of social pressure. Religious groups, university groups, and other investors used their influence as shareholders to spotlight social concerns at annual stockholders' meetings. Research and analysis were provided for many investors by the Investor Responsibility Research Center (IRRC) in Washington, D.C. A decade ago resolutions touched on a broad range of issues, some domestic—the B-1 Bomber, corporate involvement in U.S. political campaigns, strip mining and its effect on the environment—and some foreign.[45] The infant formula controversy (see Chapter Five) was a significant issue. Employment practices and wages paid by some multinationals were the subject of other resolutions. Political contributions by multinationals to other governments were challenged; Gulf Oil was charged with having spent $4 million on political contributions in South Korea alone.[46] This form of raising social issues began to influence corporate consciousness.

Apartheid in South Africa was one of the major social issues that first gave rise to stockholder resolutions. In the 1980s, apartheid became the dominant issue, but what galvanized many stockholder groups into action was the South African government's suppression of a protest demonstration by blacks in Soweto in 1976. An estimated 700 blacks were killed.

Shocked by this event, Americans became more aware of conditions in South Africa. Black Africans constitute over 70 percent of the population in South Africa, compared to 16 percent white, with "coloreds" and Asians making up the rest.[47] Though constituting a majority of the population, they were denied citizenship and had no rights. Blacks were alloted 13 percent of the poorest land for ten "homelands;" whites legally owned the rest (87 percent). Blacks had no freedom of movement. To control migration into the white cities, every black over sixteen had to carry a "pass" book. In the mid-1970s arrests for violations of passport rules averaged over 1000 a day.[48] Black workers could not freely seek work but had to apply through labor bureaus. Families were frequently separated, with husbands in male dormitories outside the urban white cities, and their wives and children left in the homelands. Wages were grossly inequitable. In 1970, whites working in mines earned twenty times the wages of blacks; in manufacturing they earned six times more.[49] By 1980, public pressure had brought a change to wage differentials: 6 to 1 in mining and 4 to 1 in manufacturing. Until public pressure brought a change, blacks were not permitted any supervisory jobs. The infant mortality rate was ten times higher among blacks. In education the government spent $940 per white child and $90 per black child.[50] All public facilities were segregated.

In 1980, about 350 U.S. companies were operating in South Africa, employing about 100,000 workers, 70 percent of them black.[51] While they constituted a small percentage of U.S. investment abroad, and ranked a distant second to Great Britain in investment in South Africa, they formed a multi-billion dollar presence. With the public conscience awakened, Rev. Leon Sullivan, a black minister elected to the Board of GM, developed a code of principles that U.S. companies in South Africa were called upon to adopt. The code called for desegregation of all public facilities at work, equal and fair employment (with the right to unionize), equal pay for equal work (and equitable wages), training programs so that more blacks could advance to skilled and managerial positions, and the improvement of housing, educational, and recreational facilities. The European Economic Community (EEC) adopted a similar code, through one which focused more on union rights and wages.[52]

The Sullivan principles did effect changes. But many challenged the extent and the effectiveness of the changes. Less than a fifth of the companies signed the first year; some 137 companies had signed by 1980. Many companies desegregated their facilities, but segregation could be effectively maintained in some instances by designating separate facilities for hourly workers and salaried employees. Equal pay could often be circumvented since 71 percent of the blacks worked in jobs in which there were no whites, and nearly all top managerial positions were held by whites.[53] But some progress was made;

blacks took on supervisory jobs for the first time, and the Arthur D. Little company was employed to monitor implementation of the principles; companies that wished to measure up ethically took pride in ratings; for example, "making good progress." Companies unsigned or with poor ratings came under greater criticism, at least at stockholders' meetings. In ensuing years the Sullivan principles were expanded, calling for efforts to promote black enterprises, and to voice public protest against government policies of apartheid.

By 1986, stockholder resolutions were urging, with greater insistence, that U.S. companies simply withdraw their operations from South Africa. They acknowledged that many U.S. multinationals had admirably changed in accord with the Sullivan principles and that many had initiated significant outside service programs. They noted that IBM, among its many efforts, had contributed $5 million to a special education program. General Motors, in its 1985 Public Interest Report, described its many efforts to aid in the education of blacks, to subsidize housing, and to promote black businesses.[54] GM also joined with many other companies and South African business leaders in publicly calling for an end to apartheid. The white business community in South Africa, it should be noted, is quite distinct from the unyielding white group in government.[55] The South African government, however, still resisted effecting significant reforms. Hence the call for withdrawal, along with calls for stronger U.S. government sanctions, to force change. Leon Sullivan joined the ranks of those calling for withdrawal if apartheid was not ended by 1987.

The immorality of apartheid is now widely acknowledged. The debate of the 1980s focused rather on the moral value and the effectiveness of withdrawal. Advocates of withdrawal argued that compliance with the Sullivan principles was not enough. It was South African government policies which had to be changed. The advocates of withdrawal argued on ethical grounds that it was wrong to do business with and in a country that practices apartheid. They argued on strategic grounds that withdrawal, together with strong U.S. economic sanctions, would force South Africa to change in order to avert economic collapse. Opponents of withdrawal argued that U.S. multinationals could be agents of change if they stayed, able to work with the more progressive forces in South Africa. Withdrawal could cause loss of jobs for blacks and might only make the South African government more recalcitrant.

By 1987, many firms had withdrawn from South Africa: General Motors, IBM, Ford, Xerox, Coca-Cola, and others. GM's move was prompted both by pressures to withdraw and by economic factors. Its automotive sales dropped to just over 5 percent of the South African car market from 12 percent five years before; it lost $200 million in 1985 and expected to do worse in 1986.[56]

These moves did not, however, end the debate over withdrawal. Some 240 companies planned to remain. Many companies that did withdraw cut their losses by moving from direct investment to licensing agreements and independent distributorships. Coca-cola continued to sell syrups to South African customers. Some critics challenged these forms of withdrawal as strategies to avoid public pressure and financial losses.

When ethical issues revolve upon strategies, moral judgments become more difficult. Withdrawal by some U.S. multinationals may help to effect change, but it may not if European companies, which already have a larger stake in South Africa, simply take up the slack. Perhaps the continued presence of U.S. multinationals could have an effect on the South African government. It appears, however, that South African hard-liners will resist change whatever the consequences. One clear and troubling ethical issue does remain, however. Apartheid is an egregious violation of the freedom and human dignity of blacks, who make up the vast majority of the population in South Africa. Why were multinationals blind to this for so long? Why did they do little or nothing to act against apartheid until public awareness pressured them to react?

LOOKING AT BOTH SIDES

The size and wealth of multinationals give them power, and power too often does corrupt. Some multinationals have corrupted local officials to gain concessions, as did United Brands in the $1.25 million dollar bribe to a Honduran official to lower taxes.[57] Some multinationals have taken advantage of cheap labor, or tried to cut its losses at home by exploiting workers abroad, as Ford did in South Africa, raising work hours there to offset the 1978 recession in the United States. Some multinationals have acted with the same insensitivity once characteristic of colonialism, creating enclaves of luxury in the midst of degrading poverty. Some multinationals have used their influence to thwart the autonomy of host countries, as in Guatemala and Chile. It would be wrong, however, to judge all multinational operations by the sins of some, or to assume that Third World countries would be better off without them. Without repeating the list of benefits that proponents of the modernization theory say accrue to Third World countries through multinationals, we do wish to add some specific comments in defense of multinationals.

In Defense of Multinationals

In discussing the dependency theory we noted some of the counter arguments to charges of excess profits and exploitation. Risk factors must be considered by multinationals before they invest. United Fruit lost $58 million when its operations were expropriated by Castro in Cuba.[58] In countries where the risk of nationalization is high, foreign companies were unlikely to invest unless they are given generous concessions that offer promise of significant gains to offset the risk. The risk factor has diminished in recent years because expropriations occur less often. One reason expropriations are less frequent is that host countries have experienced the *disadvantages* of nationalization. Zaire and Zambia experienced losses in revenues since they nationalized their mining industries; Peru and Chile also met with economic setbacks.[59] We noted earlier the process by which host countries may grow in bargaining power once initial investments are made. Competition may be the most significant equalizing factor. Twenty years ago, many U.S. firms could count on their oligopolistic status to establish contracts with provisions strongly in their favor. Now they must compete not only with Japanese and European firms, but also with successful Third World multinationals from Taiwan, India, Brazil, and other countries.

Multinationals have become more conscious of social values. Whether the change can be attributed to concern for maintaining a good public image, to public pressures, or to a new ethical awareness, new attitudes are apparent. General Motors publishes an annual report on affairs of public interest, and has adopted a "guest" philosophy to govern its relations to foreign countries. Multinationals in South Africa certainly have had to address social issues.

Multinationals may once have believed that their very presence automatically benefited poor countries by creating jobs, paying generally higher wages, bringing in new technology, and managerial skills. Now programs specifically designed to improve other social conditions in Third World countries have become more evident. One study cites several examples to illustrate the "high degree of social responsibility" shown by most multinationals. The study began by highlighting a turnabout at Gulf + Western. In the early 1970s, G + W came under sharp attack for its treatment of workers in the Dominican Republic. It answered critics with several constructive moves. It began a "Dominicanization" of its personnel in 1978, replacing top foreign-born officers with native Dominicans. From 1980–1983 it spent $24 million in programs to improve the health, housing, nutrition, and agricultural skills of Dominican workers. It donated more than 70,000 acres of company-owned land to a government program aimed at establishing small farm and ranch cooperatives. Unfortunately, a year after this study was made, G + W announced plans to pull out of the Dominican Republic. But other examples in the study are worth citing.

In Ghana, a joint-venture aluminum smelter owned by Kaiser Aluminum & Chemical Corp. and Reynolds Metals Co. made possible the construction of a long-sought hydro-electric power project that has eased the country's dependence on imported oil.

In a remote province of Indonesia, a subsidiary of New York-based Freeport-McMoRan Inc. built most of the infrastructure—including roads, a port, and an airstrip—to support a copper mining venture. In addition, the firm built a hospital that serves employees and others in the local community.

In Brazil, a pulp-and-paper operation owned by Manville Corp. creates needed employment opportunities and has provided an infusion of technological know-how that has turned a once-failing concern into a thriving venture.[60] Examples prove little about multinationals overall, but they point to some efforts by firms to take social responsibility more seriously.

The Issue of "Appropriate" Products and Technology

The modernization paradigm discussed earlier assumed a natural path of growth that all nations would follow, but which foreign firms could help to accelerate. This "natural path," as Adam Smith first described it, involves three stages: first, the development of agriculture, through "relatively" egalitarian free enterprise among land-owning classes in rural areas; second, industrial production for the urban market; third, production for international trade.[61] W. Arthur Lewis, Nobel-prize-winning economist, has stressed the need for strong agricultural development for domestic markets as a basis for industrial growth. Moreover, he believes that underdeveloped nations cannot escape from unfavorable terms of trade without greater and more efficient agricultural productivity.[62]

If progression from agriculture to industry and from domestic markets to foreign trade is the "natural path," it is not the way most Third World countries have developed. Whether external or internal forces are the cause, most of today's developing countries have not stressed agricultural development for domestic markets. Rather, they have economies often based on cash crops for exports (bananas, coffee), or they have tried to introduce industrialization at levels of high technology. Critics of the modernization model believe that the neglect of meeting basic needs first has impeded development, and that multinationals reinforce this faulty direction by bringing in inappropriate products and technology.

For the majority of their export earnings, most underdeveloped countries now depend on only one or two crops. There is nothing "natural," critics contend, about land used for one crop. Latin America had no banana trees until the late 1830s; before this the land was used to grow corn, rice, and beans for domestic consumption.[63] Concentration on one cash export crop has made these countries vulnerable to shifting world prices. They may produce food, but not for domestic consumption. When multinational agribusinesses produce food in underdeveloped countries, the food is not the basic staples of beans and rice—needed by the local population—but luxury crops such as asparagus, strawberries, and pineapples exported to richer nations.[64] "Consumer sovereignty" may be at work, since landowners—like the 1.3 percent who control 70 percent of the land in Latin America—can expect greater returns on export crops. Del Monte found that a pineapple that would only bring 8 cents locally in the Philippines can bring $1.50 exported to Tokyo. Not surprisingly, 90 percent of its Philippine pineapple production is exported. Using far cheaper labor costs, Del Monte pays Mexicans to produce asparagus for export to the United States.[65] Ethical-social values are implicit in all of these criticisms. Human dignity calls for a priority in meeting the basic human needs of local people over filling the desires of those in more affluent societies; a sense of community calls for care of those most in need.

Other analysts question the "appropriateness" of products and technologies emphasized by many multinational companies.[66] Multinationals in the electrical industry in Brazil use less labor per unit of capital than do Brazilian firms, and on the consumption side they are oriented toward supplying an elite demand locally, such as color television.[67] The multinational auto industry promotes industrialization in Third World countries, but its consumers there are a minority class whose use of autos is subsidized by government expenditures on roads and parking facilities to the neglect of more basic food-shelter needs.[68] The pharmaceutical industry offers an inappropriate mix of drugs. In India, which has the Third World's most sophisticated drug industry, the most prevalent diseases are filariasis, malaria, dysentery, leprosy, and tuberculosis. But not one of the 15 leading pharmaceutical products was used to treat these major diseases. Instead, the pharmaceuticals in India focus upon remedies for local middle-class ailments like fatigue, headaches, and constipation. This approach also supports the orientation of Third World health services, in which 80 percent of the national health expenditures go for the needs of just 20 percent of the population.[69]

Tractor production reinforces the inequities of land distribution in Third World countries. To be economically viable, even a small tractor of 40–60HP requires arable land of more than 100 to 125 acres. But in Latin America the majority of farms are less than 25 acres, and the cost of a tractor in Guatemala, for example, would require a down payment of 11 to 34 times the annual income of a small farmer.[70]

Some firms have attempted to supply goods and machines for greater mass use in developing countries. GM takes pride in its development of an inexpensive Basic Transportation Vehicle. Some Third World countries, however, insist on the most modern capital-intensive technologies. And multinationals have been frustrated in their efforts to sell more appropriate products. General Foods, criticized for promoting junk food in poor countries, developed a highly nutritious Nutribon, only to find it had few buyers.[71] Ford tried for six years to develop a simple 7HP tractor for Third World use before concluding that returns would not be high enough to justify the cost of production.[72]

U.S. companies have developed technologies and products to meet the needs of the U.S. domestic market with its more affluent consumers. That multinationals should seek to satisfy the needs of those Third World consumers who can pay for the same type of goods should not be surprising. But this may unwittingly reinforce the inequities of income distribution in these nations. The majority of the people in the Third World need economies that give priority to meeting basic needs for food, shelter, and medical care through the use of appropriate levels of technology.

SUMMARY AND CONCLUSIONS

Public awareness does not accurately measure the point at which moral issues are most serious. Earlier stages of multinational power probably were periods at which lack of social responsibility was greatest, but public outcries at the time were also infrequent. United Fruit's actions in Guatemala met with almost no opposition at the time. When criticisms of multinationals were most strident in the 1970s, shifts in bargaining power had already led to improvements. Dramatic attention has been paid to South Africa in recent years, but little attention was given for decades when conditions were just as deplorable. Public attention and concern for social values have, however, pressed multinationals to confront issues of social responsibility. We believe that corporations can and should include ethics in their strategies of decision making.[73]

How beneficial or harmful are multinationals to developing countries? Two recent studies on multinationals, both balanced and scholarly works cited in this chapter, arrive at quite different general conclusions. Theodore Moran recognizes the possibility of lopsided bargaining power and the potential for distortions in Third World development as ongoing problems. But he sees the greater number and greater spread of multinationals as improving the bargaining power of host nations and improving, rather than worsening, their prospects for development over time. Moran warns, however, against viewing multinationals as the "hope" for poor nations. They employ about 4 million persons world wide; unemployment in the Third World affects hundreds of millions. Moran also shows concern that "protectionism" in the U.S. could thwart Third World development. He concludes overall that international trade and investment still serve the best interests of the United States *and* the Third World.[74]

Richard Newfarmer reaches a different overall assessment. He believes that developing countries do rather badly under the existing market system. Imperfections in the international market system "accord economic power to relatively few corporations and these imperfections tend to result in oligopolistic conduct that works to the disadvantage of developing countries."[75]

If these differences remain in efforts to assess the overall advantages or disadvantages that multinationals bring to Third World countries, the important task of improving relations remains. While Third World countries may be gaining in bargaining power, U.S. multinationals still retain great power due to their size, their capital, their advanced technology, their control of information, and their backing by the U.S. government. Multinational corporations, we believe, bear a heavy responsibility for conscientious use of that power. We believe that protest groups have been useful in keeping attention on the social and moral aspects of that power.

We sought in this chapter to achieve a better understanding of the problems involved and to raise ethical questions about multinational operations, using some of the social and business values presented in Chapter Two. Each of the cases or issues discussed involved one or another of these values, such as the obvious violation of human dignity reflected in apartheid, the dignity of the nations of Guatemala and Chile and sensitivity to *their* common good, and the appropriateness of products produced by multinationals, given the basic needs of peoples in Third World countries. Multinationals now have available, however, the more specific and detailed guidelines proposed by the Organization for Economic Development and the ethical "code" developed by the United Nations Commission on Transnational Corporations. These guidelines and codes embrace both the general concerns (respect for Third World countries' "aims and priorities with regard to economic and social progress") and many of the particulars (avoidance of political interference, transfer pricing) that we discussed in this chapter.[76]

DISCUSSION QUESTIONS

8.1. Outline the principal contributions and dangers of multinational corporations.
8.2. What is the modernization theory of the multinational corporation? How does it compare with the dependency theory?
8.3. Describe the bargaining power theory of the multinational corporation.
8.4. What are the strengths and weaknesses of each of these models? Are there other ways to assess the contributions and dangers of the multinational firm?
8.5. Ethically evaluate U.S. actions in Guatemala using traditional business values and social values (see Figure 2-1). Evaluate the actions of United Fruit according to these norms.
8.6. Assess the operations of U.S. copper mining firms in Chile prior to 1971, using the ethical norms of Figure 2-1.
8.7. Which ethical norms (Figure 2-1) are most helpful in evaluating a firm's operations in South Africa? Pick one U.S. firm and apply the norms to its actions. What policy or action would you recommend?
8.8. What are "appropriate" products and technology? Give examples, along with examples of inappropriate products and technology. Why did you place the products on the respective lists?
8.9. How would you assess both the positive contributions and the harmful consequences of multinational operations?
8.10. A current issue is the wisdom of protective tariffs. Examine such tariffs from the standpoint of their effect on Third World peoples, using our ethical norms.

NOTES

[1]Raymond Vernon, *Storm over the Multinationals* (Cambridge, MA.: Harvard University, 1977). Vernon had drawn attention to the problems raised by multinationals in his earlier *Sovereignty at Bay* (New York: Basic Books, 1971).

Note: We have decided to stay with the term "multinationals" because of the long-standing use. The United Nations and some contemporary writers prefer "transnationals" because multinational may seem to suggest a sharing of power and decision making with host countries while control is actually kept in the home country.

The expression "Third World" originally was meant to identify countries not aligned with the First World (the United States and Western Europe) or with the Second World of communist countries. It is now used, however, more often as an economic expression for developing countries.

[2]Richard Barnet and Ronald Muller, *Global Reach, The Power of the Multinational Corporations* (New York: Simon and Schuster, 1974), p. 26.

[3]Ibid., p. 45.

[4]For a discussion and bibilography of studies on multinationals, see Peter B. Evans, "Recent Research on Multinational Corporations," in the *Annual Review of Sociology*, vol. 7, 1981, pp. 199–223. For a discussion and briefer bibliography of multinationals in the Third World, see Karen Paul and Robert Barbato, "The Multinational Corporation in the Less Developed Country: The Econoimic Development Model Versus the North-South Model," in the *Academy of Management Review*, 1985, vol. 10, no. 1, pp. 8–14.

[5]Quoted by A.W. Clausen, in an address to the Graduate School of Business Administration at the University of Southern California, June 28, 1976 (unpublished).

[6]W.W. Rostow, *The Stages of Economic Growth* (Cambridge, England: Cambridge University, 1960).

[7]A.W. Clausen, address at USC cited above.

[8]Harry Heltzer, "The World is the Business of American Business," in the *Columbia Journal of World Business*, vol. VIII, no. 1, Spring 1973, p. 32.

[9]Donald M. Kendall, "The Need for Multinationals," in the *Columbia Journal of World Business*, vol. VII, no. 1, January–February 1972, p. 105.

[10]Thomas A. Murphy, in the *General Motors 1974 Report on Progress in Areas of Public Concern* (Warren, MI: GM Technical Center, February 7, 1974).

[11]For a more thorough discussion of dependency theory and the modernization model, see Arthur F. McGovern, "Latin America and 'Dependency' Theory," in *This World*, Spring/Summer, 1986.

[12]Andre Gunder Frank is representative of the "strong" dependency theory; Fernando Henrique Cardoso is representative of the more "nuanced" approach. The best study of dependency theory, especially in its relationship to Marxism, is Gabriel Palma's, "Dependency: A Formal Theory of Development or a Methodology for the Analysis of Concrete Situations of Underdevelopment?," in *World Development*, July–August, 1978.

[13]For an excellent but technical statement and evaluation of criticisms against multinational see Theodore H. Moran, "Multinational Corporations and Dependency: A Dialogue for Dependentistas and Non-Dependentistas," in *International Organization*, Winter, 1978, vol. 32, no. 1. Confer also the summaries of research noted above by Evans and in Paul and Barbato.

[14]Barnet and Muller, *Global Reach*, p. 162.

[15]Ibid., on Exxon, p. 17; on the rubber industry and pharmaceuticals, pp. 158–159.

[16]Ibid., p. 161. In 1985, U.S.' direct investments in development countries generated earnings of $12.4 billion; $8.7 billion was repatriated in profits; $3.7 billion was reinvested. From the *Survey of Current Business*, August 1986, Table 4.

[17]Barnet and Muller, *Global Reach*, pp. 277–88.

[18]Vernon, *Storm over the Multinationals*, p. 155.

[19]Ibid., p. 156.

[20]Ibid.

[21]Theodore H. Moran, *Multinational Corporations and the Politics of Dependence, Copper in Chile* (Princeton, N.J.; Princeton University, 1974), Chapter 6.

[22]Ibid., p. 159, note.

[23]Theodore H. Moran, "Multinational Corporations and Third World Investment," in *Latin America: Dependency or Interdependence?,"* Michael Novak and Michael P. Jackson, eds. (Washington D.C.: American Enterprise Institute, 1985), pp. 16–17, and also *Multinational Corporations*, Theodore H. Moran, ed. (Lexington, MA.: Lexington Books, 1985), chapter 5 on risk assessment.

[24]On Mobutu's wealth, see Jonathan Kwitney, *Endless Enemies* (New York: Congdon & Weed, 1984), p. 87.

[25]Andre Gunder Frank, *Crisis: In the Third World* (New York: Holmes and Meier, 1981), pp. 7, 12.

[26]On the force of autonomy as an important aspiration in Third World countries, see The Conference Board, *Multinationals in Contention: Responses at Governmental and International Levels*, Robert Black et al., eds. (New York: The Conference Board, 1978), pp. ix-x, 5–6.

[27]Michael P. Todaro, *Economic Development in the Third World* (New York: Longman, 1981, 2nd ed), p. 260.

[28]Unless otherwise noted, the history of these events in Guatemala is drawn from Stephen Schlesinger and Stephen Kinzer, *Bitter Fruit, The Untold Story of the American Coup in Guatemala* (Garden City, N.Y.: Doubleday, 1982). Confer also Richard H. Immerman, *The CIA in Guatemala* (Austin, TX.: University of Texas, 1982).

[29]Schlesinger and Kinzer, *Bitter Fruit*, p. 37, 50.

[30]Thomas P. McCann, *An America Company, The Tragedy of United Fruit*, Henry Scammell, ed. (New York: Crown, 1976), p. 41.

[31]The U.S. Department of State, *Intervention of International Communism in the Americas* (Washington, D.C., 1954), pp. 55.

[32]McCann, *An American Company*, pp. 49–51; Schlesinger and Kinzer, *Bitter Fruit*, in their discussion of United Fruit's publicity campaign (Chapter 6) refer to the book as *Red Design for the Americas*.

[33]Nixon cited in Schlesinger and Kinzer, *Bitter Fruit*, p. 234.

[34]Ibid., p. 242.

[35]Ibid., pp., 246–47.

[36]On the influence of the Guatemala coup on the Cuban crisis five years later, see Paul E. Sigmund, *Multinationals in Latin America* (Madison, WI.: University of Wisconsin, 1980), pp. 89, 95, 106, 113.

[37]Moran, *Multinational Corporations and the Politics of Dependnece*. The account that follows, up to the Allende years, is taken from this study.

[38]Ibid., p. 55.

[39]Ibid., p. 87.

[40]Ibid., p. 94.

[41]Ibid., pp. 102–15.

[42]See the special advertisement statement by Chile in *The New York Times*, January 25, 1971, p. 72. For a study of Chile in the Allende years and additional references, see Arthur F. McGovern, *Marxism: An American Christian Perspective* (Maryknoll, N.Y.: Orbis, 1980), Chapter 6.

[43]See McGovern, *Marxism*, p. 218.

[44]Ibid., p. 214.

[45]Investor Responsibility Research Center (1522 K Street, N.W., Suite 806, Washington, D.C., 20005), analyses and supplements, A to S, for the year 1976.

[46]Ibid., Analysis M, Supplement No. 1, Gulf Oil Corporations, March 29, 1976.

[47]For a study of conditions in South Africa, see *South Africa: Time Running Out*, by the Report of the Study Commission on U.S. Policy Toward South Africa (Berkeley, CA.: University of California, 1981), and Desaix Meyers III, et al., (from the IRRC), *U.S. Business in South Africa* (Bloomington, IN.: Indiana University, 1980).

[48]Meyers, *U.S. Business in South Africa*, pp. 12–13.

[49]Study Commission, *South Africa*, p. 80.

[50]Ibid., p. 113.

[51]Ibid., p. 96.

[52]Ibid., pp. 96–97

[53]See John Payton, "Why the United States Corporations Should Get Out of South Africa," in *Business Ethics, Readings and Cases in Corporate Morality*, by W. Michael Hoffman and Jennifer Mills Moore (New York: McGraw-Hill, 1984), pp. 401–6.

[54]1985 General Motors Public Interest Report, pp. 44–45.

[55]Meyers, *U.S. Business in South Africa*, pp. 57–74, notes that the South African government is controlled by white Afrikaners of Dutch origin, and that few if any business leaders are chosen to occupy cabinet posts. Business, on the other hand, is controlled by the English-speaking whites, and the business community has pressed for changes and for dialogue with black leaders.

[56]"All Roads Lead Out of South Africa," *Business Week*, November 3, 1986, pp. 24–25.

[57]Frances Moore Lappe and Joseph Collins, *Food First, Beyond the Myth of Scarcity* (New York: Ballantine, 1978, revised), p. 219.

[58]McCann, *An American Company*, p. 78.

[59]Michael Schafer, "Capturing the Multinationals: Advantage or Disadvantage?," in Moran, ed., *Multinational Corporations*. Zaire and Zambia are the two main examples studied, pp. 25–49, but the author comments also on failures in Chile and Peru, pp. 46–49.

[60]Joani Nelson-Horchler, "U.S. Multinationals: Benefactors or Bandits?," in *Industry Week*, April 18, 1983, pp. 35–39. Other examples of multinationals' care for their workers and locale can be found in Lee A. Tavis, guest editor, "Multinationals as Foreign Agents of Change in the Third World," in *Business Horizons*, September–October 1983, pp. 4–5.

[61]Confer John A. Willoughby's comments on Adam Smith in "International Capital Flows, Economic Growth, and Basic Needs," in Margaret E. Crahan ed., *Human Rights and Basic Needs in the Americas* (Washington, D.C.: Georgetown University, 1982), p. 200.

[62]W. Arthur Lewis, *The Evolution of the International Economic Order* (Princeton, N.J.: Princeton University, 1978), pp. 9–10, 16–18.

[63]Lappe and Collins, *Food First*, p. 210.

[64]Ibid., p. 279.

[65]Ibid., pp. 279–81.

[66]Richard Newfarmer ed., *Profits, Progress and Poverty, Case Studies of International Industries in Latin America* (Notre Dame, IN.: University of Notre Dame, 1985).

[67]Newfarmer, Chapter 4 on the electrical industry, in *Profits* (Newfarmer, ed.), pp. 140–42.

[68]Douglass C. Bennett and Kenneth E. Scharpe, Chapter 6 on the auto industry, in *Profits*, pp. 224–25.

[69]Gary Gereffi, Chapter 8 on the pharmaceutical industry, in *Profits*, pp. 274–77.

[70]Rhys Jenkins and Peter J. West, Chapter 9 on the tractor industry, in *Profits*, p. 329.

[71]IRRC report, Analysis V on General Foods Corporation, June 30, 1976.

[72]Louis Turner, "There is no Love Lost between Multinational Corporations and the Third World," in *Business Ethics* (Hoffman and Moore), p. 398.

[73]Confer Edwin A. Murray, "Ethics and Corporate Strategy," in *Corporations and the Common Good*, Robert B. Dickie and Leroy S. Rouner, eds. (Notre Dame, IN.: University of Notre Dame, 1986), pp. 91–117, and also the essay by Kenneth Mason in the same book.

[74]Theodore Moran, Chapter 13 in *Multinational Corporations*, pp. 263–74.

[75]Newfarmer, *Profits*, pp. 3, 57, 407.

[76]Organization for Economic Cooperation and Development, *International Investment and Multinational Enterprises*, 1979; United Nations Commission on Transnational Corporations, U.N. Doc. E/C. 1984, S.Z.

Chapter Nine
GREENMAIL
AND CONCLUSIONS

There are many conscientious corporations in the United States today; we have focused on some, along with a few of their activities. Managers of corporations are more sophisticated and often more ethical today than they were two decades ago, with regard to participation in work, the physical environment, multinational operations, relations with government, and local neighborhoods. Today social responsibility issues take more of the corporate manager's time and energy.

Advertising and television have improved technically, but it seems that most ads and commercial TV programs have not improved in their respect for the dignity of the human. In addition, there remain other important problems that face society and the firm. We have discussed defense spending, lobbying and regulations, employee ownership, plant closings, the use and abuse of the physical environment, and the effect of the multinational corporation on the Third World. Although large issues, most of these problems can be influenced by the actions of an individual person; so we have offered some recommendations for the individual, where this seemed appropriate.

TAKEOVER AND GREENMAIL

Before proceeding with our conclusions, we would like to take note of a disturbing issue that deserves attention: takeovers and the influence of financial

189

analysts. Capital markets, investment bankers, and financial analysts currently have great influence over business and the corporation. Their regular inquiries of CEOs about quarterly financial performance forces management to place more attention on short-term issues, and sometimes too little attention on the long term. Outside financial analysts ask if common stock is sufficiently valued. If not, they reason that it is because of poor management; thus a takeover could replace management, restructure the firm and increase shareholder value. *If* their assessment is correct, their solution may benefit employees, customers, and shareholders.

But their assessment may be wrong: the stock may be low because management is conscientious and is building for the long term and the market has not taken this into account. Research and development, innovation, and new products and plants aimed at the long term can leave the firm open to an unfriendly takeover. Note Goodyear, which embarked on a program for long-term growth. Goodyear was forced to scrub plans to build huge energy and aerospace operations to balance its slow-growing tire business, in order to pay off the raider James Goldsmith. Long-term planning and growth were sacrificed for short-term survival.[1] If a takeover is successful, that might well mean plant closings, selling off businesses, neglect of some customers and local neighborhoods, and large demands for unproductive capital.

The activities of investment bankers are increasingly suspect. An investment banker that one consults for advice may not ethically take that information to another client. The information may be extremely valuable to the second firm, if it is considering a takeover. When the investment banker reveals data on the first firm, that banker is equivalently placing a "for sale" sign on that firm. In so doing, the investment banker violates trust and confidentiality. A veteran of a large financial firm says, "you look over your client list, picking out a company that appears vulnerable. Somebody's going to put him into play. . ., so we'd better do it first—and accordingly you shop his company around behind his back."[2] When the sale is completed, the investment banker will collect millions of dollars in fees, even if it is not in the best interest of his client. So it is in the investment banker's interest to complete the sale. This is a conflict of interest; such actions are also unjust, and do not respect confidentiality or individual responsibility.

Mergers, acquisitions, and friendly and unfriendly takeovers are not *merely* financial decisions; they involve important ethical issues. While large firms are necessary in some industries (automaking, banking), small firms are more flexible and innovative. It is from small firms that most new products, jobs, and growth come. Economies of scale are quickly compensated for by increased bureaucracy, lack of communication, and inflexibility. So, everything else being equal, small firms are better for people *and for the economy* than are large firms. A merger does not bring new products, new jobs, or new ideas; it drains capital that could be better used in financing new research and development, plant, and equipment. So on the basis of both business and social values, we discourage acquisitions, mergers, and takeovers. The moral burden of proof to show that the larger unit will be more productive, and therefore will provide lower-cost goods, more jobs, or something else beneficial to people and society, is on those proposing the merger.

Since mergers and takeovers generally lead to less innovation and efficiency and to more bureaucracy, they often violate our business norms of individual responsibility, growth, and productivity. Moreover, mergers and acquisitions generally lead to a more distant management and less knowledge about and interest in local workers, neighborhoods, and products. This often results in management rigidity, a denial of social relationships and obligations, and plant closings. This is a violation of the social values of community, justice, and the dignity of the individual.

Greenmail and golden parachutes generally do not bring greater efficiency and they are most often not ethical. Greenmail consists of paying off a threatening party so that he will cease takeover activities. A person initiating an unfriendly takeover is offered a high price for the stock they hold, in effect buying them off. While stability is retained and management's jobs are preserved, shareholders are treated unjustly, since shareholders are not given the same opportunity to sell their stock at the higher price. This results in an unjust windfall for the deal maker, while employees, customers, and other stakeholders pay the bill.

In an attempt to discourage unfriendly takeovers, management often convinces its board of directors to vote top management "golden parachutes." The top managers of the firm are thus guaranteed high salaries for a number of years. The plan is that a firm considering the takeover would cease, knowing that they must pay large severance pay to the deposed executives. The ethical defense of golden parachutes is that they discourage unfriendly takeovers. But they are also self-serving for top management. If the takeover is successful and they lose the company, executives still walk off with millions of dollars over a five- or ten-year period. Hence golden parachutes are unfair to stockholders, customers, and others who must bear the costs of these extravagant benefits for a few top managers.

COMPETITIVENESS AND THE NEEDS OF OTHERS

There are some important ethical and value needs for business in the United States today:

1. Maintaining a productive economy reflected in innovation and increasing numbers of jobs, and

2. Encouraging integrity and an awareness of the needs of other people.

Much effort in recent years has correctly gone into encouraging competitiveness, innovation, and productivity; traditional business values motivate and support this. Less effort has been directed toward encouraging integrity, justice, and a respect for other people. This book is intended to help in this latter regard.

Our free market system is supported by, and also reinforces, our traditional business values; this is not by chance but by design. Freedom, individual responsibility, and productivity are encouraged by competition and opportunity. Social values have also been recognized as essential from our earliest days as a nation. Various laws and regulations are designed to protect justice and community. The U.S. Constitution and its Bill of Rights protects the dignity of the individual. Community and solidarity are also buttressed by recent efforts at participation and involvement at work.

During the 1970s, most people, including corporate managers, predicted that we in the United States were moving from individualistic values toward a more community-based value system.[3] In the first portion of the 1980s we witnessed a resurgence of individualistic values, evidenced by an interest in cowboys, Rambo, war toys—every person wanting to be number one. Rather than moving back to an unhealthy individualism, this was but a temporary step backward. A mistake of the 1970s was expecting the federal government to provide for so many of our needs. Community and solidarity encourages the meeting of needs by other groups also: family, church, local organizations, and local governments. The federal government is appropriate when it is the best or the only agency to handle the need.

Traditional business values (see Chapter Two, Figure 2–1) have always been important and are basic. A society will not provide jobs and goods efficiently without strong traditional business values. Freedom and individual responsibility are even more important than that: They are the bedrock of democracy and stem from the dignity of each individual person.

Social values are just as essential. Without a sense of community, justice, and a respect for the individual, people cannot depend upon one another. There is then no business; there is no modern society. Community, justice, and the dignity of each individual are the foundation of any group of people and any society. A common sense of purpose, common goals, and a feeling of responsibility for others all enable a society to exist, to grow. It is the environment in which all people are able to develop and mature.

DISCUSSION QUESTIONS:

9.1. Ethically assess takeovers (friendly and unfriendly) using the values of Figure 2–1.
9.2. Is greenmail an ethically acceptable defense mechanism?
9.3. Do you agree that traditional business values and social values are equally important in the United States today? Explain.

NOTES

[1]Trying to Streamline, Some Firms May Hurt Long-Term Prospects," *Wall Street Journal,* January 8, 1987, pp. 1, 10.

[2]Myron Magnet, "The Decline and Fall of Business Ethics," *Fortune,* December 8, 1986, p. 66.

[3]George C. Lodge, "Business and the Changing Society." *Harvard Business Review* (March–April), 1974.

INDEX